Entrepreneurship in Tourism

The development of tourism has historically been characterised by enterprising individuals. Small businesses are the backbone of the tourism and hospitality industry. However, entrepreneurship and the entrepreneurial process have long been marginal topics within tourism scholarship.

This is a critical, yet accessible, introduction to the subject. Structured into twelve chapters, this book takes an intuitive step-by-step progression through entrepreneurship in tourism: context, theoretical perspectives and definitions; the entrepreneurial process from concept to reality to growth, policy context and future directions.

Featuring learning outcomes, 'reflective practice' activities and a range of international case studies that encourage critical thinking and practical applications, this is essential reading for anyone studying tourism degree programmes at undergraduate and graduate level.

Andreas Walmsley is Associate Professor (Reader) in Entrepreneurship at the University of Plymouth, UK.

D1145824

Entrepreneurship in Tourism

Andreas Walmsley

Routledge
Taylor & Francis Group

LONDON AND NEW YORK

First published 2019
by Routledge
2 Park Square, Milton Park, Abingdon, Oxon OX14 4RN

and by Routledge
52 Vanderbilt Avenue, New York, NY 10017

Routledge is an imprint of the Taylor & Francis Group, an informa business

British Library Cataloguing-in-Publication Data
A catalogue record for this book is available from the British Library

Library of Congress Cataloging-in-Publication Data
A catalog record has been requested for this book

ISBN: 978-1-138-04876-8 (hbk)
ISBN: 978-1-138-04877-5 (pbk)
ISBN: 978-1-315-16998-9 (ebk)

Typeset in Iowan Old Style BT
by Apex CoVantage, LLC

Visit the eResources: www.routledge.com/9781138048775

Printed and bound in Great Britain by
TJ International Ltd, Padstow, Cornwall

This book is dedicated to Georgina Min-Ru and Emily Min-Yen.

Contents

Figures

Tables

Case studies

Preface

'We must all become entrepreneurs' argues Hagel (2016:1028). In a similar vein, Gibb (2002:234) has claimed entrepreneurial behaviour should be displayed by 'priests, doctors, teachers, policemen, pensioners and community workers and, indeed, potentially everyone in the community'. The reason for this? The more uncertain and changing world we now live in. Thus, Gibb (2002) at the turn of the millennium justifies his position by referring to an increasingly globalised world, while Hagel (2016) goes on to argue it is driven by the 'Big Shift' we are witnessing in the business landscape, the result of 'long-term forces' such as those in digital technology infrastructure.

The finer details of changes in the business landscape may be debated, although a number of key drivers are apparent. To name just a few: climate change, the rise of artificial intelligence, an ageing population in many countries and 'pensions time bombs', as well as geopolitical turmoil as the world comes to terms (still) with the collapse of communism, as well as the rise of formerly developing economies, notably in Asia. Focusing on this latter point, as numerous pundits have argued, the twenty-first century is very likely to be 'The Asian Century' (in 1970 neither China nor India had a significant share of global gross domestic product, today China represents more than 15% of GDP and India more than 3%, with Pricewaterhouse-Coopers (2015) suggesting they will be the largest economies by mid-century[1]). Whatever the global economy looks like come mid-century, it is likely to be very different in terms of products, markets and economic structures from today. Critically, these and other changes will continue to affect tourism where we have witnessed significant shifts in source markets, consumer tastes, industry structures and supply chains already.

These turbulent times call forth many 'prophets of doom' who ignore the promise of human ingenuity and endeavour, according to Auerswald (2012:7) at least: 'the overwhelming majority clearly are deficient when it comes to paying attention to the entrepreneurial possibilities of the present'. Entrepreneurship, and its driver, innovation, may not solve all of society's ills, but without them neither would we witness any progress. We should not, of course, forget the unacceptably high levels of extreme poverty (according to the World Bank, in 2013 10.7% of the world's population lived on less than US$1.90 a day), and a new concern: growing levels of inequality. However, we cannot ignore the fact that increasing numbers of citizens of this world have better access to healthcare, education and economic means than ever before. Were it not for innovators and entrepreneurs this would not be the case.

The development of tourism has been characterised by enterprising individuals, and the history of tourism 'has been a phenomenon characterized by immense innovativeness' (Hjalager, 2010:1). Thomas Cook will spring to most people's minds, and is regularly mentioned as the archetypal tourism entrepreneur, harnessing the power of railways not to haul goods, but to allow people to partake in excursions. Plenty of other tourism luminaries exist that have led to changes in tourism markets regionally, nationally or indeed internationally. Tourism entrepreneurs such as Freddie Laker (founder of Laker Airways in 1966, pioneer of the 'no frills' business model), or Keith Williams and Bernard Elsey, who, due to their drive and 'bloody-minded tenacity', shaped the development of the Gold Coast, Australia, in the 1960s and 1970s (Barr, 1990).

However, within the broader sphere of scholarship in tourism, entrepreneurship and the entrepreneurial process remain marginal topics (Li, 2008). The academic contribution to identifying and understanding a range of issues critical to tourism entrepreneurship continues to be a largely neglected area for research (Ateljevic and Page, 2009). There is some evidence of increased research focus on entrepreneurship in tourism since Ateljevic and Page (2009) published their edited work. This includes some further books that have been published in this area, for example Brookes and Altinay's (2015) edited tome, or Weiermair et al.'s (2010) collection of case studies of tourism entrepreneurship and innovation alongside Lee-Ross and Lashley's (2009) monograph *Entrepreneurship & Small Business Management in the Hospitality Industry*. Further key articles have been published since 2009 on aspects of tourism entrepreneurship and innovation too, but it can hardly be suggested that research in tourism entrepreneurship has 'taken off'. This situation is reminiscent of Thomas, Shaw and Page's (2011) review of research trends and challenges relating to small firms in tourism where, despite promising signs at the turn of the millennium, research remains piecemeal and sporadic rather than following a clear research agenda. This is also very much the case for entrepreneurship in tourism.

Research on entrepreneurship inevitably dovetails with research on small business. Although the emphasis in this text is on entrepreneurship (we discuss issues of tourism entrepreneurship that do not necessarily have a small-firm focus), some of the discussions will relate very directly to the small-firm literature in tourism. We make no apologies for this, and even acknowledge that many small firms may not be regarded as particularly entrepreneurial (depending on how one defines or views entrepreneurship, as we shall see).

One feature of entrepreneurship is its action-orientation. A question many readers may justifiably ask then is whether this is a book for or about entrepreneurship in tourism. The 'for or about' discussion in education has occurred both in tourism (e.g., Tribe, 2002) and in entrepreneurship (e.g., Neck and Corbett, 2018). As any educator will recognise, however, the boundaries between 'for' and 'about' are less clear-cut than might initially meet the eye. Theory, which is commonly associated with being 'about', may have practical implications. In fact, Kurt Lewin, one of the leading lights in the field of psychology in the twentieth century, famously reminds us of this: 'there is nothing as practical as good theory' (Lewin, 1951). Good theory – that is, theory that displays the qualities of generality, accuracy and simplicity (Moroz and Hindle, 2012) – may offer practical outcomes, pedagogical and professional (Weick, 1995). Theory allows us to understand general principles and use these as a basis for action. Without theory, whether explicit or tacit, we would have to face each situation anew. Good theories help us make sense of the world and they are indispensable to practice. This book is both about entrepreneurship in tourism, and for entrepreneurship in tourism. In terms of discussing theories, the literature and the empirical evidence, it might be considered more 'about' entrepreneurship in tourism, although the book contains much that can be applied to practice (especially in Chapters 3–8).

One thing this text is not is a 'how-to' book. According to Down (2010:128) 'how to' books can never capture the diversity and complexity of everyday enterprise. Platitudes such as 'Your first priority is to become rich. Then, you can afford to become magnanimous' (Szycher, 2015:xix) are simplistic and indicative of the 'get-rich-quick at any cost' mentality that has come to tarnish entrepreneurship's image in many minds.[2] What simplified 'how-to' books will not do is help the reader understand the nature of entrepreneurship in any depth, and worse, they may even mislead the reader into taking ill-advised behaviour, with potentially catastrophic results (despite the value of failure, see Chapter 2, the pain that can accompany business failure should not be dismissed). I refer here to Sam Walton (the founder of Walmart) who, when pressed on his success, came up with ten very reasonable pieces of advice whereby the tenth stated 'Break all the rules. Swim upstream. Go the other way.' Clearly, Sam Walton understood that each situation needs to be assessed on its own merits and that if you just copied what everyone else did you would achieve no more than everyone else (Dollinger, 2003).

The book has been structured around 12 chapters enabling the adoption as a text for students undertaking a course on entrepreneurship in tourism. Each chapter stands alone and can therefore be read without prior knowledge of the other chapters. That said, readers with a limited background in entrepreneurship might usefully read Chapters 1–3, which cover conceptual issues in entrepreneurship. Chapters 4–8 are more individual-firm focused (or take a micro perspective), whereas subsequent chapters take a more macro perspective; that is, they largely review the place of entrepreneurship in tourism from a societal perspective. The final chapter brings together key insights provided by the book and assumes thereby a summary function, but also offers suggestions for further research.

Notes

1 On an absolute basis. Based on purchasing power parity, China's economy is already larger than that of the US (Holmes, 2017).
2 Szycher's is one of many texts that could have been chosen. To his credit, Szycher also offers some useful advice.

References

Ateljevic, J. and Page, S. 2009. Introduction. In: Ateljevic, J. and Page, S. (eds.), Tourism and Entrepreneurship: International Perspectives. Oxford: Butterworth-Heinemann.

Auerswald, P. 2012. The Coming Prosperity: How Entrepreneurs Are Transforming the Global Economy. Oxford: Oxford University Press.

Barr, T. 1990. From quirky islanders to entrepreneurial magnates: the transition of the Whitsundays. Journal of Tourism Studies, 1, 26–32.

Brookes, M. and Altinay, L. (eds.) 2015. Entrepreneurship in Hospitality and Tourism: A Global Perspective. Abingdon: Goodfellow.

Dollinger, M. J. 2003. Entrepreneurship. Strategies and Resources. New Jersey: Prentice Hall.

Down, S. 2010. Enterprise, Entrepreneurship and Small Business. London: Sage.

Gibb, A. 2002. In pursuit of a new 'enterprise' and 'entrepreneurship' paradigm for learning: creative destruction, new values, new ways of doing things and new combinations of knowledge. *International Journal of Management Reviews*, 4, 233–269.

Hagel, I. J. 2016. We need to expand our definition of entrepreneurship. *Harvard Business Review* [Online]. Available: https://hbr.org/2016/09/we-need-to-expand-our-definition-of-entrepreneurship [Accessed 28 September 2016].

Hjalager, A. M. 2010. A review of innovation research in tourism. *Tourism Management*, 31, 1–12.

Holmes, F. 15 June 2017. One easy way to invest in the 'Asian century'. *Great Speculations* [Online]. Available from: www.forbes.com/sites/greatspeculations/2017/06/15/one-easy-way-to-invest-in-the-asian-century/ [Accessed 15 June 2018].

Lee-Ross, D. and Lashley, C. 2009. *Entreprneurship & Small Business Management in the Hospitality Industry*. Oxford: Butterworth-Heinemann.

Lewin, K. 1951. *Field Theory in Social Science*. New York: Harper & Row.

Li, L. 2008. A review of entrepreneurship research published in the hospitality and tourism management journals. *Tourism Management*, 29, 1013–1022.

Moroz, P. and Hindle, K. 2012. Entrepreneurship as a process: toward harmonizing multiple perspectives. *Entrepreneurship Theory and Practice*, 36.

Neck, H. and Corbett, A. 2018. The scholarship of teaching and learning entrepreneurship. *Entrepreneurship Education and Pedagogy*, 1, 8–41.

PricewaterhouseCoopers. 2015. *The World in 2050: Will the Shift in Global Economic Power Continue?* PwC.

Szycher, M. 2015. *The Guide to Entrepreneurship: How to Create Wealth for Your Company and Stakeholders*. Boca Raton: CRC Press.

Thomas, R., Shaw, G. and Page, S. 2011. Understanding small firms in tourism: a perspective on research trends and challenges. *Tourism Management*, 32, 963–976.

Tribe, J. 2002. The philosophic practitioner. *Annals of Tourism Research*, 29, 338–357.

Weick, K. 1995. What theory is not, theorizing is. *Administrative Science Quarterly*, 40, 385–390.

Weiermair, K., Keller, P., Pechlaner, H. and Go, F. (eds.) 2010. *Innovation and Entrepreneurship: Strategies and Processes for Success in Tourism*. Berlin: Erich Schmidt Verlag.

World Bank. 2013. *How We Classify Countries* [Online]. Available: http://data.worldbank.org/about/country-classifications [Accessed 30 June 2013].

Acknowledgements

Entrepreneurship does not occur in a vacuum, nor does writing a book. I would like to extend my thanks to everyone who has directly or indirectly, wittingly or unwittingly, helped to shape my ideas. I would like in particular to thank the following: Laura Wallis (lifestyle entrepreneurship), Areej Al-Hemimah (digital marketing), Dr Ghulam Nabi and Professor Heidi Neck (entrepreneurship education).

Chapter 1

Entrepreneurship in tourism

An introduction

The innovation, flair and vision of entrepreneurs. . . shaped modern tourism.
(Russell, 2006:105)

Entrepreneurship and pornography have a lot in common: they are both hard to define.
(Mitton, 1989:9).

On opening an introductory tourism textbook, one of the first chapters will invariably contain an explanation of terms such as tourist and visitor. . . What is most interesting when perusing these texts is that the definitions listed are dissimilar. This variation is also seen in tourism research reports, articles, monographs, serials, and proceedings.
(Masberg, 1998:67)

Introduction

This chapter provides an introduction to the book suggesting why a preoccupation with entrepreneurship in tourism is timely. It draws attention to the emergence of both tourism and entrepreneurship as areas of academic study and wider societal interest. It reviews the policy context for tourism and entrepreneurship, explaining how both continue to be encouraged by those interested in economic growth and regeneration. It discusses similarities between the two concepts, how they relate to each other, clarifying also the relationship between tourism SMEs and entrepreneurship.

Learning outcomes

At the end of this chapter the reader should be able to:

- Explain policy-makers' interest in tourism and entrepreneurship as tools to promote economic development.
- Describe the similarities in the development of tourism and entrepreneurship as concepts.

- Review different approaches to defining entrepreneurship.
- Critically evaluate the connection between small firms in tourism and entrepreneurship.

Both entrepreneurship and tourism are phenomena that are witnessing increased interest from policy-makers and academics alike. From a policy-maker's perspective, entrepreneurship is frequently held up as the driver for economic development, and with it development more broadly understood, i.e., to include social and environmental dimensions. This holds for both advanced economies and developing countries, and for emerging economies and economies in transition.

Tourism likewise is frequently regarded as a tool to stimulate economic development, albeit often in countries or regions that are suffering a decline in traditional industries, or where the scope for alternative forms of economic development are limited. Tourism is sometimes regarded as a refuge sector (Vaugeois and Rollins, 2007); for some countries and regions it is their economic and social lifeline. This is true, for example, for many small island states.

Indeed, if we regard entrepreneurship as the driving force behind economic growth and diversification, and tourism as a sector of choice for under-performing regions, urban regeneration, and countries seeking to diversify their economic base, particularly a move away from a sole reliance on agriculture, then the combination of entrepreneurship and tourism presents policy-makers with a powerful means to address economic development, and with it broader societal issues such as social mobility and cohesion, employment of marginalised groups, protection of cultural heritage and the safeguarding of the natural environment.

Furthermore, both entrepreneurship and tourism share a focus on small firms. Because of their sheer numeric dominance, small firms are frequently regarded as the lifeblood of tourism (Cooper et al., 2005; Thomas et al., 2011). While it is too simplistic to equate small businesses with enterprise, tourism is unquestionably characterised by the creation of small, often lifestyle businesses (Page et al., 1999; Shaw and Williams, 2004; Getz et al., 2004) and lends itself therefore to the study of many aspects of entrepreneurship.

Moreover, the numeric dominance of small firms is added to by so-called sideline businesses. These are ventures that offer the entrepreneur an additional income next to a main job. Hatten (2016) cites figures from the USA which suggest of the 27.9 million businesses identified by the Small Business Administration, 9 million were this kind of side-line business. Tourism itself is characterised by many of these side-line businesses. In mature, emerging and developing economies alike, tourism provides additional income for farmers in rural communities, for example. Zhao et al. (2011) have described these side-line businesses in a Chinese context, offering a less glamorous view in that necessity is frequently a driver of their creation, primarily given seasonality. In these circumstances, tourism entrepreneurship offers a lifeline.

Despite their importance, research on small tourism firms has not seen anything like the attention afforded small firms within the mainstream business and management literature (Page et al., 1999; Thomas et al., 2011). Likewise, research on entrepreneurship and innovation in tourism is also regarded by some as quite limited (Li, 2008; Thomas et al., 2011; Yang and Wall, 2008). In 2009 Ateljevic and Li (2009) asked how far entrepreneurship research in tourism had come. They offered an answer to this question following a systematic review of the literature in major hospitality and tourism journals between 1986 and 2006. Of the 4,917 articles published in the seven selected journals, approximately 2% addressed entrepreneurship. An upward trend in entrepreneurship journals published in the timeframe of the review was not discernible.

Li (2008), who also investigated the publication of entrepreneurship research in tourism and hospitality journals, comes to quite a damning verdict arguing that the issue is under-researched, theoretically weak and lacking methodological sophistication. Whether the same verdict can be reached today, ten years after Li's 2008 publication, is not clear, although there are some signs that interest is growing. As this book will demonstrate, the past ten to fifteen years have witnessed a growth in entrepreneurship-related studies in tourism. The trend appears to be upwards, even if explicit studies of entrepreneurship in tourism are relatively low in number compared to other major themes within the body of tourism knowledge such as consumer behaviour and economic or environmental impacts. It is also worth noting that even though, compared to other aspects of tourism, research in the area of tourism entrepreneurship is limited, the topic itself can hardly be described as new. Yang and Wall (2008) refer to Kibedi's (1979) work, which explores the training and development of tourism entrepreneurs in Canada, for example.

One of the key challenges for tourism scholars is the looseness of the concept of tourism itself. This makes it extremely difficult to say anything definitive about tourism, and tourists for that matter. Even what should, one imagines, be relatively straightforward issues, such as providing figures of those employed in the sector, or assessing its economic contribution, present numerous challenges the starting point of which is defining tourism itself. The same can be said of entrepreneurship, where numerous definitions abound. Rather than detract from their study, the fluid and situated nature of both tourism and entrepreneurship make them more appealing, from an academic perspective at least. The remainder of this chapter will explore the above issues in more detail. It thereby serves as a context for the remainder of the book.

Entrepreneurship

According to Shane and Venkataraman (2000:217), 'entrepreneurship has become a broad label under which a hodgepodge of research is housed'. As with all complex concepts, entrepreneurship (and by implication associated terms: enterprise, entrepreneurialism) lacks a single, universally accepted definition. Ateljevic and Li (2009:22) recognise this in their chapter on concepts and issues in tourism entrepreneurship: 'Due to its complexity, the concept of entrepreneurship is almost impossible to accommodate in one single definition.' Although Ateljevic and Li (2009) review research in the area of tourism entrepreneurship, a definition of tourism entrepreneurship is not provided. This is understandable as tourism largely presents a context within which entrepreneurship takes place and in which it can be explored (although certain characteristics of tourism make this exploration particularly interesting as we shall see throughout the book).

The focus of entrepreneurship has in similar fashion been defined by its locus, where it is believed to occur, in other words by its own context, specifically the context of small, young or owner-managed businesses. Arguably, this context approach to defining entrepreneurship can be criticised because it avoids the phenomenon itself, but suggests what happens within a specific context is entrepreneurship. Wiklund et al. (2011:5), for example, support such a critique as well as adding that the focus on commercial enterprises is wrong. The phenomenon of entrepreneurship, 'the emergence of new economic activity', does not need to be solely commercially driven (see Chapter 9).

Complexity of the phenomenon aside, a further reason why there is no universal definition of entrepreneurship is because different definitions will suit different purposes; the search for a universal definition may itself then be regarded as a misguided undertaking from the outset. It is important to stress, however, that this does not mean that in common parlance entrepreneurship is bereft of meaning or a shared understanding. As Mitton (1989:9) claims about entrepreneurship, 'I can't define it to everyone else's satisfaction – but I know it when I see it'.

Most commonly, entrepreneurship has been, and still is, associated with business start-up, the creation of a commercial venture. This is reflected in many widely cited definitions of entrepreneurship, such as that provided by Timmons (1989:1) where entrepreneurship is claimed to be

> the ability to create and build something from practically nothing. It is initiating, doing, achieving, and building an enterprise or organisation, rather than just watching, analysing or describing one. It is the knack for sensing an opportunity where others see chaos, contradiction and confusion.

Or in definitions of the entrepreneur such as that given by Bygrave and Hofer, 1991:14): 'An Entrepreneur is someone who perceives an opportunity and creates an organization to pursue it.'

There is much of interest in this definition that we will discuss later in the book, from opportunity recognition to the role of resources in the entrepreneurial process, but it is the notion here that entrepreneurship is necessarily about business start-up that can be queried. It can even be argued that business start-up is neither a sufficient not a necessary condition for entrepreneurship. If an assumption underpinning entrepreneurship is the existence of innovation (see also next chapter) then setting up a business along the lines of a tried and tested business model, such as a bed and breakfast or beach café, is not entrepreneurship. Thus, while entrepreneurship has commonly been conceptualised as the creation of a business (see Shane, 2003; Gartner, 1988) this conceptualisation does not capture the full scope of entrepreneurship. This idea is now widely supported and was raised some time ago in fact; for example, by Covin and Slevin (1991:7) who argued: 'The domain of entrepreneurship is no longer restricted in a conceptual sense to the independent new venture creation.'

According to the Information Research Management Association (2017), one of the most cited definitions in the field of entrepreneurship is that offered by Shane and Venkataraman (2000:220) in their seminal article[1] 'The promise of entrepreneurship as a field of research', which states entrepreneurship is 'the identification, evaluation, and exploitation of opportunities'. First, we can see that this definition does not focus specifically on a small or new venture. Second, we can see that entrepreneurship is bound to other concepts that also require explanation, such as what constitutes an opportunity (this is the thing with definitions; they usually call for further definitions!). Chapters 2 and 3 will discuss some of entrepreneurship's sister concepts in more detail (e.g., opportunity, innovation and the entrepreneur).

Mention of entrepreneurship often conjures up images of the archetypal entrepreneur, and definitions of entrepreneurship are regularly based on the nature of individuals who demonstrate being entrepreneurial (see Lee-Ross and Lashley, 2009: Chapter 1). Public personas such as Richard Branson (Virgin empire), James Dyson (inventor and best known for cylindrical vacuum cleaners), Sam Walton (Walmart), Henry Ford (Ford motor cars), or in tourism Thomas Cook and Freddie Laker are conjured up in our mind when we hear the word 'entrepreneurship'. This person-focus has led to much research on entrepreneurial personality types and traits, which is ongoing, in fact possibly resurgent (Davis et al., 2016).

The detachment of the entrepreneur and entrepreneurship from their contexts – historical, social, cultural and economic – is questionable. As we argue throughout this book, be that for example in relation to ideation (the coming up with ideas), the venture creation process, business growth or social entrepreneurship, entrepreneurship is very much a situated affair. The go-it-alone, so-called solo-preneur is a very rare beast.

Sahlman (1996) offers an analytical framework of entrepreneurship that demonstrates this context-dependence. His framework succinctly captures the key elements that are critical considerations for commercial entrepreneurship (as opposed to social entrepreneurship). This framework stresses the creation of a dynamic fit among four interrelated components: the *people*, the *context*, the *deal* and the *opportunity* (PCDO) (Sahlman, 1996). Austin et al. (2006), who reflect on Sahlman's model, suggest that context refers to everything outside of the immediate control of the entrepreneur but that can influence success or failure. Clearly, as Austin et al. immediately recognise, choosing which contextual factors to focus on is the challenge, not the fact that one needs to focus on contextual factors. As they argue (Austin et al., 2006:5): 'Attention to everything can mean attention to nothing. On the other hand, leaving out a single critical element of context can be the precursor of failure.'

Many varied approaches have been used to describe and to analyse entrepreneurship. Stevenson and Jarillo (1991), for example, suggest entrepreneurship research falls within three main streams:

- the results of entrepreneurship (e.g., impact on the economy)
- the causes of entrepreneurship (e.g., person-specific factors such as risk-taking propensity) and
- entrepreneurial management (e.g., corporate entrepreneurship and how to foster it).

Morrison, Rimmington and Williams (1999:4–7) in the first chapter of their text on entrepreneurship in tourism suggest attempts to describe entrepreneurship have usually been undertaken in relation to:

- an economic function (stimulation of economic growth)
- ownership structure (the creator of a small business with the entrepreneur as founder)

- degrees of entrepreneurship (exploration of the extent of innovation and entrepreneurship within firms)
- size and life-cycle of the firm (tackling the view of the new dynamic firm in contrast to the stereotypical slow, large firm – see also Chapter 6), and
- as a resource base (that draws on Kirzner's 1997 [see also next chapter] view of entrepreneurship as an economic resource).

Tourism

While definitions of tourism vary (see Masberg's 1998 quote at the start of the chapter), because this text has primarily been written for those engaged in tourism, be that students, scholars, practitioners or policy-makers, we assume some familiarity with the concept of tourism. Discussions of what tourism is, or is not, abound, but it is not our intention to go into any great depth on this issue here. What is useful, and required if the phenomenon of entrepreneurship in tourism is to be adequately dealt with, is an overview of and reflection on key characteristics of tourism, especially as they relate to entrepreneurship (views on what these characteristics are may differ). Indeed, the relationship between both concepts is the dominant theme of the book.

At the outset, we can establish that tourism is an amorphous phenomenon, vast in scope with 'messy' boundaries. To illustrate, although tourism is often regarded by policy-makers primarily as an economic activity, it 'is more than an industry and an economic activity, it is a universal dynamic social phenomenon touching most countries of the world and affecting their people' (Elliott, 1997:4). From an economic vantage point, tourism may be regarded from both a demand and a supply side. It can be seen through a variety of lenses: social, economic, cultural, political, anthropological, etc. Leiper (1990) provides a geographical standpoint for understanding tourism, proposing a traveller-generating, a transit and a destination region. Moreover, tourism has variously been described as a sector, an activity, a panacea for the economic woes of certain regions, a form of neo-colonialism for others, a reflection of our society and civilisation as argued as long ago as 1947 by Pimlott (Middleton and Likoris, 2005). Debates have taken place about whether tourism is a discipline (akin to physics or philosophy) with its own theories and methods, or whether it is the 'material of the external world of events and so is the data to be examined rather than the method of evaluation' (Tribe, 1997:639).

Notwithstanding debates about the nature of tourism, as a global phenomenon that touches the lives of literally billions of people, tourism is a force to be reckoned with. According to Middleton and Likoris (2005:11) 'tourism has grown from what was derisively known as a "candy floss industry" in the 1960s to become what is often claimed to be the world's largest industry'. Travel as a prerequisite of tourism and as an activity describing the movement of people between different geographical locations has existed since time immemorial. Indeed, it is salutary to consider for an instant that, viewed through an historical lens, nomadism as opposed to sedentism is more natural of the human condition (Grant, 2003). Despite previous eras not being devoid of tourism (one could argue in somewhat paradoxical sounding terms that tourism began when sedentism began), tourism in its current guise is unquestionably a modern phenomenon.

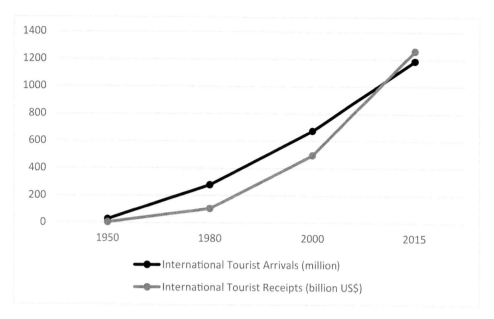

Figure 1.1 The rise of tourism

Source: Chart based on data from UNWTO (2016)

Various reasons have been advanced as to why/how tourism grew so dramatically, in scope and in scale, such as increases in leisure time, increases in disposable income, technological progress and changes in values/tastes.[2] Arguably, the search for *the* key reason for the emergence of tourism is an interesting exercise, and yet as with any modern social phenomenon, the manifestation of tourism today is dependent on a multitude of factors.

What is clear is that tourism today is in many respects quite different to the forms of tourism evidenced just 30–40 years ago, and indeed it continues to evolve. Table 1.1 has been compiled to provide an overview of a selection of current trends that illustrate the dynamic nature of modern tourism. This dynamism presents both opportunities and risks to the tourism entrepreneur. New markets, products, services, tastes and processes offer opportunities, but the speed of change also presents risks in terms of, for example, velocity of obsolescence, especially technological obsolescence (the velocity of obsolescence reflects the rate of speed at which an innovation and/or the competitive advantage of an innovation will lose its value; Gersch, 2013). The idea that in today's business environment product and business model life-cycles are shortening is not new; Hamel was writing about this, for example, in 2000 (Hamel, 2000).

For the sake of expediency, and because we should offer some boundaries as to what tourism means within the context of this text, we refer here to the United Nation's World Tourism Organization's widely used definition of tourism as:

> a social, cultural and economic phenomenon which entails the movement of people to countries or places outside their usual environment for personal or business/professional purposes.

> (UNWTO, 2014)

Table 1.1 Examples of current trends in tourism

Theme	Example/explanation
Continued rapid expansion of tourism	International tourism represents 7% of exports in goods and services, up from 6% in 2014, as tourism grows quicker than global trade overall (UNWTO, 2016).
Shifts in the structure of outbound tourism	Source markets for international tourism have traditionally been advanced economies with higher levels of disposable income. Many emerging economies are now showing higher rates of growth of outbound travel. China continues to consolidate its position as the number one source market in the world since 2012, following a trend of double-digit growth in tourism expenditure every year since 2004 (UNWTO, 2017a). The Chinese outbound travel market will continue to grow strongly but will gradually mature into a more recognisable Western-style market. It is predicted that Chinese tourists, who are known for their lavish holiday shopping in many parts of the world, will reduce this 'crazy' spending to more 'rational' levels (IPK International, 2016).
Shifts in the share of international tourist arrivals	It is estimated that international arrivals will grow at twice the rate in emerging compared to advanced economies (+4.4% and +2.2% a year respectively), albeit from a lower base (UNWTO, 2016).
Increasing awareness of sustainability	Travellers choosing destinations closer to home to reduce carbon footprint, and choosing companies with a strong social focus (Burkhard et al., 2016). More generally, the 2015 Cone Communications/Ebiquity Global CSR Study of 9,709 adults in nine countries claims 91% of global consumers expect companies to do more than make a profit, but also operate responsibly to address social and environmental issues (Cone, 2015).
Growth in the sharing economy	The likes of Airbnb and Uber and are now household names. Gallagher (2017) writing for *Fortune* estimates Airbnb's profits are to exceed US$3 billion by 2020. It is worth remembering the company was only founded in 2008. Uber Technology Inc. is an even more recent company, having only been established in 2009. In 2016 its revenue amounted to US$6.5 billion.
Continued growth in user-generated content	According to TripAdvisor's annual report (TripAdvisor Inc., 2017) there were 48 localised versions of the TripAdvisor website in 28 languages in 2016. TripAdvisor-branded websites reached nearly 390 million unique users per month and offered 465 million reviews of more than 7 million places to stay, places to eat and things to do.
Increased travel by baby boomers (born 1946–1964)	According to Patterson et al. (2017) the number of baby boomers who are aged 60 years and over are expected to more than double, from 841 million people in 2013 to more than 2 billion in 2050. They also provide an overview of studies that support the idea that travel propensity is increasing among baby boomers, as well as their characteristics such as (Patterson et al., 2017:357): • Perceiving themselves to be younger and more physically active. • Being more adventurous and requiring authentic learning experiences. • Living longer, and being better educated, and more affluent than previous generations.

Theme	Example/explanation
More women taking on solo travel	Booking.com (2014) reports that 72% of American women are taking solo journeys empowered by social media. According to Condé Nast Traveler (Lippe-McGraw, 2017), not only are more women travelling on their own, they are also engaging in more adventurous activities: 'Women are choosing mountaineering over pampering, and they don't mind going solo.'
Increase in multigenerational travel	Defined as travel that includes three or more generations. According to research conducted by Preferred Hotel Group (2011), 40% of all active leisure travellers have taken at least one multigenerational trip during the previous 12 months. The reasons for this are: families living geographically farther apart, the hyper-fast pace of life in the twenty-first century means evenings and weekends are no longer untouchable family time, and baby boomers are trading in their briefcases for a roller bag. Boomers now have the time, health and disposable income to make travel with their families a top priority (Preferred Hotel Group, 2011).
Increased interest in health and wellness	As Alisha Bhagat (2017) writes in the Huffington Post, the focus of health and wellness is no longer just about exercise and nutrition but also on mental health, itself part of a trend towards 'holistic consumerism'. According to the Global Wellness Institute (2017), the value of the global wellness industry in 2015 was said to be US$3.7 trillion, of which wellness tourism accounted for US$563 billion.
Crowdsourcing	Crowdsourcing of luxury hotels is something mentioned by Ashley Rayner of Escape Here (Rayner, 2017). She provides the example of Prodigy Network crowdfunding real estate firm, which is currently planning to construct a 194-unit space in downtown New York.
The emergence and growth of smart destinations	Developments in ICT continue to have significant implications for tourism. This is reflected also in the emergence of the so-called smart destination, an innovative tourist destination that draws on state-of-the-art technology to improve sustainability, the visitor experience and residents' quality of life (Lopez de Avila, 2015).

Widespread use aside, the benefit of this definition is also its simplicity, although what constitutes someone's usual environment is a matter of debate (e.g., Govers et al., 2008). This definition includes day trippers or excursionists, an overnight stay is not necessary to be classified as a tourist. What the reader will also note is the frequent reference to the hospitality sector. Although tourism and hospitality are not wholly congruent, there is a substantial overlap, which is furthermore compounded in international statistics where the closest one frequently gets to measures of tourism are subsectors of the hospitality sector (e.g., accommodation providers and restaurants).

The primary focus of the book will be on the supply side of tourism as an economic phenomenon; that is, the provision of tourism products and services by tourism entrepreneurs, as well as the implications of this for economic development. Tourism entrepreneurs can be defined in straightforward terms as those engaging in entrepreneurial activity within tourism, whether creating a tourism enterprise, or displaying entrepreneurship within an existing organisation (the distinction between entrepreneurship and intrapreneurship is defined elsewhere in the text).

We regard entrepreneurship foremost as an activity that can be undertaken by anyone; it is the act that determines entrepreneurship, not the individual.

Furthermore, the focus of this text will predominantly be at micro and meso levels. In other words, the text will look at the behaviour of individual firms and entrepreneurs, and the behaviour of firms within a sector (here tourism), although at times it will be necessary to look at the macro context, particularly in Chapter 10 where we look at public policy and tourism entrepreneurship. As has been acknowledged, the boundaries of tourism are anything but clear-cut, and the impacts of tourism, even when defined narrowly as an economic activity, will extend far beyond the economic sphere.

Tourism and entrepreneurship: the path most travelled

It is interesting to note that the development of tourism and entrepreneurship in academia have followed similar paths. Entrepreneurship is a new domain or field of scholarly enquiry, just as tourism is. According to Brazeal and Herbert (1999), at the close of the century, the study of entrepreneurship was still regarded as being in its infancy. Eight years prior to this, however, Bygrave and Hofer (1991:13) claimed that increased research in the 1980s led to entrepreneurship being recognised in the 1990s as a legitimate field of academic inquiry. Shane and Venkataraman writing in 2000 still queried its legitimacy as did Low (2001). These concerns about legitimacy as a field of academic enquiry have similarly plagued tourism scholars where a key concern has been the lack of a body of theory unique to the 'discipline' (Tribe, 1997). More recently Wiklund et al. (2011:1) strengthened the case for entrepreneurship, claiming: 'The field has emerged as one of the most vital, dynamic, and relevant in management, economics, regional science, and other social sciences.' Whether the same can be said for tourism is a moot point and yet, as an economic activity contributing 10% of global GDP (UNWTO, 2017b), tourism is unquestionably a force to be reckoned with.

Both tourism and entrepreneurship are multidisciplinary. Although debates as to whether tourism is a discipline in its own right are likely to continue, the fact that tourism draws on numerous disciplines is commonly argued (Graburn and Jafari, 1991; Gunn, 1994). The same interdisciplinary/multidisciplinary focus applies to entrepreneurship as Bygrave and Hofer (1991:17) aver: 'And yet any theory of entrepreneurship must be rooted in the social sciences, such as anthropology, psychology, sociology, economics, and politics, because these are the sciences that describe the key variables that underlie the process of venture creation.' Again, we can identify that as areas of academic enquiry tourism and entrepreneurship share a number of features.

Small firms in tourism

Entrepreneurship and small firms are often mentioned in the same breath. Because of the dominance of small firms in tourism one could argue therefore that entrepreneurship and tourism are, by their very nature, strongly intertwined. Small firms are not unique to tourism of course but predominate economy-wide. Data from the European Commission (2012) suggest that 99.8% of firms across the EU28 countries are classified as SMEs (those employing up to 250 employees). These firms were responsible for employing 67% of employees (full-time equivalent) and contributing 57.5% of gross value added. According to Hatten (2016), who refers to Small Business Administration data, these figures broadly reflect the situation in the USA also. While there is little variation in the proportion of SMEs across EU countries, greater variation exists in relation to their role in generating jobs (SMEs provide 86.5% of jobs in Greece, but only 53% in the UK) and in providing Gross Value Added[3] (almost 75% in Estonia and Malta, but just 50.1% in Poland). At a global level, the International Finance Corporation (2017) provides estimates on the number of micro, small and medium-sized enterprises (MSMEs) for 132 countries. Although definitions vary, and the IFC's figures are estimates, their data point clearly to the preponderance of particularly micro and small enterprises in the global economy, but also a great deal of variation relating to MSMEs' contribution to employment, and also to their economic contribution more generally.

A common distinction, one for example adopted by the EU (Eurostat, 2016), between micro, small and medium-sized enterprises is as follows:

- Micro enterprise: fewer than ten persons employed.
- Small enterprise: fewer than 50 but more than nine persons employed.
- Medium-sized enterprise: fewer than 250 but more than 49 persons employed.

Other ways of measuring firm size include balance sheet totals, sales and profits, but frequently only persons employed is considered. There is a debate as to how useful the above distinction is for tourism and hospitality as here the vast majority of firms are not only small but micro in size, in which case a finer distinction could be made at the lower end. However, in practice the above definition is most frequently adopted.

Furthermore, using number of employees as the gauge of size, many tourism firms grow and shrink as they hire and lay off staff according to seasonal demand cycles. Tourism firms employing just a handful of staff in the off-season might treble or quadruple their employees during the peak season indicating a distinction between core and peripheral workers (Johnson, 1981). Managing demand in tourism is a key challenge for the tourism entrepreneur in fact as it is often unpredictable and susceptible to supply- and demand-side shocks (Frechtling, 2001).

Beyond the recognition of their prominence, there still exists a paucity of research into tourism SMEs (Page et al., 1999; Thomas et al., 2011), where contradictory perspectives are occasionally encountered. For example, paradoxically, small firms are seen as engines of growth while simultaneously they have been accused of being reactionary, staid in their business practices and anti-growth. Thomas et al. (2011) have reviewed trends and challenges relating to the topic of small firms in tourism, thereby also taking stock of what we know in this area. The following summarises some of their main insights:

- While we can no longer regard research on small firms in tourism to be 'terra incognita' (Page et al., 1999) research efforts are still piecemeal. There is no clearly developing research agenda and the promise of a strong research base, as was intimated might arise in the late 1990s and early 2000s, has not materialised. A key purpose of Thomas et al.'s (2011) paper was precisely to rejuvenate academic interest in small tourism firms.

- The role of small tourism firms in local economic development remains contested. Moreover, a lack of understanding of tourism SMEs is likely to be hampering many key issues in tourism, such as the impact of policy initiatives, the social and cultural role of tourism, and moves towards more sustainable and responsible forms of tourism.
- One thing stands out from their analysis, if tourism is to be better understood, and if policy is consequently to be successfully designed and implemented, then an increased focus on tourism SMEs is crucial. This book aims to contribute to this via its exploration of entrepreneurship in tourism.

Summary

This chapter has discussed the nature of entrepreneurship primarily, but also touched upon the nature of tourism. Commonalities between the two concepts were identified also in relation to their historic development. It was shown that both tourism and entrepreneurship are complex phenomena lacking universal definitions. Both tourism and entrepreneurship are of interest to policy-makers because of their potential in supporting economic development. Both are relatively new as standalone academic subjects. Both tourism and entrepreneurship have grappled for recognition within the academic community. Both can be viewed through a number of lenses, although both are regularly viewed through an economic one (and this is also the primary lens adopted in this book). Finally, the most direct overlap between entrepreneurship and tourism is the small-firm focus. As we have noted, however, and as shall be further discussed in the next chapter, even here opinions differ as to the extent to which small firms share entrepreneurial characteristics.

Entrepreneurship is often defined by the context within which it is assumed to occur; for example, small and/or young firms. A more recent approach is to focus on the activity of entrepreneurship, which then can be identified as occurring in a range of contexts. This approach is, for example, found in the frequently cited definition of entrepreneurship provided by Shane and Venkataraman (2000), which does not specify a context (e.g., business start-up). However, what we also identified is that definitions of entrepreneurship such as the one provided by Shane and Venkataraman (2000) then also draw on further constructs, that in their own turn call for further definitions. Both entrepreneurship and tourism are then social constructs, consequently with meanings dependent on the situations in which they are being defined. Nonetheless, the search for the 'essence' of both tourism and entrepreneurship allows us to better appreciate their interconnectedness, or 'close coupling' (Langley, 1999). The remainder of this book is engaged in this endeavour.

Review questions/discussion points

1   Does it matter that there is not a universally agreed definition of either tourism or entrepreneurship?

2   Why has it been argued that the combination of tourism and entrepreneurship is a 'potent mix'?

3   Given the importance of entrepreneurship to economic growth and development, why is it that studies of entrepreneurship in tourism are relatively limited?

4   Do you think starting a small business should be classified as entrepreneurship? Explain your position.

5   What do you understand by 'the velocity of obsolescence'? What factors might contribute to an increased rate of obsolescence?

6   In a group, come up with your own list of five key factors that are going to shape tourism in the next decade. Rank them by importance.

Notes

1 '[T]he best-cited – by far – article of the decade in the *Academy of Management Review*' (Wiklund et al., 2011:1)

2 Interestingly, as well as worryingly, increases in leisure time have now stalled and in much of the developed world real incomes have stagnated.

3 Gross Value Added is a measure of the value of goods and services produced in an area, industry or sector of an economy.

References

Ateljevic, J. and Li, L. 2009. Tourism entrepreneurship – concepts and issues. *In:* Page, S. and Ateljevic, J. (eds.), *Tourism and Entrepreneurship: International Perspectives*. London: Routledge.

Austin, J., Stevenson, H. and Wei-Silkern, J. 2006. Social and commercial entrepreneurship: same, different or both? *Entrepreneurship Theory and Practice*, 30, 1–22.

Bhagat, A. 2017. A little is a lot: health and wellness trends [Online]. *The Blog*. Available: www.huffingtonpost.com/alisha-bhagat/a-little-is-a-lot-health-and-wellness-trends-2016_b_9393638.html [Accessed 7 March 2017].

Booking.com. 2014. *Do Not Disturb: More Than Half of American Women Travelers Are Going Solo* [Online]. https://news.booking.com/do-not-disturb-more-than-half-of-american-women-travelers-are-going-solo/ [Accessed 22 August 2018].

Brazeal, D. and Herbert, T. 1999. The genesis of entrepreneurship. *Entrepreneurship Theory and Practice*, 23, 29–45.

Burkhard, S., Kow, N. and Fuggle, L. 2016. *Travel Trend Report 2017*. Trekksoft.

Bygrave, W. and Hofer, C. 1991. Theorizing about entrepreneurship. *Entrepreneurship Theory and Practice*, 16, 13–22.

Cone. 2015. *2015 Cone Communications/Ebiquity Global CSR Study* [Online]. Available: www.conecomm.com/research-blog/2015-cone-communications-ebiquity-global-csr-study [Accessed 22 April 2018].

Cooper, C., Fletcher, J., Fyall, A., Gilbert, D. and Wanhill, S. 2005. *Tourism Principles and Practice*. Harlow: Pearson.

Covin, J. and Slevin, D. 1991. A conceptual model of entrepreneurship as firm behaviour. *Entrepreneurship Theory and Practice*, 16, 7–26.

Davis, M. H., Hall, J. and Mayer, P. 2016. Developing a new measure of entrepreneurial mindset: reliability, validity and implications for practitioners. *Counseling Psychology Journal: Practice and Research*, 68, 21–48.

Elliott, J. 1997. *Tourism, Politics and Public Sector Management*. London: Routledge.

European Commission. 2012. *Number of Enterprises, Persons Employed and Gross Value Added (GVA) and the Share of SMEs, 2012* [Online]. Available: http://ec.europa.eu/eurostat/statistics-explained/index.php/File:Number_of_enterprises,_persons_employed_and_gross_value_added_(GVA)_and_the_share_of_SMEs,_2012.png [Accessed 17 April 2017].

Eurostat. 2016. *Glossary: Enterprise Size* [Online]. European Commission. Available: http://ec.europa.eu/eurostat/statistics-explained/index.php/Glossary:Enterprise_size [Accessed 21.09.2017 2017].

Frechtling, D. 2001. *Forecasting Tourism Demand: Methods and Strategies*. Oxford: Butterworth-Heinemann.

Gallagher, L. 2017. Airbnb's profits to top $3 billion by 2020. *Fortune* [Online]. Available: http://fortune.com/2017/02/15/airbnb-profits/ [Accessed 29 June 2017].

Gartner, W. 1988. 'Who is an entrepreneur?' is the wrong question. *American Journal of Small Business*, 12, 11–32.

Gersch, L. 2013. The velocity of obsolescence. *Forbes* [Online]. Available: www.forbes.com/sites/lewisgersh/2013/07/29/the-velocity-of-obsolescence/#448513c96596 [Accessed 07 January 2018].

Getz, D., Carlsen, J. and Morrison, A. 2004. *The Family Business in Tourism and Hospitality*. Wallingford: CABI Publishing.

Global Wellness Institute. 2017. *Statistics and Facts* [Online]. Global Wellness Institute. Available: www.globalwellnessinstitute.org/press-room/statistics-and-facts/ [Accessed 17 May 2017].

Govers, R., Van Hecke, E. and Cabus, P. 2008. Delineating tourism: defining the usual environment. *Annals of Tourism Research*, 35, 1053–1073.

Graburn, N. and Jafari, J. 1991. Introduction: tourism social science. *Annals of Tourism Research*, 18, 1–11.

Grant, R. 2003. *Ghost Riders: Travels with American Nomads*. London: Abacus.

Gunn, C. 1994. A perspective on the purpose and nature of tourism research methods. *In:* Richie, J. B. R. and Goeldner, C. R. (eds.), *Travel, Tourism and Hospitality Research: A Handbook for Managers and Researchers*, 2nd ed. New York: Wiley.

Hamel, G. 2000. *Leading the Revolution*. Cambridge, MA: Harvard University Press.

Hatten, T. S. 2016. *Small Business Management: Entrepreneurship and Beyond*. Boston, MA: Cengage Learning.

Information Research Management Association. 2017. *Entrepreneurship: Concepts, Methodologies, Tools, and Applications*. Hershey, PA: IGI Global.

International Finance Corporation. 2017. *MSME Country Indicators*. International Finance Corporation.

IPK International. 2016. *ITB World Travel Trends Report 2016–17*. Berlin: Messe Berlin GmbH.

Johnson, K. 1981. Towards an understanding of labour turnover. *Service Industries Review*, 4–17.

Kibedi, G. 1979. Development of tourism entrepreneurs in Canada. *The Tourist Review*, 34, 9–11.

Kirzner, I. M. 1997. Entrepreneurial discovery and the competitive market process: an Austrian approach. *Journal of Economic Literature*, 35, 60–85.

Langley, A. 1999. Strategies for theorizing from process data. *Academy of Management Review*, 24, 691–710.

Lee-Ross, D. and Lashley, C. 2009. *Entreprneurship and Small Business Management in the Hospitality Industry*. Oxford: Butterworth-Heinemann.

Leiper, N. 1990. Tourist attraction systems. *Annals of Tourism Research*, 17.

Li, L. 2008. A review of entrepreneurship research published in the hospitality and tourism management journals. *Tourism Management*, 29, 1013–1022.

Lippe-McGraw, J. 2017. Women are becoming more adventurous travelers – and doing it alone. *Condé Nast Traveler* [Online]. Available: www.cntraveler.com/story/solo-female-adventure-travel-is-on-the-rise [Accessed 4 January 2018].

Lopez de Avila, A. 2015. Smart destinations: XXI century tourism. *ENTER2015 Conference on Information and Communication Technologies in Tourism*. Lugano, Switzerland.

Low, M. 2001. The adolescence of entrepreneurship research: specification of purpose. *Entrepreneurship Theory and Practice*, 25.

Masberg, B. 1998. Defining the tourist: is it possible? A view from the Convention and Visitors Bureau. *Journal of Travel Research*, 37, 67–71.

Middleton, V. and Likoris, L. 2005. *British Tourism: The Remarkable Story of Growth*. Oxford: Elsevier Butterworth-Heinemann.

Mitton, D. 1989. The compleat entrepreneur. *Entrepreneurship Theory and Practice*, 13, 9–19.

Morrison, A., Rimmington, M. and Williams, C. 1999. *Entrepreneurship in the Hospitality, Tourism and Leisure Industries*. Oxford: Butterworth-Heinemann.

Page, S., Forer, P. and Lawton, G. R. 1999. Small business development and tourism: terra incognita? *Tourism Management*, 20, 435–459.

Patterson, I., Sie, L., Balderas-Cejudo, A. and Rivera-Hernaez, O. 2017. Changing trends in the baby boomer travel market: importance of memorable experiences. *Journal of Hospitality Marketing and Management*, 26, 347–360.

Preferred Hotel Group. 2011. *Multigenerational Travel. The Next Powerful Growth Opportunity in the Travel Industry*. Preferred Hotel Group.

Rayner, A. 2017. *The Top 7 Tourism Trends for 2016* [Online]. Available: www.escapehere.com/travel-tips/the-top-7-tourism-trends-for-2016/# [Accessed 17 May 2017].

Russell, R. 2006. The contribution of entrepreneurship theory to the TALC model. *In:* Butler, R. (ed.), *The Tourism Area Life Cycle, Vol. 2, Conceptual and Theoretical Issues*. Clevedon: Channel View.

Sahlman, W. A. 1996. Some thoughts on business plans. *In:* Sahlman, W. A., Stevenson, H., Roberts, M. J. and Bhide, A. V. (eds.), *The Entrepreneurial Venture*. Boston, MA: Harvard Business School Press.

Shane, S. 2003. *A General Theory of Entrepreneurship: The Individual-Opportunity Nexus*. Cheltenham: Edward Elgar.

Shane, S. and Venkataraman, S. 2000. The promise of entrepreneurship as a field of research. *Academy of Management Review*, 25, 217–226.

Shaw, G. and Williams, A. 2004. From lifestyle consumption to lifestyle production: changing patterns of tourism entrepreneurship. *In:* Thomas, R. (ed.), *Small Firms in Tourism: International Perspectives*. London: Elsevier.

Stevenson, H. and Jarillo, C. 1991. A new entrepreneurial paradigm. *In:* Etzioni, A. and Lawrence, P. (eds.), *Socio-economics: Toward a New Synthesis*. New York: M. E. Sharpe.

Thomas, R., Shaw, G. and Page, S. 2011. Understanding small firms in tourism: a perspective on research trends and challenges. *Tourism Management*, 32, 963–976.

Timmons, J. A. 1989. *The Entrepreneurial Mind*. Andover, MA: Brick House Publishing.

Tribe, J. 1997. The indiscipline of tourism. *Annals of Tourism Research*, 24, 638–657.

TripAdvisor Inc. 2017. *2016 Annual Report*.

UNWTO. 2014. *Glossary of Tourism Terms*. Geneva: UNWTO.

UNWTO. 2016. *UNWTO Tourism Highlights*. Geneva: UNWTO.

UNWTO. 2017a. Chinese tourists spent 12% more in travelling abroad in 2016. PR 17046. Geneva: UNWTO.

UNWTO 2017b. *UNWTO Tourism Highlights*. Madrid: UNWTO.

Vaugeois, N. and Rollins, R. 2007. Mobility into tourism refuge employer. *Annals of Tourism Research*, 34, 630–648.

Wiklund, J., Davidsson, P., Audretsch, D. and Karlsson, C. 2011. The future of entrepreneurship research. *Entrepreneurship Theory and Practice*, 35, 1–9.

Yang, L. and Wall, G. 2008. Ethnic tourism and entrepreneurship: Xishuangbanna, Yunnan, China. *Tourism Geographies*, 10, 522–544.

Zhao, W., Brent Ritchie, J. and Echtner, C. 2011. Social capital and tourism entrepreneurship. *Annals of Tourism Research*, 38, 1570–1593.

Chapter 2

Conceptual foundations of entrepreneurship

> There is probably no group of individuals that have received more discussion and have been assumed to be more heterogeneous from the rest of the population than entrepreneurs.
>
> (Alvarez and Busenitz, 2001:757)

> Although an opportunity for entrepreneurial profit might exist, an individual can earn this profit only if he or she recognizes that the opportunity exists and has value.
>
> (Shane and Venkataraman, 2000:221)

Introduction

Theorising about entrepreneurship, Bygrave and Hofer (1991:13) write 'Good science has to begin with good definitions. Perhaps some empiricists believe they can function without precise definitions, but we doubt it.' Bygrave and Hofer are right in their claim where the aim is to collect data, particularly quantitative data, but science and knowledge progress via reflection as well as empiricism; witness the plethora of conceptual papers in leading tourism and entrepreneurship journals.[1] The aim of this and the next chapter is not to provide ultimate definitions of the entrepreneur, the entrepreneurial process, innovation or an opportunity, but to provide different perspectives on all of these so that we may better appreciate the nature of entrepreneurship and its relationship with tourism.

More specifically, this chapter introduces key concepts within the field of entrepreneurship that will help make sense of entrepreneurship in tourism. Specifically the chapter will explore the personality of the entrepreneur, which – as the quotation by Alvarez and Busenitz (2001:757) suggests – is the most studied aspect of entrepreneurship. The nature of the entrepreneurial mindset is reviewed because of its currency, and because of its value as an extension to the entrepreneurial personality debates. How entrepreneurs deal with failure and how failure has been conceptualised provides a further point for discussion in relation to the entrepreneur. The chapter then moves on to opportunity, its role in entrepreneurship and why some individuals and not others recognise and then act on opportunities, an issue of immediate and ongoing concern to scholars of entrepreneurship, which, if understood better, may also present some practical implications for latent entrepreneurs and policy-makers. The chapter concludes with a review of the concept of new venture creation and entrepreneurship within existing organisations, or intrapreneurship.

Learning outcomes

At the end of this chapter the reader should be able to:

- Discuss the existence of entrepreneurial traits and how the concept of the entrepreneurial mindset offers a new perspective on the personality of the entrepreneur.
- Critically evaluate the concept of failure in entrepreneurship.
- Understand the nature of opportunity, why some opportunities remain undiscovered by some, and how opportunities can be created.
- Explain how entrepreneurship can manifest itself within tourism organisations in the form of tourism intrapreneurship.

The entrepreneur

Just what characterises entrepreneurs, what distinguishes them from non-entrepreneurs and what motivates them is one of the most discussed issues in entrepreneurship, although the same may not be said of entrepreneurs in tourism (Ahmad, 2015). This may add to the mystique surrounding entrepreneurs, who are regularly held up as heroes (Gibb, 2002), as the generators of economic growth, the torchbearers of economic renewal bringing about, as Schumpeter (1934) famously argued, gales of creative destruction. The Schumpeterian entrepreneur is not necessarily representative of all entrepreneurs as Bygrave and Hofer (1991:18) suggest:

> The destiny of emerging industries is determined by Schumpeterian entrepreneurs who, above all else, are anything but average! They are truly exceptional, but population ecology is unable to recognize them.

The difficulty in agreeing what, if any, characteristic entrepreneurs share is demonstrated by de Vries who asks (1985:160) 'What are entrepreneurs like? What distinguishes them from other businesspeople? Although as a group they are not easy to get a handle on, some characteristics seem to be common to all of them.' Then, at the same time, de Vries also claims (1985:161): 'let's keep in mind that entrepreneurs are not a homogeneous group. They come in all sizes, each with his or her own characteristics.' So, what de Vries is suggesting is that as a group entrepreneurs share certain characteristics, but each entrepreneur is unique in his/her own individual way. Effectively what he is warning against is the so-called ecological fallacy of drawing conclusions about an individual based on group characteristics.

It is still very common to encounter the belief that all entrepreneurs, as individuals, share certain characteristics, and there exists a vast body of literature that tries to establish what these characteristics are – indeed, research in this area is now so abundant that a number of meta-analyses such as that by Rauch and Frese (2007) exist. The popular press is particularly prone to draw, uncritically, conclusions about the relevance of personality traits to entrepreneurs and entrepreneurial success. Popular articles that seek to promote action – such as the one by Smale (2015) entitled '10 traits all successful entrepreneurs share' – are indicative of this trait approach to entrepreneurship where he suggests successful entrepreneurs are characterised by the following:

1   Full of determination
2   Not afraid to take risks
3   High level of confidence
4   Craves learning
5   Understands failure is part of the game
6   Passionate about his or her business
7   Highly adaptable
8   Good understanding of money management
9   Expert at networking
10 Ability to sell and promote

It seems fairly evident that any of these traits are likely to enhance an entrepreneur's success, just as they would assist anyone's career development more generally. It is not then that we argue specifically against any of these traits (or characteristics) of successful entrepreneurs (however success may be defined – it need not be the same for everyone – see the section on lifestyle entrepreneurship); it is just that the evidence provided to support them is anecdotal in Smale's (2015) case. Just as it is possible to find entrepreneurs that fit these characteristics, we can find successful entrepreneurs that are risk-averse, that perhaps are not good at networking but that have set up as a partnership where the partner has this skill, where determination means they are highly inflexible and so forth.

Early writings such as those by McClelland and Winter (1969) popularised the trait approach to entrepreneurship and in fact it is precisely the nature of what an entrepreneur does as a result of what s/he is (leading, organising resources, seeking opportunities for innovation) that has been discussed by notable economic luminaries in the past (e.g., Richard Cantillon, Jean-Baptiste Say, Alfred Marshall, Joseph Schumpeter). While there have been critiques of measures frequently employed to measure entrepreneurial traits (Caird, 1993) this has not prevented the proliferation of entrepreneurial trait studies. Examples of traits or characteristics that characterise entrepreneurs frequently found in the literature are:

• High need for autonomy
• High need for achievement/self-actualisation
• Inability to submit to authority (similar to high need for autonomy)
• High in social competence or strong persuasive powers
• Enjoying uncertainty or 'high stress tolerance' or tolerance for ambiguity
• Risk-taking, or moderate risk-taking
• Commitment to making things happen, or a 'proactive personality', or 'initiative', or 'action orientation'
• Creativity
• High locus of control/belief in control of one's own destiny

- Leadership
- Optimism
- Persistence
- Passion

While the trait approach to entrepreneurship sometimes ignores issues surrounding entrepreneurial success, attempting only to identify who becomes an entrepreneur, Bygrave and Hofer (1991) suggest that research on the entrepreneur also encompasses:

1   Why people become entrepreneurs.
2   What the characteristics are of successful entrepreneurs.
3   What the characteristics are of unsuccessful entrepreneurs.

Typically, points 2 and 3 above are tackled by the 'self-help' literature as demonstrated in the example by above by Smale (2015). The answer to the question as to why people become entrepreneurs is indeed intricate and will depend on both individual and environmental factors. As we have seen, even if we were to focus solely on personality factors, i.e., factors unique to the individual, the question as to the 'why' of entrepreneurship will not have a single answer. In terms of motives for engaging in entrepreneurship, as long ago as 1963 Cyert and March (1963:9) noted: 'Entrepreneurs, like anyone else, have a host of personal motives.' There now exists a substantial body of literature on necessity versus opportunity entrepreneurship (also push versus pull factors) (e.g., Valdez and Richardson, 2013; Verheul et al., 2010; Giacomin et al., 2011; Nabi et al., 2013), which indicates the interplay of person and environment when it comes to explaining entrepreneurship at the level of the individual, as well as at the macro level.

In writing of *becoming*, Bygrave and Hofer (1991) refute the notion that entrepreneurs are born and not made, and the recognition that entrepreneurship is situational, i.e., that it happens in a particular context, suggests that entrepreneurship can be promoted. This might seem a rather banal 'insight' and yet its implications are profound if we consider entrepreneurship education, for instance. At its extreme it would mean no amount of education will help you if you do not have the 'entrepreneurial gene'. In fact, the failure of many studies to identify outcomes associated with entrepreneurial personality traits led to Gartner's (1988) view that attempts to identify an entrepreneurial personality were fundamentally misguided.

In contrast to the 'born not made' view of the entrepreneur we have definitions such as that by Rae (1999), which stresses how the individual will develop over time a set of thinking patterns or personal theories that enable him or her to perceive, filter, analyse, decide and act on opportunities more effectively than others. Here the link to learning is provided very directly, regardless of whether one focuses on learning that involves a change in knowledge or the outcome of that change, i.e., a change in actual behaviour (Lachman, 2010).

Shane and Venkataraman's (2000) conceptual framework for entrepreneurship similarly criticises the excessive focus on the characteristics of the entrepreneur. Rather than looking, however, solely at *becoming* an entrepreneur, they focus on the role of opportunities as presented by the environment. Theirs is a context-dependent view of entrepreneurship. In their own words (Shane and Venkataraman, 2000:218):

> Since a large and diverse group of people engage in the transitory process of entrepreneurship, it is improbable that entrepreneurship can be explained solely by

reference to a characteristic of certain people independent of the situations in which they find themselves.

Entrepreneurial mindset

Despite the criticism levied against the trait approach to understanding entrepreneurs, today, some researchers such as Davis et al. (2016) argue there is a renewed interest in personality traits of entrepreneurs. They recognise that entrepreneurs are likely to be characterised by a combination of personality traits, and furthermore, that personality traits may be mediated by other variables. Based on this understanding they have looked at how an 'entrepreneurial mindset' defined as motives, skills and thought processes may distinguish entrepreneurs from non-entrepreneurs. By including skills and motives, Davis et al. (2016) are moving the definition of personality traits beyond their usual scope. They developed their Entrepreneurial Mindset Profile (EMP) based on 14 scales divided into traits (personality factors that are unlikely to change much) and skills (dimensions that can be altered by training, practice or intervention).

Developing an entrepreneurial mindset is of concern to tourism organisations that seek to foster an entrepreneurial orientation and as such is further discussed in Chapter 7.

Table 2.1 Dimensions of the Entrepreneurial Mindset Profile

Traits	Skills
Independence	Future focus
Preference for limited structure	Idea generation
Non-conformity	Execution
Risk acceptance	Self-confidence
Action orientation	Optimism
Passion	Persistence
Need to achieve	Interpersonal sensitivity

Source: Davis et al. (2016)

Types of entrepreneur

Just as Bygrave and Hofer (1991) have pointed to a distinction between successful and non-successful entrepreneurs, others have identified a range of entrepreneurial types. Table 2.2 provides an overview of different types of entrepreneur.

Failure and entrepreneurship

The concept of failure in entrepreneurship is something of a paradox. One imagines failure would in most, if not all, circumstances be something to avoid. It comes with liabilities such as stigma and damaged reputation of individuals associated with previously unsuccessful ventures (Amankwah-Amoah, 2016), let alone sunk costs (time and money). But, at the same time, failure provides much scope for

Table 2.2 Types of entrepreneur

Entrepreneur type	Definition
Entrepreneur	Is someone who perceives an opportunity and creates an organisation to pursue it (Bygrave and Hofer, 1991:14).
Serial entrepreneur	Someone who takes on one project at a time (Ucbasaran et al., 2011:26).
Nascent entrepreneur	Those individuals who start to commit time and resources to founding a new firm (Wagner, 2007).
Portfolio entrepreneur	Those who hold multiple businesses simultaneously (Ucbasaran et al., 2011:26).
Latent entrepreneur	Those who state that they would prefer being self-employed over being an employee (Blanchflower, 2004).
Lifestyle entrepreneur	Entrepreneurs who *seek* lifestyle opportunities. . . around which a business can be built (Ateljevic and Doorne, 2000; see also Chapter 11).

learning and improvement. Constant failure is clearly not a good thing, but if the entrepreneur learns from failure then good may, ultimately, come out of it (Ucbasaran et al., 2011).

Fear of failure defined by Wyrwich et al. (2016:469) as 'the perceived risk of experiencing failure and its consequences when engaging in entrepreneurship' can serve both as a driver and as an inhibitor of entrepreneurship, although commonly it is the latter that features in the entrepreneurship literature (Cacciotti et al., 2016). Fear of failure is a socio-cultural trait. This means that in some cultures more than in others, failure is stigmatised and therefore seen as something to be ashamed of. Within this cultural context, fear of failure is closely related to risk aversion.

Fear of failure as an inhibitor of entrepreneurship features in the Global Entrepreneurship Monitor's (GEM) evaluation of nations' entrepreneurial ecosystems. The GEM fear of failure rate reflects the percentage of 18–64 population who indicate that fear of failure would prevent them from setting up a business. Data from 2013 indicate that the country with the highest rate at 69% is Greece and the country with the lowest score at 17% is Malawi (the mean rate is 38%). There is evidently a great deal of variation in attitudes towards fear of failure globally.

Rather than inhibiting entrepreneurship, fear of failure can also serve as a motivator in an attempt to avoid failure. However, at times in fact it seems as though there is now almost a 'cult of failure' (Isenberg, 2011). There are those that suggest failure should be embraced rather than avoided. However, Isenberg (2011) is very clear: failure should not be celebrated. It is inevitable that at some point failure in one form or another will occur, but clearly failure is to be avoided and only has value if we do in fact then learn from it. As Ucbasaran et al. (2011) argue, serial entrepreneurs are regularly admired for their pluck and courage but come under scrutiny from venture capitalists to see if they have actually learned anything from past failures. Failure should keep over-optimism in check, but if it does not one is liable to commit the same mistakes repeatedly.

Opportunity

Opportunity represents the cornerstone of entrepreneurship. 'To have entrepreneurship, you must first have entrepreneurial opportunities' (Shane and Venkataraman, 2000:220). Unsurprisingly, Bygrave and Hofer (1991:14) therefore refer to the entrepreneur as 'someone who perceives an opportunity and creates an organization to pursue it', which aligns with Kirzner's (1973) view of entrepreneurship as 'alertness to opportunity'. In tourism, opportunities are frequently seen in markets that are expanding rapidly (e.g., growing middle class in emerging economies) or in destinations that have yet to be 'tapped'. As a growing number of the world's population travel, these 'undiscovered' destinations are becoming increasingly rare. Frequently, destinations are victims of their own success, with unscrupulous marketing sharing some of the blame (e.g., urging tourists to visit before the destination 'becomes spoilt'; Goodwin, 2011).

One of the key discussion points in entrepreneurship is whether opportunities are created, or already exist and therefore just need to be discovered. For Shane and Venkataraman (2000), as for others (Schumpeter, 1934; Kirzner, 1997), opportunities are objective, they exist, waiting to be exploited. One reason why some individuals and not others discover opportunities is therefore provided by 'asymmetrical distribution of information'; this means not everyone has equal access to the same information. As opportunities begin to be exploited more information about them becomes available, information asymmetries break down and the process goes on until there is no longer any opportunity to exploit (in economic-speak, marginal rates of return are zero[2]).

However, opportunity discovery differs between individuals on the basis of unequal access to information, but also because people interpret the same information in different ways. This is what Alvarez and Busenitz (2001:756) refer to when they claim: 'Entrepreneurial opportunities exist primarily because different agents have different beliefs about the relative value of resources when they are converted from inputs into outputs.' What is subjective is people's ability to recognise opportunities as summarised in this quote attributed to Albert Szent-Gyorgyi (a Hungarian biochemist credited with 'discovering' vitamin C): 'Discovery is seeing what everybody else has seen, and thinking what nobody else has thought.'

Butler's (1980) Tourism Area Lifecycle (TALC) lends itself very well to illustrate how information about commercial opportunities in tourism is recognised at different rates by tourism entrepreneurs. TALC is one of the most, possibly *the* most cited model in tourism. The model posits destinations go through stages of development: exploration, involvement, development, consolidation, stagnation followed by rejuvenation or decline. Development (tourist numbers over time) takes the shape of an 'S-curve'. Tourism growth is initially slow (few people recognise the commercial opportunity, perhaps because few people are aware of demand for their destination from tourists as this is latent). A few forward-thinking individuals, perhaps only one, recognise a commercial opportunity by providing a guesthouse to travellers who had previously stayed with friends and family, or who had stayed informally with accommodating locals. The guesthouse is quite successful, news spreads and other individuals start to take note, recognising and then deciding to act on the opportunity. The process repeats itself, and growth in terms of tourist arrivals speeds up. Soon the opportunity is so obvious, and examples of how to exploit the opportunity abound, that the market floods, returns start to fall as prices come down as competition grows and supply of accommodation and facilities outstrips demand, ultimately to the point where the opportunity no longer exists or is so small the opportunity costs are too high. In theory at least this is what happens.

In support of the notion above that even with the same access to information individuals will respond differently to opportunities, Kirzner (1997:62) argues entrepreneurial discovery is about more than overcoming imperfect information but about 'gradually and systematically pushing back the boundaries of sheer ignorance. It is about discovering our ignorance and therefore should contain an element of surprise; "one had hitherto not realised one's ignorance".' A question that arises therefore is how are opportunities discovered, or how do we 'wake up' and realise our ignorance? The question as to why some individuals see opportunities where others see none is so fundamental to entrepreneurship that Herbert and Link (1988) describe the traditional economist's view of an entrepreneur as an opportunity seeker (not dissimilar to Von Mises, 1949).

A crucial distinction in entrepreneurship which helps us understand how some people become entrepreneurs and others do not is that between opportunity discovery and opportunity exploitation. Thus, why is it that some individuals will see an opportunity, recognise it for what it is (i.e., recognise its potential) and yet still not seize or exploit it? In fact, it is often following through with an idea that is the hurdle to new venture creation and perhaps unsurprisingly therefore Von Mises (1949) regards the entrepreneur as an 'acting man [sic]' (not just a discoverer of opportunities), the same idea Shane and Venkataraman (2000) adopt in their seminal article: discovery, evaluation *and* exploitation of profitable opportunities.

It is very easy to fall into the trap of explaining why some opportunities are exploited and others are not, solely on the basis of the characteristics of the entrepreneur such as attitudes to risk, fear of failure, and self-efficacy, for example. Any explanation should, however, also take into account the nature of the opportunity itself. It stands to reason that the greater the potential returns, the greater the likelihood of an opportunity being acted upon. Pursuing an opportunity involves costs, financial usually, but also in terms of an individual's time. Opportunity costs will also be considered; that is, what other opportunity could have been invested in (both in terms of time and money, including leisure). In fact, there is some literature that suggests the relationship between levels of education and levels of entrepreneurship is shaped like an inverted 'U' curve: as education levels increase, individuals feel more able to start a business and this becomes more attractive to them. However, at some point an individual's education level means they can command high salaries in the labour market and therefore the opportunity cost of starting a business is also higher – i.e., the business start-up option becomes less attractive (Giacomin et al., 2011). The value of what appears to be an objective opportunity will be perceived subjectively by different individuals (how much does an individual value his/her time, what other opportunities are available and so forth). Thus, not only is information not equally available, even where it is individuals will have subjective preferences resulting in varying rates of opportunity exploitation.

The requirement for action as well as the subjectivity surrounding opportunities is recognised in Shapero's (1982) model of the entrepreneurial event (commonly referred to as SEE), which has been used to explain entrepreneurial intent in tourism (e.g., Walmsley and Thomas, 2009). SEE hypothesises that the intent to start a business derives from perceptions of desirability and feasibility and, crucially, from a propensity to act upon opportunities. Even furnished with the same information surrounding an opportunity, individuals will respond differently to it depending on how attractive (desirable) the opportunity is to them personally (yes, I would like to run a yacht charter business), how feasible it is to them personally (as much as I'd like to own a yacht charter business, the extent of my knowledge of yachts is close to zero!), and finally the propensity to act, or the readiness for action.

Case study 2.1: Opportunity discovery, evaluation and exploitation at Deliveroo

Deliveroo, a London-based delivery service, has entered the world of 'dark kitchens'. Deliveroo has spotted a market for high-end dining at home on the back of a dramatic rise in demand for home delivery (in 2016 demand for home delivery grew ten times faster than for dining out). At Deliveroo Editions, food from around the world is prepared by chefs from different London restaurants but there are no diners. The restaurants provide the meals (chefs and menus) and Deliveroo then coordinates orders and delivery.

The food-delivery market itself is not new. In the UK, Chinese and Indian takeaways began offering a delivery option in the 1950s. However, things remained largely unchanged for decades with a focus at the lower end of the market. Then, just over a decade ago Just Eat provided a website offering a platform to access restaurant food available for home delivery. In 2013 Deliveroo then took this a step further when it assumed responsibility for delivery too. This opened the option to restaurants that traditionally did not deliver to be integrated into the home delivery market.

The opportunity as perceived by Deliveroo relies not just on changing market trends; changes in technology are key too. A key problem that has prevented expansion of the idea previously was distance of the customer to the food source. If you lived too far away, quality would suffer. Deliveroo's 'real time dispatch algorithm' has overcome the issue by being able to coordinate chefs and delivery better. An order comes in from a customer straight to the chef via a tablet. The chef then prepares the food. As soon as it is ready the chef presses a buzzer and a 'runner' collects the food, takes it to a despatch watch where it is repackaged and kept warm momentarily under a heater. Outside, couriers monitor a screen for the signal that they are to collect their charge.

It also helps that Deliveroo select which restaurants to include in which area based on a mass of data at their disposal. They are able to share data with restaurants and do so on a daily basis, for example on number of re-ordered dishes. It is not all plain sailing, however; other companies have failed with similar concepts (e.g., SpoonRocket, Sprig, Munchery and Maple). For now, however, it is 'The restaurant is dead. Long live the restaurant.'

Source: Adapted from Garlick (2017).

New venture creation

As we have seen, frequently entrepreneurship is equated with business start-up. Although we recognise that business start-up does not sufficiently describe entrepreneurship (the salaried managing director of a fast-growing, medium-size firm may be much more entrepreneurial than the owner-manager of a small 'lifestyle' firm; Casson and Della Giusta, 2007:223), entrepreneurship is frequently understood to mean business start-up. The process of venture creation, here referring to setting up a new business, has been widely studied and this is the focus of this section.

Gartner (1985) has gone to some trouble in conceptualising the phenomenon of new venture creation. At the outset Gartner (1985:696) clarifies that differences among entrepreneurs and among their ventures are 'as great as the variation between entrepreneurs and non-entrepreneurs and between new firms and established firms'. In fact, if the creation of new ventures followed a standard procedure, there would be no use for a framework; one would simply describe the process and be done with it. The fact that Gartner's (1985) framework identifies interrelationships between four distinct dimensions (Figure 2.1) signals that new venture creation is complex. For Gartner (1985) no new venture can be comprehensively described until each one of these four elements, and the way they interact, is explored.

According to Figure 2.1, the four dimensions comprise: individual(s) – the person(s) involved in starting a new organisation; (b) organisation – the kind of firm that is started; (c) environment – the situation surrounding and influencing the

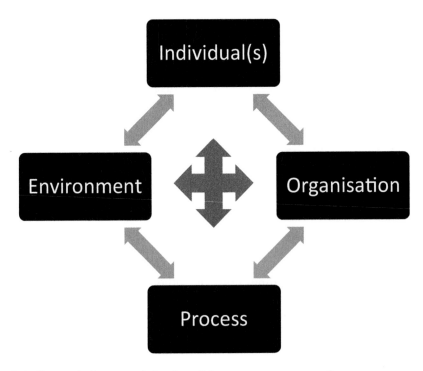

Figure 2.1 Gartner's framework for describing new venture creation

new organisation; and (d) new venture process – the actions undertaken by the individual(s) to start the venture.

Examples of variables associated with the dimensions are:

- Individual: need for achievement, locus of control, risk-taking propensity.
- Environment: venture capital availability, proximity of universities, levels of competitive rivalry.
- Organisation: overall cost leadership, licensing, the new product or service.
- Process: the entrepreneur locates a business opportunity, the entrepreneur accumulates resources, the entrepreneur produces the product/offers the service.

If we were to consider the application of Gartner's framework to the creation of a new tourism venture we could suggest the following:

- Individual: values a particular geographic location, values a hobby or activity associated with the tourism venture that has been created (these examples relate to lifestyle entrepreneurs).
- Environment: availability of migrant labour, infrastructure that meets the need of tourists, existence of a destination management/marketing organisation (DMO).
- Organisation: focused on service quality, perishability of the product/service that will involve revenue management.
- Process: initial outlay before income is generated, which can be small (e.g., selling souvenirs) or substantial (running an owned hotel), liaising with a DMO, undertaking legally required training (e.g., food handling or health and safety).

Intrapreneurship

'What you need is a corporate culture that nurtures its intrapreneurs, which I deem to be the lifeblood of any well-run hospitality organization', argues Larry Mogelonsky, owner of a hotel management consultancy (Mogelonsky, 2016). It is often suggested that to succeed in today's competitive environment tourism firms, whether large or small, established or new, must be entrepreneurial. Table 1.1 in Chapter 1 offered examples of trends that are changing the tourism business landscape. These changes, which are ongoing, present opportunities to entrepreneurs but also carry risks for those firms unwilling to change. Being able to identify changes in the marketplace, in the competitive environment, is not something that concerns only new businesses, but in equal measure should be of concern to existing tourism firms. That said, corporate entrepreneurship was found to be the least studied aspect of entrepreneurship in tourism and hospitality by Li (2008).

As Parker (2011) has pointed out, the term 'new venture creation' can in fact refer to a new venture in an existing organisation (although in the previous section this was conveniently ignored and commonly the expression is taken to mean the creation of a new business). Indeed, entrepreneurship as we have argued previously is not restricted to business start-up. In Shane and Venkataraman's words (2000:219): 'entrepreneurship does not require, but can include, the creation of new organizations' and likewise therefore the entrepreneur 'may indeed exist in all types and sizes of private and public sector organisation' (Gibb, 1996:312). Entrepreneurship, if manifesting itself in an existing firm, is frequently referred to as intrapreneurship, corporate entrepreneurship or corporate venturing (see for example Kuratko and Hodgetts, 2001). The term intrapreneur and corporate entrepreneur are in turn defined by Kuratko et al. (1990:5) as 'corporate managers who exhibit entrepreneurial spirit in terms of idea generation, creativity and drive in the course of carrying out their work: marshalling resources and influencing and championing . . . new ideas from development to complete profitable reality'. Covin and Miles (1999:50) offer a broader remit to corporate entrepreneurship by suggesting it is 'the presence of innovation with the objective of rejuvenating or redefining organizations, markets, or industries in order to create or sustain competitive superiority'. Dess et al. (1999) distinguish two types of corporate entrepreneurship: one is linked to the birth of new businesses within an existing organisation, akin to Parker's (2011) definition of intrapreneurship; the other one refers to a much broader issue, the transformation of organisations through strategic renewal (we review this latter issue in more detail in Chapters 7 and 8).

The idea that intrapreneurship is an important factor in a firm's success gained traction in the 1980s with the publication of titles such as those by Pinchot (1985), *Intrapreneuring: Why You Don't Have to Leave the Corporation to Become an Entrepreneur*, or Lessem (1986), *Intrapreneurship: How to be an Enterprising Individual in a Successful Business*. The recognition that firms can be distinguished based on whether they are entrepreneurial or not predates this (Collins and St Moore, 1970; Cooper, 1979; Smith, 1967). For Stevenson and Jarillo (1991) the issue of intrapreneurship is so important that they claim how to foster entrepreneurship in existing organisations is one of three predominant approaches to the analysis of entrepreneurship itself (the other two being the results of entrepreneurship and the causes of entrepreneurship).

The academic study of intrapreneurship in tourism is quite limited. Getz et al.'s (2004) work on the family business in tourism suggests that the intrapreneur displays entrepreneurship within the limits of an existing organisation, mirroring the definitions provided by many entrepreneurship scholars previously. Lee-Ross and Lashley's (2009:51) text describes managers that are able to generate growth and a profitable business as entrepreneurial. They reserve the term intrapreneurs for those who only have a 'tangential' relationship with the owners of the tourism firm (the idea here is that the owner of the firm will have created the venture and is therefore an entrepreneur). As intrapreneurship is something driven by individuals, the focus is understandably on the human resources function, including leadership within the organisation. These issues are so important they will be discussed separately in Chapter 7.

Summary

Chapter 2 has offered a discussion of some key concepts in entrepreneurship. The chapter began by reviewing the entrepreneur him/herself, not least because characteristics of the entrepreneur have been the most studied issue in entrepreneurship research. Even though many entrepreneurs share certain traits, it should not be forgotten that entrepreneurs are a diverse group of individuals. There is no magic formula or list of traits one must display to be an entrepreneur. A review of the concept of the entrepreneurial mindset offers a view that accepts some of the ideas behind the notion of an entrepreneurial personality, but recognises that many of these traits are mediated and that motivation and skills will play an equally important role in determining entrepreneurial behaviour.

The chapter also reviewed the concept of failure as it is a good example of a concept that, depending on context, can both stymie or foster entrepreneurship. Fear of failure may prevent some from starting a firm, but it may also encourage the nascent entrepreneur, driving him/her forward in the quest to establish a successful firm.

Opportunity – its identification, evaluation and exploitation – plays a fundamental role in entrepreneurship and has been the focus of much research by economists in particular. Opportunities are not recognised in equal measure by everyone. Individuals do not have the same access to information, and even where they do, the information is interpreted subjectively. This evaluation will depend on a number of personal factors, not least opportunity costs (here we provided an example of how levels of education are related to the opportunity cost of being a salaried employee – the higher the level of education, the higher the level of opportunity cost).

The final sections of the chapter looked at the framework for new venture creation and intrapreneurship. Drawing on Gartner's (1985) work, the framework for new venture creation was posited to consist of four elements: the individual (entrepreneur), the new venture that s/he is trying to set up, the process of setting up the venture and the environment surrounding the venture. All of these factors will come together to shape the characteristics of the new venture. Intrapreneurship was discussed to support the view that entrepreneurship itself extends beyond the creation of a new business. In fact, intrapreneurship is regarded by many as key to a firm's success in the turbulent, competitive environment engulfing many tourism firms. The issue is so important that Chapters 7 and 8 will discuss a firm's entrepreneurial orientation in greater detail.

Review questions/discussion points

1   Identify a tourism entrepreneur. What do you think are his or her traits that have led to success/failure? If working with others, compare your results.
2   Identify a commercial opportunity in tourism. Consider why this might present a good opportunity, what the challenges with the opportunity might be. Do you think this opportunity could be discovered by anyone? Why/why not?
3   How do you view failure? Does it motivate you to try harder, or does it have the opposite effect?
4   What do you think is the key characteristic of an entrepreneur? Discuss this with others.
5   Think of a work situation; for example, your current employer or somewhere you have worked in the past. Can you identify examples of intrapreneurship within this organisation? Who, if anyone, was driving the intrapreneurship? What could be done to increase greater levels of intrapreneurship in this organisation?

Notes

1 A whole branch of philosophy is dedicated to knowledge, the nature of the world (ontology) and how we can know about the world (epistemology) – it is definitively not the intention to engage in this here!

2 The marginal rate of return is zero when the cost of production of an additional unit (let's use the provision of an additional holiday as an example here) is the same as the revenue achieved by that additional unit.

References

Ahmad, S. Z. 2015. Entrepreneurship in the small and medium-sized hotel sector. *Current Issues in Tourism*, 18, 328–349.

Alvarez, S. and Busenitz, L. 2001. The entrepreneurship of resource-based theory. *Journal of Management*, 27, 755–775.

Amankwah-Amoah, J. 2016. An integrative process model of organisational failure. *Journal of Business Research*, 69.

Ateljevic, I. and Doorne, S. 2000. 'Staying within the fence': lifestyle entrepreneurship in tourism. *Journal of Sustainable Tourism*, 8, 378–392.

Blanchflower, D. G. 2004. Self-employment: more may not be better. *Swedish Economic Policy Review*, 11, 15–74.

Butler, D. 1980. The concept of a tourist area cycle of evolution: implications for management of resources. *Canadian Geographer*, 24, 5–12.

Bygrave, W. and Hofer, C. 1991. Theorizing about entrepreneurship. *Entrepreneurship Theory and Practice*, 16, 13–22.

Cacciotti, G., Haytn, J., Mitchell, R. and Giazitzoglu, A. 2016. A reconceptualization of fear of failure in entrepreneurship. *Journal of Business Venturing*, 31, 302–325.

Caird, S. 1993. What do psychological tests say about entrepreneurs? *Journal of Managerial Psychology*, 8, 11–20.

Casson, M. and Della Giusta, M. 2007. Entrepreneurship and social capital: analysing the impact of social networks on entrepreneurial activity from a rational action perspective. *International Small Business Journal*, 25, 220–244.

Collins, O. F. and St Moore, D. G. 1970. *The Organization Makers*. New York: Appleton-Century-Crofts.

Cooper, A. C. 1979. Strategic management: new ventures and small business. *In:* Schendel, D. E. and Hofer, C. W. (eds.), *Strategic Management*. Boston: Little, Brown.

Covin, J. and Miles, P. M. 1999. Corporate entrepreneurship and the pursuit of competitive advantage. *Entrepreneurship Theory and Practice*, 23, 47–63.

Cyert, R. M. and March, J. G. 1963. *A Behavioral Theory of the Firm*. Englewood Cliffs, NJ: Prentice Hall.

Davey, L. 2014. Strengthen your strategic thinking muscles. *Harvard Business Review*, 2–4.

Davis, M. H., Hall, J. and Mayer, P. 2016. Developing a new measure of entrepreneurial mindset: reliability, validity and implications for practitioners. *Counseling Psychology Journal: Practice And Research*, 68, 21–48.

de Vries, K. 1985. The dark side of entrepreneurship. *Harvard Business Review*, 63, 160–167.

Dess, G., Lumpkin, G. T. and Mcgee, J. 1999. Linking corporate entrepreneurship to strategy, structure, and process: suggested research directions. *Entrepreneurship Theory and Practice*, 23, 85–102.

Garlick, H. 2017. Dark kitchens: is this the future of takeway? *Financial Times Magazine*, 8 June 2017.

Gartner, W. 1985. A conceptual framework for describing the phenomenon of new venture creation. *Academy of Management Review*, 10, 696–706.

Gartner, W. 1988. 'Who is an entrepreneur?' is the wrong question. *American Journal of Small Business*, 12, 11–32.

Getz, D., Carlsen, J. and Morrison, A. 2004. *The Family Business in Tourism and Hospitality*. Wallingford: CABI Publishing.

Giacomin, O., Janssen, F., Guyot, J.-L. and Lohest, O. 2011. Opportunity and/or necessity entrepreneurship? The impact of the socio-economic characteristics of entrepreneurs. *MPRA Munich Personal Repec Archive*. Munich: University Of Munich.

Gibb, A. 1996. Entrepreneurship and small business management: can we afford to neglect them in the twenty-first century business school? *British Journal of Management*, 7, 309–321.

Gibb, A. 2002. In pursuit of a new 'enterprise' and 'entrepreneurship' paradigm for learning: creative destruction, new values, new ways of doing things and new combinations of knowledge. *International Journal of Management Reviews*, 4, 233–269.

Goodwin, H. 2011. *Taking Responsibility For Tourism*. Oxford: Goodfellow Publishing Ltd.

Herbert, R. F. and Link, A. N. 1988. *The Entrepreneur: Mainstream Views and Radical Critiques*. New York: Praeger.

Isenberg, D. 2011. Entrepreneurs and the cult of failure. *Harvard Business Review*, 89, 36.

Kirzner, I. M. 1973. *Competition and Entrepreneurship,* Chicago: University of Chicago Press.

Kirzner, I. M. 1997. Entrepreneurial discovery and the competitive market process: an Austrian approach. *Journal of Economic Literature*, 35, 60–85.

Kuratko, D. and Hodgetts, R. 2001. *Entrepreneurship – A Contemporary Approach*. Orlando: Harcourt College Publishers.

Kuratko, D., Montagno, R. and Hornsby, J. 1990. Developing an intrapreneurial assessment instrument for an effective corporate entrepreneurial environment. *Strategic Management Journal*, 11, 49–58.

Lachman, S. 2010. Learning is a process: toward an improved definition of learning. *Journal of Psychology*, 131, 477–480.

Lee-Ross, D. and Lashley, C. 2009. *Entreprneurship & Small Business Management in the Hospitality Industry*. Oxford: Butterworth-Heinemann.

Lessem, R. 1986. *Intrapreneurship: How to be an Enterprising Indvidual in a Successful Business*. Aldershot, Hants: Wildwood.

Li, L. 2008. A review of entrepreneurship research published in the hospitality and tourism management journals. *Tourism Management*, 29, 1013–1022.

McClelland, D. and Winter, D. 1969. *Economic Achievement*. New York: Free Press.

Mogelonsky, L. 2016. *Opinion Piece: Intrapreneurs are the Lifeblood of a Hotel* [Online]. Available: www.hospitalitynet.org/opinion/4075102.html [Accessed 12 January 2018].

Nabi, G., Walmsley, A. and Holden, R. 2013. Pushed or pulled? Exploring the factors underpinning graduate start-ups and non-start-ups. *Journal of Education and Work*, 10, 1–26.

Parker, S. 2011. Intrapreneurship or entrepreneurship? *Journal Of Business Venturing*, 26, 19–34.

Pinchot, G. 1985. *Intrapreneuring: Why You Don't Have to Leave the Corporation to Become an Entrepreneur*. New York: Harper and Row.

Rae, D. 1999. *The Entrepreneurial Spirit*. Dublin: Blackhall Publishing.

Rauch, A. and Frese, M. 2007. Let's put the person back into entrepreneurship research: a meta-analysis on the relationship between business owners' personality traits, business creation, and success. *European Journal of Work and Organizational Psychology*, 16, 353–385.

Schumpeter, J. 1934. *The Theory of Economic Development*. New York: Oxford University Press/Galaxy 1961.

Shane, S. and Venkataraman, S. 2000. The promise of entrepreneurship as a field of research. *Academy of Management Review*, 25, 217–226.

Shapero, A. 1982. Social dimensions of entrepreneurship. *In:* Kent, C. et al. (eds.), *The Encyclopedia of Entrepreneurship*. Englewood Cliffs, NJ: Prentice Hall.

Smale, T. 2015. 10 traits all successful entrepeneurs share. *Entrepreneur* [Online]. Available: www.entrepreneur.com/article/243792 [Accessed 1 March 2017].

Smith, N. 1967. *The Entrepreneur and His Firm: The Relationship Between Type of Man and Type of Company.* East Lansing: Michigan State University.

Stevenson, H. and Jarillo, C. 1991. A new entrepreneurial paradigm. *In:* Etzioni, A. and Lawrence, P. (eds.), *Socio-Economics: Toward a New Synthesis.* New York: M. E. Sharpe.

Ucbasaran, D., Westhead, P. and Wright, M. 2011. Why serial entrepreneurs don't learn from failure. *Harvard Business Review*, 89, 26.

Valdez, M. and Richardson, J. 2013. Institutional determinants of macro-level entrepreneurship. *Entrepreneurship Theory and Practice*, 37, 1149–1175.

Verheul, I., Thurik, R., Hessels, J. and Van Der Zwan, P. 2010. Factors influencing the entrepreneurial engagement of opportunity and necessity entrepreneurs. *EIM Research Reports.*

Von Mises, L. 1949. *Human Action.* New Haven: Yale University Press.

Wagner, J. 2007. Nascent entrepreneurs. *In:* Parker, S. (ed.), *The Lifecycle of Entrepreneurial Ventures.* Berlin: Springer Verlag.

Walmsley, A. and Thomas, R. 2009. Understanding and influencing entrepreneurial intentions of tourism students. *In:* Ateljevic, J. and Page, S. (eds.), *Tourism and Entrepreneurship: International Perspectives.* Oxford: Elsevier.

Wyrwich, M., Stuetzer, M. and Sternberg, R. 2016. Entrepreneurial role models, fear of failure, and institutional approval of entrepreneurship: a tale of two regions. *Small Business Economics*, 46, 467–492.

Chapter 3

Innovation

Under capitalism, innovative activity – which in other types of economy is for-tuitous and optional – becomes mandatory, a life-and-death matter for the firm.

(Baumol, 2002:1)

Tourism firms operate in a business environment where innovation is important for survival.

(Sorensen, 2007:22)

There's a way to do it better – find it.

(Thomas Edison)

Introduction

Building on Chapter 2, this chapter discusses the nature of innovation in tourism. Different types of innovation will be discussed including radical and incremental innovation. The chapter will make reference to Schumpeter's five areas in which companies can introduce innovation: (1) generation of new or improved products, (2) introduction of new production processes, (3) development of new sales markets, (4) development of new supply markets, and (5) reorganisation and/or restructuring of the company. It will also make reference to other categorisations of innovation, such as Drucker's work in this area. The chapter will look at the relationship between small firms and innovation as well as the concepts of effectuation and ideation before closing with a review of the role of crowdsourcing as a means to foster innovation.

Learning outcomes

At the end of this chapter the reader will have a critical awareness of:

- The nature of and types of innovation, from incremental to radical, and how innovation relates to entrepreneurship in tourism.
- How businesses can adopt a systematic approach to innovation.
- The difference between the logic of causation and effectuation as these relate to entrepreneurship.

Innovation

Comments that apply across sectors such as the following, 'Organizations operating under the present conditions of global competition, rapid technological advances, and resource scarcity must innovate in order to grow, to be effective, and even to survive' (Damanpour and Wischnevsky, 2006:270), are now commonplace. In tourism too, the sentiment that an increasingly competitive business environment requires increasing levels of innovation is regularly found (e.g., Kallmuenzer, 2018). There appears to be broad agreement about the importance of innovation to business growth and even survival.

Any book on entrepreneurship cannot fail to mention innovation; the two concepts are regularly uttered in the same breath. Joseph Schumpeter himself defined the entrepreneur as an innovator and others were quick to follow: 'Innovation is the activity or function of a particular set of individuals called entrepreneurs' (Sweezy, 1943:93). It was the entrepreneur as innovator who brought about 'creative destruction', who revolutionised the economic structure from within, and although often attributed to Schumpeter, other notable economists such as Von Mises have advocated a focus on the entrepreneur to explain this market process of creative destruction.

Although 'enterprise' and 'innovation' are often used interchangeably, the terms are distinct. First, whereas entrepreneurship is frequently equated with business start-up, there is little such bias surrounding the term innovation, which is applied as much to existing organisations as to new businesses. As was noted previously, entrepreneurship can also take place within the confines of an existing enterprise, i.e., intrapreneurship or corporate entrepreneurship. More than enterprise, it can be argued that innovation implies novelty. Kallmuenzer (2018:1979) makes reference to Hjalager's (2010:2) definition of innovation in tourism as 'everything that differs from business as usual or which represents a discontinuance of previous practice in some sense for the innovating firm'.[1] Hjalager (2010), however, recognises that innovation has become something of a 'buzzword' in tourism, associated with anything that is novel, but that novelty on its own is not enough. Hjalager (2010) confirms that innovation goes beyond novelty but also includes implementation. In other words, coming up with an idea is not innovation.

More than entrepreneurship, innovation must involve the introduction of something new. This view finds early recognition in Sweezy's (1943:93) work who, commenting on Schumpeter's work, asks: 'What are the characteristics of the entrepreneur? First, understandably, the ability to appreciate the possibilities of an innovation; whether or not he is also the discoverer or "inventor" of the innovation is a matter of minor consequence.' More important for the entrepreneur than coming up with something new is the desire and ability to do something with the innovation (or invention). Just as Shane and Venkataraman (2000) distinguish between opportunity discovery, evaluation and exploitation, it is possible to distinguish an innovation from entrepreneurship, the latter being the commercialisation of the innovation. This is reinforced by Rosenberg (1994, cited in Shane and Venkataraman, 2000), who points to the many inventors who failed to see the commercial application of their inventions.

Innovation, opportunity and classic economic theory

It is perhaps surprising that the role of the entrepreneur and with it the processes of opportunity discovery and exploitation have remained largely absent from standard (neoclassical) microeconomics. Kirzner (1997) argues the reason for this is that the general equilibrium model at the heart of classical microeconomics (where supply and demand are in balance) offers no room for the entrepreneur. It is a model based on equilibrium, not disruption. By way of contrast, the Austrian school of economics sees the role of the entrepreneur as fundamental to the market process. We have already encountered Schumpeter's (1934) notion of creative destruction as the driving force for change, and we point to Baumol's (2002) quotation at the start of the chapter in recognition that firm survival is predicated on innovation, an issue picked up by Sorensen (2007) for tourism firms specifically. Similarly, Von Mises (1949:325–326) suggests: 'The driving force of the market process is provided neither by the consumers nor by the owners of the means of production – land, capital goods, and labour – but by the promoting and speculating entrepreneurs.' The need to understand entrepreneurship as a driving force for change at both micro (i.e., at the level of the individual firm) and at macro (i.e., economy-wide) levels is increasingly recognised.

Types and sources of innovation

Reflecting on types of innovation offers an insight into the sources of innovation and to begin this section we draw on Schumpeter's work who proposed five types of innovation:

- Technological innovation (often this involves new production processes/new methods of production)
- Marketing innovation (sometimes referred to as product innovation)
- Opening a new export market (or simply: new markets)
- Exploiting a new source of supply (new materials or resources, new inputs)
- The creation of a new type of institution (new forms of organisations).

Hjalager (2010) comments in an article on innovation in tourism that product, process, organisational/managerial and market innovations constitute the main body of innovation categories, and that distribution innovations and institutional innovations are examples of attempts to consider particularities of innovation in tourism. What we can see if we compare Schumpeter's types of innovation with those in Hjalager's review is that there is considerable overlap, just at times a different use of terminology. The key message to take away here is that far from the common view of innovations revolving around product innovations as a result of technological developments in particular, innovations can be found in a variety of forms. Innovations are more than technological developments.

Case Study 3.1: Code sharing in the airline industry

Innovations in the airline industry are common. Many have resulted from advances in technology that have manifested themselves in the design of planes. The Boeing 707 that transformed transatlantic air travel in the 1950s, 'kicking the jet age into top gear' (Glancey, 2014), for example, or more recent developments in the shape of the Airbus380 which have disrupted seat mile costs (although the A380's fortunes have turned a little sour more recently; Goldstein, 2017). Innovations do not have to be dramatic to have impact, in fact, they are often unassuming. Few people outside the airline industry will be familiar with code sharing and yet it is a key innovation for the industry. Code sharing is an arrangement between airlines to share flights. It involves cooperation but at a lower level than full membership of the airline alliances (which is another innovation). Taneja (2018) reflects that it is a form of sharing that was taking place long before anyone mentioned the sharing economy. Code sharing became popular with the deregulation of the airline industry in the United States at the end of the 1970s (it is not considered a vital public service and is therefore under less stringent regulations). Similarly, in Europe code sharing became more popular in 1993 with the deregulation of the sector (Steer Davies Gleave, 2007). Code sharing allows airlines to expand their networks, to offer their customers more destinations and schedules without having to make expensive capital investments. It has the potential to increase revenue by increasing confidence and increasing market presence. However, concerns have also been raised about a reduction in competition where airlines code share to dominate a market, allowing capacity to be restricted or prices to be raised. Today, the vast majority of airlines have code-share arrangements in place, usually with several airlines (Steer Davies Gleave, 2007).

It is interesting to consider how code sharing first came about as it demonstrates how serendipitous innovations can be. In the case of code sharing, the attempt to circumvent or manipulate a system led to the discovery of additional, unanticipated benefits. A report on the impact on competition of code sharing (Steer Davies Gleave, 2007) reports how code sharing arose in the United States with the widespread use of Computer Reservation Systems (CRS, more commonly known now as Global Distribution Systems, GDS). One of the rules governing the GDS was the prioritising of 'online' connections (these are connections operated by the same airline) above interline connections (those between different airlines). Because the GDS used codes to identify flights, airlines realised that if they shared a code, the GDS would assume connecting flights belonged to the same airline and give this higher priority. Effectively, this meant giving the flight a higher chance of being sold. Today, because of a removal of the GDS display rules in the US, and with the reduction in importance of GDS as a direct selling channel, the original reason for code sharing has largely disappeared. Because of its other advantages, however, airlines have kept the practice.

A further distinction that can be made to help us understand the nature of innovation is that between radical and incremental innovation. Radical innovation – sometimes referred to as discontinuous innovation, disruptive innovation or breakthrough innovation – has been the subject of a substantial amount of research. This is to be expected where technological innovations abound, and where rates of technological obsolescence are high. Increasingly, technological forces are pushing companies to either innovate or disappear: 88% of firms in the 1955 Fortune 500 were not on the 2014 list, and the rate of turnover is accelerating, while the duration of product life-cycles declined across all industries by 24% between 1997 and 2012 (World Economic Forum, 2016:51).

As we can see in Ettlie et al. (1984), radical innovation can be seen to distinguish itself from incremental innovation in that it involves:

* Greater risk
* The incorporation of technology that represents a clear departure from existing practice
* Novelty in the market (not just for the individual firm)
* Changes in both throughput (process) as well as output (product or service)
* High costs or high magnitude of change.

Bessant et al. (2014) provide a very clear, because not encased in jargon, definition of incremental and radical innovation. The former is where we 'do what we do but better', and the latter is 'do-different' innovation (Bessant et al., 2014:1284). Radical innovations are more likely to occur where a firm is no longer able to meet the challenges the market presents. In simple terms, it is a case of 'innovate or die'.

A further type of innovation that is radical as it involves 'a fundamental reconceptualization of what the business is all about. . . a dramatically different way of playing the game in an existing business' (Markides, 1998:32) is strategic innovation. This type of innovation is akin to business repositioning, or a change of strategic direction. It is rare for established companies to demonstrate strategic innovation for a variety of reasons; for example, fear of cannibalising existing products or cultural inertia.

The tourism industry offers plenty of examples of innovation although it is not always recognised by policy-makers as being a particularly innovative sector (Hall, 2009). Finding examples of innovation in tourism is not difficult although Hjalager (2002) makes the case that it is often the suppliers to the tourism industry that demonstrate innovation rather than the sector itself. That said, Hjalager (2010:6) also raises the question: 'in practice, and on balance, how much is tourism innovating?' to which she provides the inevitable answer: 'No matter how crucial, there is still no ultimate answer to this question.' The reason for this according to Hjalager (2010) resides in measurement difficulties relating to innovation. Beyond difficulties in measuring innovation, we also encounter the perennial difficulty in defining tourism – so an 'ultimate answer' is likely to remain elusive.

Certain individuals are commonly held up to support the claim that the tourism and hospitality sectors are particularly innovative, from Thomas Cook's first excursion in 1841, to Ray Kroc's innovation in the fast food sector resulting in McDonald's, to Freddie Laker, who pioneered cheap air travel, and Walt Disney, the creator of Disneyland. Arguably, every industry has its mavericks, those individuals keen to push boundaries and try something new. Hjalager (2010) notes, however, that whereas examples and discussions of innovation historically focused on manufacturing, with the rise in the importance of the service industry, recognition of innovation in services has also grown. It is easy to see why even today much initial focus on innovation considers product-innovation; that is, the change in the design or nature of a product. Something tangible, a product, can be visualised and changing something physical therefore might be easier to imagine (visualise even!) than changing something intangible, such as a process. But this is not to say that non-product innovations are less important.

Ottenbacher (2007) in a review of innovation success in hospitality distinguishes between new product development (NPD) and new service development (NSD). NSD can include the development of a new product, but crucially it is the way it is delivered (the service element) that can make or break the success of the innovation. In fact, he outlines the high failure rate of service innovations in hospitality, estimating it to be more than four in ten, which at least feels right given the number of new hotel and restaurant concepts that fail (Kotler et al., 2014). Ottenbacher (2007) and Hall (2009:4) distinguish between four NSD success factors (Hall, 2009, suggests these factors are derived from the OECD's work):

- Product-related
- Market-related
- Process-related
- Organisation-related

In tourism – commonly regarded as a service, and without question featuring as part of the wider service sector – product innovation can refer to the intelligent bundling of new issues and new market segments (Hjalager, 2010). In the sense, however, that tourism from the supply side is about the bundling of services for tourists, the scope for innovations is considerable. Because these improvements in processes are so important to the customer, they do in fact become part of the service. Disentangling process from service from product in tourism is not always obvious.

Examples of process innovations abound. Drawing on Toast's (2016) report on developments in restaurant technology, which relates to data from 1,115 diners, 60% of whom were millennials, in the US the following issues were noted, which provides examples of process innovation:

- Kiosk ordering, where guests order and pay at a kiosk, is becoming increasingly popular in fast casual restaurants. When a kiosk is available, 55% of customers use it sometimes and 10% every time.
- Server tablets, where the server takes an order using a handheld tablet, which then sends the order straight to the kitchen; 68% of diners agreed that tablets improved their dining experience.

Hotel chains such as Hilton and Louvre have started to introduce the use of smartphones to replace room key cards. By downloading an appropriate app, guests will be able to enter hotel rooms by pressing a button on their phones, receive notifications of when their room is ready and select particular room features at the touch of a virtual button.

Notwithstanding the potential benefits of technological innovation, technology should be used judiciously. It is a means to an end, not the end itself. This is demonstrated in the aforementioned report by the following quote:

> I think that restaurant technology, and technology in particular really takes away from the human experience. A good part of the experience at restaurants is the social interaction with the workers, the waiter/waitress, and that is being taken away more and more with technology.
>
> (Toast, 2016:10)

The adoption of technology that leads to less human interaction may work in some settings such as in fast food or fast casual dining environments, but not in others such as in fine dining. It is also conceivable that some customers may balk at the idea of solving minimum wage pressures in this way (Restaurantbusinessonline, 2017). The report provides results of an open-ended question on what dining trends customers wanted to see introduced more widely in 2017. The list includes:

- Progress bars letting the diner know at what stage of the cooking process their meal was.
- Better 'wait time' technology including texts alerting diners to when the restaurant is ready to seat them.
- Easier means of leaving feedback while still at the restaurant.
- Menu information being more readily accessible (which could be achieved via a tablet).
- A server call button, which reduces waiting times for the bill.

A further use of technological innovation in the tourism industry relates to robotics. While we may be some time off witnessing the wholesale replacement of service staff by robots as in the Henn-na Hotel in Nagasaki (Murison, 2016), the increased adoption of artificial intelligence (AI) is a very real phenomenon. In fact, reporting on 352 expert views from the 2015 Conference on Neural Information Processing Systems, an article in *Newsweek* (Bort, 2017) predicts that AI will 'best humans at everything' by 2060. The pace of change is indeed striking (see also Chapter 7).

The importance of innovation has not passed tourism educators by – there even exist courses in tourism that focus specifically on innovation. For example, a collaboration between three universities (Universitat Rovira I Virgili, Université de Bordeau and the University of Porto, which can itself be considered innovative) has led to the offer of a Master's on Wine Tourism Innovation. Alongside modules on wine production, the programme included at the time of writing a module featuring entrepreneurship, and another called 'ICT and wine tourism' which covers things such as website design, social media and online promotion (Wintour, 2018).

Case study 3.2: Artificial intelligence: pizza robot

The European Union has offered €2.5 million for the development of a robot that can make pizza. Formerly, the development of a robot with the dexterity to knead, stretch, toss and twirl dough, and then add ingredients before sliding it into an oven might have been regarded as an impossible challenge, even for the most technologically minded. Today, the dream of the robot-making pizzaiolo (the traditional name for a pizza baker) is turning into reality.

RoDyMan, short for Robotic Dynamic Manipulation, is a five-year project sponsored to the tune of a €2.5 million grant from the European Research Council. The team of scientists led by Bruno Siciliano from the University of Naples Federico II called upon the assistance of a master pizza chef, Enzo Coccia, in their quest to create RoDyMan. They requested Coccia don a suit of movement-tracking sensors to help RoDyMan simulate these movements. Coccia himself was less enamoured with the robot pizzaiolo idea, quoting: 'I would never eat a pizza made by a robot. It would not have the taste a real piz-zaiolo, with his soul, would put into it' (Crisp, 2017).

Product and process innovations aside, Hjalager (2010) mentions three other forms of innovation in tourism: managerial, management and institutional innovation. Managerial innovation relates to the typical human resource functions (e.g., recruitment, selection, training, retention). Based on Hjalager's (2010) explanation, management innovation appears similar to marketing innovation (see also below). For example, she mentions the introduction of loyalty cards, or a destination management organisation's focus on new market segments. Arguably, the most trenchant management innovation/marketing innovations have resulted from advances in ICT, which have led to a revolution in booking patterns. The high street travel agent has not been consigned to history but the era of the high street travel agent has. The ability to source information independently, tied to the ability to book from the comfort of your own home has largely removed the need for travel agents.

Another marketing/management-related area that has seen rapid advances as a result of technological innovations is social media, itself part of the wider impact of the internet, which Buhalis and Law (2008) determine has wholly redefined the distribution of information related to tourism consumption. Developments in ICT (also digitisation) and their application in tourism have been revolutionary in many respects. The increased use of technology, and resultant innovations, has fundamentally changed many aspects of tourism, especially in relation to distribution channels and market structures.

Whether they belong to the public or private sector, many tourism organisations are tapping into the potential of social media to attract and retain customers. An example is the growing use of instant messaging platforms such as WhatsApp, Facebook Messenger and WeChat. According to Statista (2018), the number of monthly active WhatsApp users worldwide grew from 200 million in June 2013 to 1,300 million in July 2017 (growth of 850%). Skift, which defines itself as 'the largest industry intelligence platform providing media, insights and marketing to key sectors of travel' (https://skift.com/about/)[2] confirms travel companies' increasing reliance on third-party messaging platforms such as Facebook Messenger, WhatsApp, and others. Particularly among the 18–29 age group it is a 'rapidly evolving and nearly primary method of electronic communications' (Skift, 2018), highlighting companies such as Southwest Airlines, Silvercar, Hyatt, Nomad List and Travel Noire that are trying to make the most of these developments. Messaging services provide a means of communication between the customer and the tourism firm that is direct and personal. Being able to make hassle-free contact directly with the service provider is of enormous convenience (for example, in a situation where your transfer has not arrived). Companies such as Hyatt and KLM have trialled the use of instant messaging for these purposes, and others such as Shangri-La Hotels are using it for marketing purposes also.

Identifying innovative opportunities and opportunities for innovation

Innovation and opportunity are easy bedfellows. Innovations frequently provide opportunities for the entrepreneur as we have seen (think about the impact of technological innovation on bricks and mortar travel agents), and sometimes innovations are introduced by individuals in the pursuit of opportunities. In the past, the ability to innovate as well as to spot opportunities was frequently regarded as some inherent quality of the entrepreneur. Either you had this ability, or you did not. Given the fundamental role innovation plays in the Schumpeterian/Austrian school of economics, as well as the personal rewards achievable to those who are able to spot commercially valuable opportunities, it is not surprising that a great deal of effort has been made to understand sources of innovation, and the nature of opportunities and how to spot them.

Renowned business guru Peter Drucker has, for example, attempted to promote systematic innovation (he writes also of purposeful and managed innovation). Innovation then does not have to be some magical thing that happens inexplicably and spontaneously: 'Systematic innovation therefore consists in the purposeful and organized search for changes, and in the systematic analysis of the opportunities such changes might offer for economic or social innovation' (Drucker, 1985:31). Because, for Drucker, innovation is about exploiting change, his systematic method to identify innovative opportunities resides in a systematic scanning of sources of change. He identifies seven such sources, four inside the organisation or industry, and three outside the organisation/industry (see Table 3.1).

Table 3.1 Drucker's sources of innovative opportunities

	Source of innovative opportunity	Explanation
Inside sources	The unexpected	The innovative opportunity can result from both an unexpected success or an unexpected failure. Organisations may focus so much on planned outcomes that they do not recognise the unexpected success. They may recognise success but not want to acknowledge it because it goes against 'the plan' or accepted wisdom. Failures are unlikely to go unnoticed but may not be regarded as offering an opportunity. Failure can indicate an underlying change such as in consumer preferences or spending habits.
	The incongruity	An incongruity between reality as it is and reality as it is assumed to be. An incongruity is a symptom of change. It can relate to, for example, an incongruity between perceived and actual customer value, or in economic realities (e.g., growing demand leads to less profitability). There could also be an incongruity within a process, something everyone is aware of that does not feel right, but that is accepted just because 'this is the way it's always been'.
	Process need	Here the starting point is a need with regard to a process as opposed to an opportunity that leads to innovation. Innovations based on process needs require: a self-contained process; one 'weak' or 'missing' link; a clear definition of the objective; that the specifications for the solution can be defined clearly; widespread realisation that 'there ought to be a better way', i.e., high receptivity.

(Continued)

Table 3.1 Continued

	Source of innovative opportunity	Explanation
	Changes in industry or market structure	Market and industry structures are quite brittle. Frequently it is industry outsiders who recognise the opportunity; insiders see changes as a threat. Indicators of impending change include: rapid growth of an industry; convergence of technologies that were hitherto regarded as separate. Often opportunities are large where there is only one or few large providers of the product or service. Given their size, these incumbents are often complacent, offering greater scope to exploit the opportunity for smaller, more nimble firms.
Outside sources	Demographics	Of all external changes, those relating to population changes are the clearest. Changes can relate to, for example, size, age structure, educational status and income. While the business community and politicians regularly acknowledge the importance of population trends, day-to-day decisions do not often draw on these considerations, partly because it is believed that these changes are very gradual, occurring over a lengthy period of time. Its neglect by decision-makers makes demographic changes such a rewarding opportunity for the entrepreneur.
	Changes in perception, mood and meaning	This is all about the human need to interpret and 'make sense' of the world. In other words, facts may not change, but what these facts mean or how they are interpreted might. Critical to success in perception-based innovation is timing. Both diving in too early and waiting too long to jump on the bandwagon can prove fatal. It is key to move early, imitation will not work, but at the same time there is uncertainty around whether a change in perception is just a fad or has staying power.
	New knowledge	Drucker describes knowledge-based innovation as the 'superstar' of innovation. It is frequently what people think about when they talk of innovation, especially technological innovation, although new knowledge can be found in all areas with dramatic consequences. Clayton Christensen's (1997) classic *The Innovator's Dilemma* describes the dangers to incumbent firms of technical innovations that are easily ignored, for all the right reasons! The dilemma is whether incumbent firms should pursue opportunities at the margins, which only interest a small section of the market, at the expense of more profitable and larger market segments. The obvious answer would be 'no'. However, knowledge-based innovations that only have a small following initially can, within a relatively short space of time, become the dominant technology in the market. By adopting a 'rational' approach, i.e., not investing in an uncertain technology at the expense of a tried-and-tested technology, large incumbent firms could be jeopardising their future. There is usually a lengthy lead time between the creation of knowledge and its commercial application; Drucker estimates between 25 and 35 years, but this is likely to be shorter now. Crucially, most innovations based on new knowledge depend on the convergence of several areas of knowledge. The risks associated with knowledge-based innovation are high (the window of opportunity is narrow and is often crowded), but so are the potential rewards.

At times it is difficult to distinguish between Drucker's different sources of opportunities for innovation; the unexpected success points to an incongruity, that between expectation and reality. Demographic changes frequently go hand-in-hand with changes in mood, perception and meaning. Furthermore, how are changes in perception, mood or meaning different to an incongruity between what the enterprise believes consumers want and what consumers actually want given changes in perception? Nonetheless, as a means of systematically seeking opportunities for innovation, Drucker provides a very useful starting point.

Case study 3.3: Morgan's Wonderland

Morgan's Wonderland, a fully accessible theme park in Texas, provides an example of an incongruity that led to an innovative opportunity (Bates, 2017). The park cost $34 million (£26 million) and opened in 2010. Its founder, Gordon Hartman, realised there were no theme parks where his disabled daughter could play. Speaking to other parents, Hartman and his wife, Maggie, were after a theme park that was not only fully accessible, but that also offered a warm and inclusive environment. In 2005 the Gordon Hartman Family Foundation was established to help people with disabilities, which included the creation of the world's first 'ultra-accessible' theme park. Attractions include a fully accessible Ferris wheel, adventure playground and miniature train. Since it opened, Morgan's Wonderland has received over a million visitors from 67 countries and from all 50 American states. A third of its staff have disabilities and entrance is free to any guest with a condition.

The incongruity that led to the establishment of the theme park is an example of something everyone is aware of but that does not feel right, something that is accepted just because this is the way things have always been done (i.e., the needs of people with disabilities – although even here one could argue that not everyone is in fact aware of them although awareness is growing). This could then also be an example of an innovation opportunity as a result of a change in perception, mood or meaning.

Case study 3.4: Marriott

An example of an unexpected success: a classic example dates back to the early days when Marriott was still a restaurant chain before it diversified into hotels. Management observed that one of their restaurants in Washington, DC, was outperforming all others in their chain in terms of monthly revenues. Upon investigation, they found the restaurant was located across from the National Airport. This was before airlines served meals on planes and they discovered that airline passengers would stop by the restaurant and purchase sandwiches and snacks to take on the plane with them. Marriott met with Eastern Airlines and suggested they provide food to be served on the plane – thus the beginning of the airline catering business. Of course, now many airlines, in an attempt to control costs, have eliminated meals and passengers are left to bring their own snacks with them again (Swaim, 2011).

Within tourism, Hjalager (2010) points to three sources of innovation: the entrepreneur, technological developments and innovation clusters.

1. **The characteristics of the entrepreneur:** Here the idea is that the entrepreneur as the origin of 'creative destruction' is key. It is not the case that individuals engaged in the tourism industry are necessarily any more innovative than others; however, often 'chaos makers' – as Russell and Faulkner (1999) term tourism entrepreneurs – are certainly one of the driving forces for the development of destinations. Russell and Faulkner (1999) also suggest that different kinds of tourism entrepreneurs will prevail at different stages of the destination lifecycle (Butler, 1980); for example, local entrepreneurs in the *exploration* stage and migrant entrepreneurs in the *involvement* stage (Barr, 1990). They provide examples of two archetypal maverick entrepreneurs, Keith Williams and Bernard Elsey, who, due to their drive and 'bloody-minded tenacity', shaped the development of the Gold Coast, Australia, in the 1960s and 1970s.
2. **The technology-push/demand-pull paradigm:** Technological developments provide a major source of innovation in tourism as in many industries. At the same time as technological developments push the adoption of innovations in tourism, the market, i.e., consumers, constantly pull in different directions offering opportunities for the entrepreneur to adopt technology to meet this changing demand.
3. **The Marshallian innovation systems or innovation cluster approach:** In the 1920s Alfred Marshall developed the concept of industrial districts, whereby the development of individual businesses will depend on the specifics of the localities in which they are embedded. This aligns with Gartner's (1985) framework of new venture creation as discussed in the previous chapter, which suggests the environment around the new venture is crucial to understanding the nature of the new venture. Hjalager (2010) acknowledges that research on innovation systems in tourism is still at an embryonic stage. What we know, however, is that particularly given the structure of the tourism sector, one made up predominantly of small businesses, having a supportive regulative environment and an environment where firms can cooperate, particularly in marketing terms, can be key to success.

Parallel to Hjalager's (2010) notion of the 'Marshallian innovation system', Novelli et al. (2006) have explored the impact of clusters and innovation in tourism SMEs. Their research, which focused on the south east of the UK, found that combined marketing efforts were a benefit of the cluster (it created a unique selling point for the region) as well the creation of opportunities to find out about the market, the environment, potential partnerships and possible value chain establishment and enrichment. However, Novelli et al. (2006) also point to the perennial problem of diversity in the tourism SME population, which can make clusters and collaboration difficult, as well as hampering policy efforts in supporting tourism SMEs (Thomas et al., 2011).

An example of how, within a region, tourism associations contribute to a support system is the case of the south west of the UK where two tourism associations, the Tourism Society Westcountry and the South West Tourism Alliance, collaborated to offer workshops to assist tourism firms in tackling emerging challenges to the sector. Thus, when the UK government announced a ban on term-time holidays for children, with the possibility of fines for breaches of this rule, many local tourism firms that depended heavily on the family market felt very aggrieved. In a series of events, these regional tourism associations provided examples of how firms were changing their product offer to accommodate for the trying situations, such as providing a pet-friendly form of accommodation or seeking new markets (e.g., overseas) where the regulations were not in effect. This is an example where industry came together to share ideas and best practice (Walmsley, 2018).

Case study 3.5: Airbnb

Airbnb, founded in 2008, is possibly the best-known firm operating in what is referred to as the 'sharing economy', the 'collaborative economy', 'peer to peer' (P2P) economy or new platform tourism services (another contender is Uber, founded in 2009 and boasting revenue of US$6.5 billion in 2016, it made losses in every year between 2012 and 2017). At the time of writing Airbnb was still a private company, i.e., not yet having gone public. It is estimated it made a profit upwards of US$100 million on turnover of US$1.7 billion in 2016, with further profits estimated to grow to US$3 billion by 2020 (Gallagher, 2017). It is increasingly the focus of research attention within the broader scope of the sharing economy and how this relates to tourism. To illustrate, a recent special issue of the *International Journal of Contemporary Hospitality Management* (Volume 29, Issue 9) on the sharing economy offered 14 papers, eight of which focused directly on Airbnb.

Airbnb's main metric for user growth is guest arrivals, which refers to the number of times an individual traveller checks into an Airbnb listing. In 2016 this figure grew from 40 million to almost 80 million. 'Thriving on innovation', the company is already broadening its activities to include trips, restaurant bookings and 'meetups', and according to CEO Brian Chesky is planning to add more travel services (e.g., ground transportation and grocery delivery). It is foreseeable that revenue from accommodations will eventually represent less than half of Airbnb's overall revenue (Gallagher, 2017).

The impact of Airbnb is a contentious issue, particularly for traditional providers of short-term accommodation who fear losing business. Zervas et al. (2017), who focus on the impact of Airbnb in Texas, estimate that in Austin, where Airbnb supply was highest, the impact on hotel revenue was in the 8–10% range. Zervas et al. (2017) also reveal that the impact of Airbnb is non-uniform, with lower-priced hotels and those hotels not catering to business travellers being the most affected.

Airbnb has also faced accusations of exacerbating housing shortages and pushing up property prices. This has resulted in cities like Berlin curtailing the short-term lettings market. In 2016 the City of Berlin upheld a ban on people letting more than 50% of their apartment on a short-term basis without a permit. Those who do risk a fine of €100,000. The fear is that other cities, not just in Germany, could see this as setting a precedent and adopt a similar stance (Oltermann, 2016).

Small firms and innovation

As we have seen, small firms are regularly set on a par with entrepreneurship and innovation. In fact, large firms, by way of contrast, are regarded as slow to innovate and adopt innovation as Markides (1998:33) summarises:

Compared to new entrants or niche players, established companies find it hard to innovate because of structural and cultural inertia, internal politics, complacency, fear of cannibalizing existing products, fear of destroying existing competencies, satisfaction with the status quo, and a general lack of incentive to abandon a certain present (which is profitable) for an uncertain future.

Paradoxically, small firms can also be considered the least enterprising, however. Hjalager (2010:7) summarises a number of studies in tourism claiming: 'A major and broadly recognised impediment for tourism innovation is the small size of many enterprises.' As has been mentioned previously, lifestyle/non-financial goals drive many tourism entrepreneurs. Innovation that leads to growth of the small tourism firm is not necessarily something many owners/managers desire.

Nonetheless, much is made of the fast-paced, constantly evolving business environment that puts pressure on companies of whatever size to change and adapt. Competitive pressures are such that one has to innovate simply to 'stand still', whether we are considering tourism firms or destinations:

In an environment of strong international competition and rapidly changing customer needs, tourist destinations must continuously perform product, process, and market innovation.

(Beritelli et al., 2007:96)

The major challenge facing today's hospitality companies is knowing how to build and maintain healthy businesses in the face of a rapidly changing marketplace and environment.

(Kotler et al., 2014:98)

Hall and Williams (2008) link innovativeness with the propensity to survive as an enterprise. These are not the only scholars who believe this to be the case (e.g., Kelling and Entebang, 2017; Weiermaier, 2006). Reasons for this include rapid technological changes, changes in consumer tastes, global economic restructuring and environmental limits to growth (in fact these issues are not new and have been mentioned within a tourism context by Poon a quarter of a century ago (Poon, 1993)). Boella and Goss-Turner (2013:38) (with a focus on the hospitality industry) likewise highlight 'a proliferation of competing brands, shorter business and product life cycles with many different business models all make the world's business environment more complex and challenging'. The term 'hypercompetition', first coined by D'Aveni in 1994, describes a 'new' reality for firms. According to D'Aveni, traditional strategies of defining an industry, reducing the level of competition and then avoiding competition where possible are now obsolete. The notion of sustained competitive advantage is defunct. In such an environment is it even possible to be anything but innovative and entrepreneurial (D'Aveni and Gunther, 1994)?

Levels of competition will differ in different markets. This is certainly true for tourism, which covers a vast array of products and services, spread across an equally vast array of markets globally. Levels of competition tend to be lower in rural than in urban areas, for example, and small rural tourism firms are sometimes set aside as a special case because of their unique characteristics (e.g., Kallmuenzer and Peters, 2018; Zhao and Getz, 2008). To provide broad-brushed claims that competition in tourism is fierce would ignore this fact. This should not detract, however, from the dramatic changes that have affected many tourism firms, from the very small to the very large.

The impact of developments in ICT, and among these the role of ratings systems, is a case in point. Mitas et al.'s (2015) report on the digitisation of tourism enterprises, written for the European Parliament as an aid to guide policy-makers, highlights the threats posed to tourism SMEs that are unable to keep up with the rapid pace of change. The report writes of 'existential risks' to tourism SMEs that use traditional business models.

Another reason why it is important for small firms to innovate is the potential disadvantages that accrue to firms because of their small size and/or because of their newness (if recently established). Whether a small tourism firm is old or new, it may be at a disadvantage compared to large firms because it is unable to benefit from economies of scale, it may have difficulty attracting suitable staff (it is said small firms are less attractive workplaces, although the issue is debatable; see also Chapter 7). Small firms may find it harder to gain access to finance and are in a weaker bargaining position than their large counterparts.

The literature on start-ups frequently mentions the concept of 'liability of newness' (originally coined by Stinchcombe, 1965), which suggests small start-ups are frequently at a competitive disadvantage, hence higher failure rates, because of things like a lack of market knowledge and experience, or the absence of competencies and capabilities that are more likely to be found in an established team. Because of their newness they lack a track record of past performance, which can affect legitimacy claims (Choi and Shepherd, 2005) or claims of being competent or worthy (Zimmerman and Zeitz, 2002). The issues of legitimacy and reputation are compounded by the ubiquity of social media, where potential customers can draw on online consumer reviews to judge a firm's products or services. Just a handful of negative reviews can prove fatal for a new firm.

Effectuation, causation and ideation

Two key concepts that should feature in any chapter on opportunity recognition and innovation in entrepreneurship are effectuation and ideation.[3] Effectuation applies a different logic to opportunity recognition and by implication to the start-up process (as such it could equally feature in Chapter 4). What is meant by a 'different logic' is explained by Sarasvathy (2001) in an article that has served as the cornerstone of the effectuation literature as it applies to entrepreneurship (for much of the below explanation we refer to Sarasvathy's work).

The traditional explanation of entrepreneurship involves a causal logic whereby an end is envisaged and a search for means follows. This is summarised neatly in Stevenson and Jarillo's (1991:23) definition of entrepreneurship as: 'The pursuit of opportunity beyond the tangible resources that you currently control.'

So, a business plan will offer a defined market and a defined product that meets the need of that target market as well as the steps required to achieve the profit/sales forecasts in the business plan (see also Chapter 4). The target is set, the question is 'how do we get there?' Effectuation on the other hand does not envisage a clear end. With a given set of means (resources) it seeks to explore different ends (or opportunities). As Sarasvathy (2001) suggests, however, the two logics usually work together, both are integral parts of human reasoning.

The implications for the discussion of the entrepreneurial process (see Chapter 4), particularly for the traditional view as explained in Shane and Venkatarman's (2000) 'discovery, evaluation, exploitation' framework, are profound. The traditional view relies on opportunities that exist, that are perceived before action takes place; they are acted upon. Effectuation on the other hand sees action as creating opportunities. At this point readers versed in the principles of strategic management will recognise parallels to emergent and prescriptive notions of strategy (e.g., Mintzberg and Waters, 1985; Lynch, 2009), causation logic referring to the former, effectuation to the latter. As with strategic management, the prescriptive/deliberate approach works better in predictable and stable environments, effectuation better in situations of uncertainty and dynamism.

Ideation is linked to creativity, which itself is often regarded as the cornerstone of entrepreneurship (the link being made very strongly by Schumpeter's notion of 'creative destruction' and creativity being included by some as an entrepreneurial personality trait). Ideation, simply put, is the generation of ideas. Different kinds of ideation exist. Ames and Runco (2005) distinguish between ideational fluency, the ability to come up with many ideas, and ideational originality, the ability to come up with unique, novel or unusual ideas. According to their research, more successful entrepreneurs (those who created more businesses – arguably not a sophisticated measure) had higher ideation scores.

Ideas may abound but successful ideas are rare and valuable as Stevens and Burley (1997) have demonstrated with reference to industrial products where they estimate 3,000 raw ideas are needed to come up with one substantially new commercially successful product. Success curves will vary by industry, whereby Stevens and Burley (1997) suggest that drug companies typically require a higher number of starting ideas (6,000–8,000). Product extensions as opposed to substantially new products would not require as many ideas, one imagines. Whether it takes 60 or 3,000 new ideas to achieve one successful product will also depend where on the success curve, or new product development curve, one starts counting. The point is to underline the challenge involved in coming up with a commercially successful new idea, and that having an idea, however original, does not guarantee a successful outcome.

A layperson's view of the entrepreneur is commonly one of the lone individual, coming up with an idea on his/her own, having a so-called 'eureka moment'. As we have argued before, this heroic view is now somewhat outdated and there is substantial evidence that points to the entrepreneurial process (the process of setting up a new business), including ideation, being a situated affair.

Although research on the impact of social networks on entrepreneurial creativity and ideation are limited, there is evidence that these do have an effect (e.g., Baron and Markman, 2000). Gemmel et al.'s (2012:1054) study is a case in point. They interviewed 32 entrepreneurs regarding their ideational experiences and concluded that:

> Our data shatter the traditional over-simplistic view of ideation as the first in a linear series of progressive activities to form a new business. We observed entrepreneurs consciously engaging in an ongoing complex, cyclical, and recursive social process of problem solving and learning, which is integral to and inseparable from the larger cycle of innovation and new business formation. These findings illuminate methodologies and skills that nascent entrepreneurs can master, challenging the conventional wisdom that only certain individuals are 'born' to be entrepreneurs.

More specifically, Gemmel et al. (2012) establish three ideational processes:[4]

1 The utilisation of complex and sophisticated social networks as sources of ideas and to test, refine and validate trial ideas.
2 The exhibition of extraordinary domain specificity by filtering ideas outside specific markets and technologies (they pursue almost exclusively ideas within their area of expertise).
3 Active experimentation and iteration of ideas rather than engagement in protracted conceptual analysis.

Whether these three processes map onto tourism entrepreneurs perfectly is a moot point (Gemmel et al.'s sample were all highly educated, and the majority highly successful with companies achieving sales of over $10 million per year, so unlike your typical small tourism firm). However, there is no reason to believe that what is exhibited here in terms of point 1 in particular should not hold for tourism entrepreneurs also.

Crowdsourcing

Many innovative firms now use crowdsourcing as means to obtain and explore new product ideas. The term crowdsourcing was popularised by Jeff Howe in a 2006 magazine article for *Wired*. Originally the term referred to businesses outsourcing tasks to 'the crowd' undertaken by employees through an open call to online communities. Today, the definition of crowdsourcing has evolved to encompass 'an online, distributed problem-solving and production model that leverages the collective intelligence of online communities to serve specific organizational goals' (Brabham, 2013:xix).

Crowdsourcing based on this extended meaning has proven to be an effective means of harnessing collective intelligence, of using the power of many minds to solve problems. This 'crowd' can be composed of a very heterogeneous group of individuals, from experts in various fields to novices. This way a firm can draw on a vast range of experience and ideas. According to Brabham (2013:100), 'crowdsourcing is a process for connecting organizations to online communities and exchanging information between them'. This is not what everyone understands by the term, however. It has, for example, been applied by Kotler et al. (2014) to 4Food's (a restaurant in New York) initiative to serve hamburgers with a hole in the middle. This hole is then filled by the customers themselves from a selection of different vegetarian dishes, such as humus or salsa. By creating their own combinations of these ingredients, customers can develop their unique filling. If 4Food is able to get others to order 'its' hamburger, it will get 20 cents for every burger sold (Kotler et al., 2014:266–267). The crowd one sources does not have to be internet-based; it effectively extends to anyone and everyone outside the organisation who wants to engage with the firm.

Crowdsourcing is becoming more common because of its associated advantages, which extend beyond benefiting from others' ideas. It is also a means of transferring risk, and only paying for products and services that meet the firm's expectations. Crowdsourcing tends to involve three kinds of actors:

- The providers, or 'the crowd'
- The firm, or client, who has put out the call
- A crowdsourcing enabler, i.e., those providing the intermediation platform between the client and the providers (Schenk and Guittard, 2011).

Schenk and Guittard (2011) also distinguish between integrative crowdsourcing and selective crowdsourcing. This points to an important distinction as it exemplifies the diversity of approaches within crowdsourcing itself. Selective crowdsourcing is akin to a competition where providers offer solutions to the client (firm). It is crucial that the client organisation provides a clear brief or problem to be solved. Integrative crowdsourcing on the other hand is not so much a competition to find 'the' best solution, but a means of collecting information and building a database; a form of content crowdsourcing. Integrative crowdsourcing can be quite resource-intensive and there are a number of issues that need to be considered in relation to obtaining redundant data, data that do not meet requirements and data from unreliable sources.

We can see examples of integrative and selective crowdsourcing in the way destination management organisations (DMOs) draw on individuals' photo contributions to Facebook, or the way they can vote on cover images (see Chapter 5 for Mariani, di Felice and Mura's, 2016, examples of regional DMOs in Italy). This user-submitted content approach is not unique to Italian DMOs of course. In 2012 the Canadian Tourism Commission asked the public to submit their own videos while undertaking 'fun activities' (e.g., hiking, skiing, kayaking). The Commission received more than 65 hours of footage and from this compiled a two-minute promotional video capturing the essence of what Canada is.[5]

Summary

This chapter began by reviewing the similarities and differences between entrepreneurship and innovation. A key distinction here was the notion of novelty, which was a prerequisite for innovation but not necessarily for entrepreneurship. The concept of innovation was then discussed in more detail with taxonomies of innovation being offered, such as Drucker's five types of innovation, which overlap with Hjalager's (2010) innovation categories in tourism. Another way of looking at innovation was the extent to which the innovation presented a departure from 'the norm' for the entire business. Here we distinguished between radical and incremental innovation. We also made reference to Ottenbacher's (2007) distinction between new product development and new service development, to remind ourselves that innovations do not always have to relate to the physical product, but that they can also relate to intangible aspects including service, a key consideration for tourism. Technological innovations have shaped the nature of tourism and a number of case studies were offered by way of illustration.

Inevitably, a chapter on innovation in tourism will focus on developments in ICT, especially the role of social media, which continues to shape consumer choices and preferences. Rather than stumbling across innovations by chance, many management theorists, including Peter Drucker, have tried to conceptualise the discovery of innovations. Here we have discussed the systematic search for innovations using Drucker's sources of innovative opportunities. The chapter also looked at the relationship between small firms and innovation on the backdrop of a general notion that small firms are more innovative than large. However, we also recognised that in tourism much of the innovation is found in large organisations as opposed to the typical small tourism firm. The final two themes of the chapter relate to the distinction between effectuation and ideation, and the role of crowdsourcing in aiding the innovation process. Focusing on the latter, it is easier today than ever before to draw on a global community of expertise to assist in developing and testing innovations. Today, tourism firms frequently use consumers to come up with innovations for them, as do DMOs. Finally, the distinction between a causation and an effectuation logic is based on a consideration of means–ends relationships. In ideation the entrepreneur starts with the idea, the goal, and an entrepreneur who marshals resources to achieve a set goal. This is very much akin to the prescriptive view of strategy (see also Chapter 8). Effectuation, however, starts with means and sees what ends might be achieved. In reality there is usually neither a focus on one, without a concern for the other. The two approaches work together.

Review questions/discussion points

1   In pairs, or in a group, identify five innovations in tourism. Then, on a scale of 1 to 10, where 1 is incremental innovation and 10 is a radical innovation, score each innovation. Explain your choice.
2   Can you identify examples of crowdsourcing in tourism?
3   'Innovation is key to the successful tourism firm' – discuss this within a group. Alternatively, create two teams and debate this from opposite perspectives.
4   What do you believe are the key barriers to innovation within the tourism firm? Do you believe small tourism firms are more or less innovative than large firms?

> 5 In your own words, explain the difference between effectuation logic and causal logic.

Notes

1 Hjalager (2010:2) uses this definition but attributes it to Johannesson et al. (2001).
2 Accessed 29 January 2018.
3 Interestingly, neither term is mentioned in recent books that cover entrepreneurship in tourism and hospitality (Lee-Ross and Lashley, 2009; Ateljevic and Page, 2009), which can be interpreted in a number of ways: as the rapid development of theory in the field, as the breadth of theory in the field of entrepreneurship, or as the very early stages of academic engagement with entrepreneurship in tourism. Considering Perry et al. (2012) believe the application of effectuation in entrepreneurship is still relatively new, we are prone to side with the first suggestion.
4 The study relates to technology entrepreneurs.
5 See www.trendhunter.com/trends/canadian-tourism-commission (accessed 14 August 2017).

References

Ames, M. and Runco, M. A. 2005. Predicting entrepreneurship from ideation and divergent thinking. *Creativity and Innovation Management*, 14, 311–315.

Ateljevic, J. and Page, S. (eds.) 2009. *Tourism and Entrepreneurship: International Perspectives*. Oxford: Elsevier.

Baron, R. A. and Markman, G. 2000. Beyond social capital: how social skills can enhance entrepreneurs' success. *Academy of Management Perspectives*, 14, 106–116.

Barr, T. 1990. From quirky islanders to entrepreneurial magnates: the transition of the Whitsundays. *Journal of Tourism Studies*, 1, 26–32.

Bates, S. 2017. How one man built a $51m theme park for his daughter. *BBC Magazine* [Online]. Available: www.bbc.co.uk/news/magazine-40742586 [Accessed 23 August 2018].

Baumol, W. 2002. *The Free-Market Innovation Machine: Analyzing the Growth Miracle of Capitalism*. Princeton: Princeton University Press.

Beritelli, P., Bieger, T. and Laesser, C. 2007. Destination governance: using corporate governance theories as a foundation for effective destination management. *Journal of Travel Research*, 46, 96–107.

Bessant, J., Öberg, C. and Trifilova, A. 2014. Framing problems in radical innovation. *Industrial Marketing Management*, 43, 1284–1292.

Boella, M. and Goss-Turner, S. 2013. *Human Resource Management in the Hospitality Industry: A Guide to Best Practice*. London: Routledge.

Bort, R. 2017. Will AI take over? Artificial intelligence will best humans at everything by 2060, experts say [Online]. *Newsweek*. Available: www.newsweek.com/artificial-intelligence-will-take-our-jobs-2060-618259 [Accessed 11 July 2017].

Brabham, D. C. 2013. *Crowdsourcing*. Cambridge, MA: MIT Press.

Buhalis, D. and Law, R. 2008. Progress in information technology and tourism management: 20 years on and 10 years after the internet – the state of e-tourism research. *Tourism Management*, 29, 609–623.

Butler, D. 1980. The concept of a tourist area cycle of evolution: implications for management of resources. *Canadian Geographer*, 24, 5–12.

Choi, Y. R. and Shepherd, D. A. 2005. Stakeholder perceptions of age and other dimensions of newness. *Journal of Management*, 31, 573–596.

Christensen, C. 1997. *The Innovator's Dilemma: When New Technologies Cause Great Firms to Fail*. Boston: Harvard Business School Press.

Crisp, J. 2017. Pizza robot has £2.3m slice of EU science fund. *The Daily Telegraph*, 12 August 2017.

D'Aveni, R. and Gunther, R. 1994. *Hypercompetition: Managing the Dynamics of Strategic Maneuvering*. New York: Free Press.

Damanpour, F. and Wischnevsky, D. 2006. Research on innovation in organizations: Distinguishing innovation-generating from innovation-adopting organizations. *Journal of Engineering and Technology Management*, 23, 269–291.

Drucker, P. 1985. *Innovation and Entreprneurship: Practice and Principles*. London: Elsevier.

Ettlie, J., Bridges, W. and O'Keefe, R. 1984. Organization strategy and structural differences for radical versus incremental innovation. *Management Science*, 30, 682–695.

Gallagher, L. 2017. Airbnb's profits to top $3 billion by 2020. *Fortune* [Online]. Available: http://fortune.com/2017/02/15/airbnb-profits/ [Accessed 29 June 2017].

Gartner, W. B. 1985. A conceptual framework for describing the phenomenon of new venture creation. *Academy of Management Review*, 10, 696–706.

Gemmel, R., Boland, R. and Kolb, D. 2012. The socio-cognitive dynamics of entrepreneurial ideation. *Entrepreneurship Theory and Practice*, 36, 1053–1073.

Glancey, J. 2014. Boeing 707: the aircraft that changed the way we fly [Online]. *BBC*. Available: www.bbc.com/culture/story/20141020-the-plane-that-changed-air-travel [Accessed 19 January 2018].

Goldstein, M. 2017. Operating costs killing jumbo jets as airlines profit from smaller planes [Online]. *Forbes*. Available: www.forbes.com/sites/michaelgoldstein/2017/10/05/operating-costs-killing-jumbo-jets-as-airlines-profit-from-smaller-planes/#410fecfe336a [Accessed 20 January 2018].

Hall, C. M. 2009. Innovation and tourism policy in Australia and New Zealand: never the twain shall meet? *Journal of Policy Research in Tourism, Hospitality and Events*, 1, 2–18.

Hall, C. M. and Williams, A. 2008. *Tourism and Innovation*. London: Routledge.

Hjalager, A. M. 2002. Repairing innovation defectiveness in tourism. *Tourism Management*, 23, 465–474.

Hjalager, A. M. 2010. A review of innovation research in tourism. *Tourism Management*, 31, 1–12.

Johannesson, J. A., Olsen, B. and Lumpkin, G. T. (2001). Innovation as newness: what is new, how new, and new to whom? *European Journal of Innovation Management*, 4(1), 20–31.

Kallmuenzer, A. 2018. Exploring drivers of innovation in hospitality family firms. *International Journal of Contemporary Hospitality Management*, 30, 1978–1995.

Kallmuenzer, A. and Peters, M. 2018. Entrepreneurial behaviour, firm size and financial performance: the case of rural tourism firms. *Tourism Recreation Research*, 43, 2–14.

Kelling, W. and Entebang, H. 2017. Dayak homestay entrepreneurs innovation characteristics. *Ottoman Journal of Tourism and Management Research*, 2.

Kirzner, I. M. 1997. Entrepreneurial discovery and the competitive market process: an Austrian approach. *Journal of Economic Literature*, 35, 60–85.

Kotler, P., Bowen, J. and Makens, J. 2014. *Marketing for Hospitality and Tourism*. Harlow: Pearson.

Lee-Ross, D. and Lashley, C. 2009. *Entreprneurship & Small Business Management in the Hospitality Industry*. Oxford: Butterworth-Heinemann.

Lynch, R. 2009. *Strategic Management*. Harlow: Prentice Hall.

Mariani, M., di Felice, M. and Mura, M. 2016. Facebook as a destination marketing tool: evidence from Italian regional destination management organizations. *Tourism Management*, 54, 321–343.

Markides, C. 1998. Strategic innovation in established companies. *Sloan Management Review*, 39, 31–42.

Mintzberg, H. and Waters, J. 1985. Of strategies, deliberate and emergent. *Strategic Management Journal*, 6, 257–272.

Mitas, O., van der Ent, M., Peeters, P. and Weston, R. 2015. *Research for Tran Committee – The Digitisation of Tourism Enterprises*. Brussels: Directorate General for Internal Policies, Policy Department B, European Parliament.

Murison, M. 2016. *5 Technology Trends Transforming the Travel Industry* [Online]. Travelshift. Available: www.travelshift.com/5-technology-trends-transforming-the-travel-industry/ [Accessed 24 June 2017].

Novelli, M., Schmitz, B. and Spencer, T. 2006. Networks, clusters and innovation in tourism: a UK perspective. *Tourism Management*, 27, 1141–1152.

Oltermann, P. 2016. Berlin ban on Airbnb short-term rentals upheld by city court. *The Guardian*, 8 June 2016.

Ottenbacher, M. 2007. Innovation management in the hospitality industry: different strategies for achieving success. *Journal of Hospitality and Tourism Research*, 31, 431–454.

Perry, J. T., Chandler, G. N. and Markova, G. 2012. Entrepreneurial effectuation: a review and suggestions for future research. *Entrepreneurship Theory and Practice*, 36, 837–861.

Poon, A. 1993. *Tourism, Technology and Competitive Strategies*. Wallingford: CAB.

Restaurantbusinessonline. 2017. To kiosk or not to kiosk? [Online]. *Restaurantbusinessonline*. Available: www.restaurantbusinessonline.com/operations/technology/kiosk-or-not-kiosk#page=0 [Accessed 24 June 2017].

Russell, R. and Faulkner, B. 1999. Movers and shakers: chaos makers in tourism development. *Tourism Management*, 20, 411–423.

Sarasvathy, S. 2001. Causation and effectuation: toward a theoretical shift from economic inevitability to entrepreneurial contingency. *Entrepreneurship Theory and Practice*, 26, 243–263.

Schenk, E. and Guittard, C. 2011. Towards a characterization of crowdsourcing practices. *Journal of Innovation Economics*, 1, 93–107.

Schumpeter, J. 1934. *The Theory of Economic Development*. New York: Oxford University Press/Galaxy 1961.

Shane, S. and Venkataraman, S. 2000. The promise of entrepreneurship as a field of research. *Academy of Management Review*, 25, 217–226.

Skift. 2018. *The Future of Messaging Technology in the Travel Industry: Part 1* [Online]. Available: https://research.skift.com/reports/future-of-messaging-technology-in-the-travel-industry-pt-1/ [Accessed 29 January 2018].

Sorensen, F. 2007. The geographies of social networks and innovation in tourism. *Tourism Geographies*, 9, 22–48.

Statista. 2018. Number of monthly active WhatsApp users worldwide from April 2013 to December 2017 (in millions) [Online]. *Statista*. Available: www.statista.com/statistics/260819/number-of-monthly-active-whatsapp-users/ [Accessed 23 August 2018].

Steer Davies Gleave. 2007. *Competition Impact of Airline Code Sharing Agreements*. Final Report. Brussels: European Commission

Stevens, G. A. and Burley, J. 1997. 3,000 raw ideas = 1 commercial success! *Research-Technology Management*, 40, 16–27.

Stevenson, H. and Jarillo, C. 1991. A new entrepreneurial paradigm. *In:* Etzioni, A. and Lawrence, P. (eds.), *Socio-Economics: Toward a New Synthesis*. New York: M. E. Sharpe.

Stinchcombe, A. L. 1965. Social structure and organizations. *In:* March, J. G. (ed.), *Handbook of Organizations*. Chicago, IL: Rand McNally.

Swaim, R. 2011. *Failure and the Seven Sources of Innovation* [Online]. Available: www.proces-sexcellencenetwork.com/innovation/columns/failure-and-the-seven-sources-of-innova-tion/ [Accessed 21 June 2017].

Sweezy, P. M. 1943. Professor Schumpeter's theory of innovation. *The Review of Economics and Statistics*, 25, 93–96.

Taneja, N. 2018. Professor Nawal Taneja knows airlines well – but makes sure his plane arrives on time. *Perspectives* [Online]. Available: www.accenture.com/gb-en/insight-per-spectives-travel-nawal-taneja [Accessed 18 January 2018].

Thomas, R., Shaw, G. and Page, S. 2011. Understanding small firms in tourism: a perspec-tive on research trends and challenges. *Tourism Management*, 32, 963–976.

Toast. 2016. *Restaurant Technology in 2016: Dining Edition*. Toast.

Von Mises, L. 1949. *Human Action*. New Haven: Yale University Press.

Walmsley, A. 2018. Policy decisions and tourism: unintended consequences or deliberate neglect – reactions to the ban on term time holidays in the UK's south west. *Journal of Policy Research in Tourism, Hospitality and Events*.

Weiermaier, K. 2006. Product improvement or innovation: what is the key to success in tourism? In: OECD (ed.), *Innovation and Growth in Tourism*. Paris: OECD.

Wintour. 2018. *Erasmus Mundus Master on Wine Tourism Innovation* [Online]. Available: www.wintour-master.eu/what-is-wintour/en_index/ [Accessed 29 January 2018].

World Economic Forum. 2016. *The World Global Competitiveness Report 2016–2017*. Geneva: World Economic Forum.

Zervas, G., Proserpio, D. and Byers, J. 2017. The rise of the sharing economy: estimating the impact of Airbnb on the hotel industry. *Journal of Marketing Research*, 54, 687–705.

Zhao, W. and Getz, D. 2008. Characteristics and goals of rural family business owners in tourism and hospitality: a developing country perspective. *Tourism Recreation Research*, 33, 313–326.

Zimmerman, M. A. and Zeitz, G. J. 2002. Beyond survival: achieving new venture growth by building legitimacy. *Academy of Management Review*, 27, 414–431.

Chapter 4

Initial steps
The role of the business plan

The beginning is the most important part of the work.

(Plato)

Every new beginning comes from some other beginning's end.

(Seneca)

A journey of a thousand miles begins with a single step.

(Laozi/Lao-Tzu)

Introduction

Starting something involves effort. Businesses are not created by accident, they require sustained attention and intention (Bird, 1988). Many people think about starting a business but almost as many never actually start one. The three quotations above, drawn from antiquity, were selected to demonstrate that there is something very human about struggling to 'get going'. Entrepreneurship is about action, however, as we have seen already, and so this chapter explores these initial steps on the entrepreneurial journey.

Compared to the previous chapters, this chapter is more typical of texts on entrepreneurship that are aimed at a practitioner audience. It does begin with a focus on the theory surrounding venture creation as a process but then moves on to discussing business plans. It outlines the typical contents and purpose of business plans, and offers some fundamental financial considerations that no business plan would be complete without. A brief overview of financial statements is followed by a section on raising finance. A frequently neglected facet of entrepreneurship, the role of social capital and networks, is then also discussed.

Learning outcomes

At the end of this chapter the reader should be able to:

- Outline features of the entrepreneurial process.

- Appreciate the uses but also the limitations of business plans.
- Understand why new and small firms face a finance gap.
- Evaluate different forms of finance available to the entrepreneur.
- Gauge the importance of networks and start-up support to the entrepreneur.

The process of new venture creation

> Two weeks in and things still weren't running very smoothly. But that's the nature of starting up. It's not really designed to be smooth. It wasn't really designed at all.
>
> (Cheung and Norton, 2016:136, on starting their social enterprise 'Foodcycle').

Bygrave and Hofer (1991:16) in an early review of theorising in entrepreneurship suggested that the traditional focus of much entrepreneurship research had been on the individual. They then went on to highlight a redefined definition of the field of entrepreneurship to include the entrepreneurial process. This they defined as involving 'all the functions, activities, and actions associated with the perceiving of opportunities and the creation of organizations to pursue them' (Bygrave and Hofer, 1991:14). In fact, the entrepreneurial process is possibly the defining feature of entrepreneurship as its own discipline (Moroz and Hindle, 2012), and it has been suggested that it should feature more prominently in tourism research (Peters, 2005). Bygrave and Hofer (1991) suggest that a focus on the entrepreneurial process typically addresses the following:

1   What's involved in perceiving opportunities effectively and efficiently?
2   What are the key tasks in successfully establishing new organisations?
3   How are these tasks different from those involved in successfully managing ongoing organisations?
4   What are the entrepreneur's unique contributions to this process?

Whereas previous chapters dealt with the first of these questions, this chapter will focus predominantly on the second.

Turning again to Bygrave and Hofer (1991:17) the entrepreneurial process is characterised by the following:

- It is *initiated* by an act of *human volition*
- It occurs at the level of the *individual* firm
- It involves a *change of state*
- It involves a *discontinuity*
- It is a *holistic process*
- It is a *dynamic process*
- It is *unique*
- It involves *numerous antecedent variables*
- Its outcomes are extremely *sensitive to the initial conditions of these variables*

The point to note here is that the entrepreneurial process is frequently complex but always context-specific. It is not algorithmic, although it is sometimes portrayed as such. This has not stopped academics in their attempts to conceptualise the entrepreneurial process and admittedly the debate as to whether a general model of the entrepreneurial process can exist (e.g., Moroz and Hindle, 2012) is ongoing. Nonetheless, we contend that care needs to be taken in prescribing practical solutions to what can be complex problems. What will work in one situation may not in another as we can infer from Bygrave and Hofer (1991). In reading the guidelines provided in this chapter, it should therefore be borne in mind that familiarity with context, and one's own, independent appraisal thereof, should always be applied.

A common view of the entrepreneurial process is given in Figure 4.1:

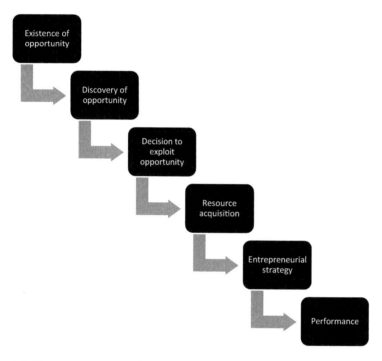

Figure 4.1 The entrepreneurial process

(Adapted from Shane, 2003)

That the process of business creation is not necessarily linear, smooth and continuous (Bygrave, 1989), that it does not follow a causation logic but a logic of effectuation (Sarasvathy, 2001) has, however, also been recognised. Indeed, some of our own research on graduate entrepreneurs (Nabi et al., 2010, 2013) shows that far from following a clear plan, the entrepreneurial process is characterised by experimentation. Some individuals do almost 'slide' into entrepreneurship. Gemmel et al. (2012) reach a similar conclusion in relation to technology entrepreneurs' processes of ideation (see previous chapter).

The business plan

In the general spirit of this book, we start this section on business plans with an air of criticality, one could even say scepticism. The warning here specifically relates to the value of business plans. Hannon and Atherton (1998:102) write: 'There is an ongoing debate within the academic literature about the value of the business plan in the development of the small firm.' We should hasten to add that Hannon and Atherton's (1998) review of research in this area reveals a great deal of value in the use of business planning as a process, mirroring Napoleon Bonaparte's 'The plan is nothing: planning is everything' (according to Bridge et al., 2003:236). Anyone interested in setting up a business and writing a business plan will stumble across commentary such as that provided by Monroy (cited in Hannon and Atherton, 1998:104) who in relation to business plans argues that:

- They are very rarely referred to after preparation
- They are written to impress not to accurately describe
- 56% of successful businesses have written plans, therefore 44% have not; the benefit is marginal
- There is no evidence of causality between business plan creation and successful venture management.

Nonetheless, as much as they have been critiqued, business plans have also been endorsed:

> Perhaps the most important step in launching any new venture or expanding an existing one is the construction of a business plan.
>
> (Barrow et al., 2001:6)

> The creation of your business plan is the first step on your path to financial success.
>
> (Szycher, 2015:273)

Hannon and Atherton (1998), although less complimentary about business plans as an output, recognise that there are situations when they are required (mainly when seeking financial support; e.g., from banks or funding agencies/bodies). Lenders will want to see a business plan because:

- It allows the business/fledgling business to set and monitor quantifiable targets. Where targets are not met, the causes and subsequent courses of action can be negotiated with support agencies/lenders.
- It assists the support agency to understand the impact its support is having on the organisation/business.
- It provides a means to assess the risk inherent in a project/business proposal. This is critical for funders because the cost of borrowing is determined by levels of risk; the higher the risk, the higher the return lenders will demand.

The business plan should be considered a kind of sales document by the entrepreneur. It should convey 'your irrepressible excitement and vision to potential investors and stakeholders' (Szycher, 2015:273). That said, a balance does need to be reached between exuberance and realism. The business plan should be underpinned by realistic assumptions;[1] it should reassure the potential investor. The business plan serves as a means to clarify an entrepreneur's thoughts about their new business/business idea. Indeed, the number of things one could, or arguably should consider (not everyone does, of course) is vast. The business plan can be viewed as a device to organise thinking and to thereby assist in answering the following types of question:

- Is there a market for my product/service?
- Where is my competitive advantage?
- How much is all this going to cost?
- How soon can I expect to be making money and will it be enough to cover costs?

One of the dangers inherent in business plans is to regard them as a fool-proof, i.e., guaranteed, path to success. Drawing on Mintzberg and Waters' (1985) seminal article on strategic management, a distinction is made between deliberate strategies – realised as intended – from emergent strategies – patterns or consistencies realised despite, or in the absence of, intentions. As Mintzberg and Waters (1985) point out, for a strategy to be perfectly deliberate, for the realised strategy to form exactly as intended, no external force (market, technological, political, etc.) could have interfered with them. In other words: 'The environment. . . must have been either perfectly predictable, totally benign, or else under the full control of the organization' (Mintzberg and Waters, 1985:258).

Evidently, this situation is highly unlikely to arise in the real world and as a consequence we recognise that there is going to be some divergence between a plan as intended and a plan as realised. Precisely because of this, the business plan should be a working document, subject to revisions as required.

The structure of a business plan

There is no set format for a business plan, although it would be a peculiar business plan that did not cover key aspects of the fledgling business such as sales and profit forecasts, a description of the product/service, sources of anticipated finance and an overview of who is involved.

To provide examples of what could, and commonly is, included in a business plan we offer the following from a range of sources:

According to Friend and Zehle (2004) a business plan:

- Will identify the market, its growth prospects, the target customers and the main competitors
- Must be based upon a credible set of assumptions and should identify the assumptions to which the success of the business is most sensitive
- Should also identify the risks facing the business, the potential downsides and the actions that will be taken to mitigate the risks
- Should describe what makes the business different from its competitors: its source of competitive advantage and how it will be sustained in the longer term.

They also provide more general advice when writing a business plan, which is that it needs to tell a story, it needs to be consistent, and at its core should be the customer.

Table 4.1 provides an overview of three different business plan templates. Szycher's (2015) was chosen because it is not sector-specific, whereas Lee-Ross and Lashley's (2009) relates to the hospitality industry. The Prince's Trust is a UK charity that offers support to young people (18–30-year-olds) including a free template on its website.[2]

Table 4.1 Elements of a business plan

Szycher (2015)	Lee-Ross and Lashley (2009)	The Prince's Trust 2017 (abridged)
Executive summary	Executive summary	Executive summary
		Elevator pitch
Company description Business concept	The business and management - History - Current mission - Objectives - The team	Owner's background - Why you want to start your own business - Previous work experience - Qualifications and Education - Training - Hobbies and interests
	Products and services - Products and services - Current sales mix	Products and services - What are you going to sell? - Describe the basic product/service - Describe the different types of product/service you are going to be selling
Marketing plan Market analysis Industry analysis and trends Competition Sales strategy	Market and competition - Description of customers - Customer occasions, needs and benefits - Market segments - Market size in the area - Location of customers and flows - Market projects over the period - Competition	The market - Describe your customer (business/individual/both) - Where are your customers based? - What prompts your customers to buy your product/service? - Have you sold any products/services already?
Management team and organisation		Market research - Key findings from desk research - Key findings from field research – questionnaires - Key findings from field research – test trading
Technology and innovation Risk assessment Operations and management plan		Marketing strategy - What are you going to do? - Why have you chosen this marketing method? - How much will it cost?
Milestones and exit plan		Competitor analysis - Overview of competitors (named) with a description of their product/service, price, strengths and weaknesses - SWOT analysis - Unique selling point

Szycher (2015)	Lee-Ross and Lashley (2009)	The Prince's Trust 2017 (abridged)
Financial plan	Operations - Critical success factors - Quality management and control - Organisation structure - Employee management and motivation	Operations and logistics - Production - Delivery to customers - Payment methods and terms - Suppliers - Premises - Equipment (with costs) - Transport - Legal requirements - Insurance requirements - Management and staff
Supporting documents	Competitive business strategy - Pricing policy - Promotional plans - Premises - Competitor responses	Costs and pricing strategy - Product/service name - Number of units in calculation - Cost per unit, price per unit, profit margin, mark up
	Forecasts and results - Sales forecasts - Operational budget - Business objectives and action plans	Financial forecasts (by month) - Sales forecasts - Costs forecast - Assumptions - Estimated costs - Estimated income - Cashflow forecast
		Back-up plan - Short-term plan - Long-term plan - Plan B

Mason and Stark (2004) helpfully point out that a range of investors will seek a variety of things in a business plan. Their study compared what bankers, business angels (BAs) and venture capital fund managers (VCFMs) were particularly interested in ascertaining prior to deciding whether to invest in a company or lend it money. Bankers were more interested in the financial aspects of the business rather than the market conditions or the entrepreneur. Although differences between VCFMs and BAs were less pronounced, they still existed. Whereas both focused on market and finance issues, BAs placed more emphasis on the entrepreneur and 'investor fit' considerations (the investor's background and relation to the sector being targeted).

'Accounting 101' for business start-up

Break-even point

Without wanting to go into too much detail here, as finance and accounting textbooks exist that cover these issues, we feel it would be remiss not to cover some basic financial concepts that would normally be required in any business plan. All business plans will need to include projected sales and costs, for example. Profit is only made once costs have been deducted from sales (therefore, if costs are greater than sales we would be looking at negative profit or, put simply, a loss). One of the most common sayings in business is 'sales are vanity, profit is sanity' (and variations thereof, such as 'turnover is vanity, profit is sanity but cash is reality'). This may sound obvious but there are many businesses that are so keen to make additional sales and grow market share that associated cost of sales are readily forgotten. Then, a rude awakening occurs when the period's financial reports indicate a loss, especially when the break-even projections indicated a profit was to be expected. Small firms, especially start-ups, are less experienced in making predictions surrounding sales and costs, certainly compared to larger firms that can draw on a wealth of historical data, and experience, to make their estimates. A frequent error in business plans is over-optimistic sales forecasts (remember, the assumptions underpinning the figures need to be sound).

The break-even point is that point at which sales equal costs and therefore profits equal zero:

SALES – COSTS = ZERO

Costs themselves comprise fixed costs (that do not change with the volume of sales, such as rent, manager's salary) and variable costs, which rise and fall in proportion with sales volume (e.g., the ingredients required to serve a meal in a restaurant). As is noted later on, many tourism services are characterised by high fixed costs and low variable costs. This means that once the break-even point is reached, profits rise quite rapidly (but the reverse is also true, losses accumulate quite rapidly the further one moves away from the break-even point in the opposite direction). This is demonstrated in Figure 4.2 and the accompanying data in Table 4.2.

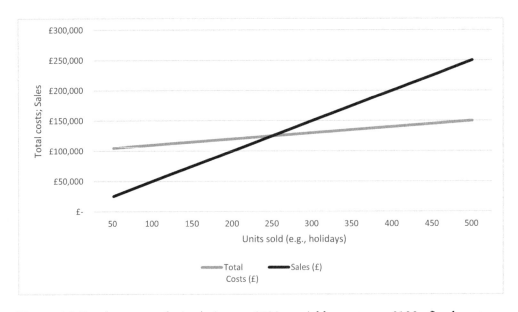

Figure 4.2 Break-even analysis (price = £500; variable costs = £100; fixed costs = £100,000)

Table 4.2 Break-even analysis

Sales volume (e.g.holidays sold)	Fixed costs (£)	Variable costs (£)	Total costs (£)	Sales (£)	Profit (loss) (£)
50	100,000	5,000	105,000	25,000	−80,000
100	100,000	10,000	110,000	50,000	−60,000
150	100,000	15,000	115,000	75,000	−40,000
200	100,000	20,000	120,000	100,000	−20,000
250	100,000	25,000	125,000	125,000	0
300	100,000	30,000	130,000	150,000	20,000
350	100,000	35,000	135,000	175,000	40,000
400	100,000	40,000	140,000	200,000	60,000
450	100,000	45,000	145,000	225,000	80,000
500	100,000	50,000	150,000	250,000	100,000

In the above example, we are able to estimate the break-even point visually (i.e., at about 250 units/holidays). Rather than representing the break-even point graphically, and then trying to work out visually where this point lies, we are equally able to work this out using elementary calculus as shown here using the above example:

Profit is defined as: Sales – Costs. The Breakeven Point (BP) is where profits equal zero. Therefore, BP occurs where:

Sales – Costs = [price x units sold] – [fixed costs + variable costs x units sold]
= 0

Inserting our data this results in: £500x – [£100,000 + £100x] = 0
→ £500x = £100,000 + £100x
→ £400x = £100,000
→ x = 250

Financial statements

The three most important financial statements of a firm are the balance sheet, the income statement (or profit and loss account), and the cash flow statement. Although we are not going to go into detail here, as plenty of introductory accounting and finance textbooks already exist (including some that focus specifically on the tourism and/or hospitality sectors), we felt a necessarily brief overview appropriate given their importance in business, and as elements of a business plan.

The balance sheet tells us about the total wealth of a company (assets) and what it owes ('debt and equity' or 'liabilities and capital'). The two sides of the balance sheet must balance (no surprises there!) as a company cannot own more assets than its sources of finance have permitted it to own (even if amongst these sources are included contributions from family/the owner). The basic balance sheet equation is therefore:

ASSETS = CAPITAL + LIABILITIES or ASSETS = EQUITY + DEBT

In a start-up firm capital (or equity) represents the owner's contribution whereas liabilities are the sources others have contributed. The debt-to-equity ratio (D/E) therefore is a financial ratio indicating the relative proportion of the owner's contribution and debt to finance the company's assets. It is important to consider, as it serves as a measure of risk for those providing funds to the start-up. If, for example, the D/E ratio is 3, this would mean that three-quarters of the assets have been funded by debt finance, and a quarter by equity (the owner's contribution). So what is considered a good D/E ratio? There is no agreement, which should not be surprising because of other contextual factors that should be taken into account (notably industry context). In reviewing the gearing ratio[3] (closely associated to the D/E ratio), McLaney (2011:58) states: 'It is not particularly easy to say whether a particular figure represents a high figure. "High" is probably defined as significantly larger than is typically found in the industry in which the business operates.'

The balance sheet offers many insights into a company's financial position but it should be remembered that it only provides a snapshot; to understand changes one would need to compare balance sheets across accounting periods. At the end of the financial year (or accounting period) profits that are not otherwise spent (e.g., dividend payments or withdrawals by the owner) will be added to the firm's capital (a loss would reduce its capital).

The income statement provides crucial information on the operating activities of a firm. It answers the question 'how much wealth (profit) has the business generated (over a predetermined period)?' and is therefore a crucial measure of a firm's performance. For the start-up that has only just started trading, or perhaps has not yet even started trading, the income statement provided in the business plan is based on estimates and supporting assumptions. It is very important, vital in fact, to offer evidence to support one's anticipated sales figures (e.g., by providing evidence of orders).

The principle behind the income statement is to deduct costs from income (or revenue; see Table 4.3). Revenue might arise for the firm via various sources; for example, sales, interest, fees for services and subscriptions (raising finance to support the firm via loans, equity, etc. is not classified as revenue, these do not relate to operating activities). For the start-up, revenue is likely to derive mainly from sales. Coming up with an anticipated revenue figure can be tricky (just how many products or services will we sell?). Likewise, anticipating costs associated with sales can be tricky too but these figures need to be estimated if we are to offer an anticipated profit forecast. Because the income statement covers the operating activities of the firm – for example, selling holidays, selling tours, selling hotel rooms, etc. – only costs associated with these operating activities, i.e., costs incurred as a result of generating revenues, should be taken into account.

Table 4.3 offers the first part of an income statement, which will suffice for the purposes of understanding gross and net profit – two key financial metrics that should feature in any business plan. Gross profit margin is calculated by dividing gross profit by revenues expressed as a percentage, in our example £30,000 divided by £100,000 which is 30%. This figure is very useful in understanding the relationship between revenue and the costs directly associated with producing that revenue. The business owner might think of this as indicating that for every £1 earned, 30 pence remain as gross profit. It also gives investors an indication of how able a company will be to cover operating expenses (the smaller the GP margin, the less is left of the original revenue to cover these expenses). Many financial metrics really only begin to make sense when compared with the same metrics from other businesses, or comparisons are made across time. While the latter is not possible with

Table 4.3 Gross and net profit

Turnover (revenue)	£100,000.00
Cost of sales (= direct costs)	£70,000.00
Gross profit	£30,000.00
Other operating expenses (= indirect costs)	£15,000.00
Operating profit (= net profit)	£15,000.00

the start-up, it is possible to compare this data across similar firms. This kind of information is of use to both the entrepreneur and potential investors.

Once the cost of sales (or direct costs) has been deducted from turnover, we still need to deduct indirect costs (or other operating expenses) to determine our net profit figure. Although this figure is then closer to what might be considered 'profit' in layman's terms, it is not the same as what is left to invest back in the firm or to withdraw for the owner's personal use. Examples of other operating expenses, which need to be deducted from gross profit to arrive at a net profit figure, include things such as utilities, salaries and wages, rent and rates, insurance and depreciation. Similar to the calculation of the gross profit margin, the net profit margin is determined by taking net profit and dividing this by turnover. In our example above, this would result in £15,000 divided by £100,000 = 15%. Again, a useful way of thinking about net profit margin is to consider it as what remains from every £1 the new firm makes in sales (e.g., 15 pence).

Cash is often described as the lifeblood of a business (see also Case study 4.2 on cash flow and the foot and mouth disease outbreak in the UK). It is critical for the start-up to ensure it has sufficient cash (or working capital) to manage its day-to-day operations. The cash flow statement is a summary of the cash receipts and payments over the period concerned. Because of accrual accounting, where income is not the same as cash received (a company might sell some of its goods and services on credit) cash flow statements can be very important, ensuring the company does not run out of cash while still generating profits. We will cover the importance of cash flow again in the next section on raising finance and financial management.

Raising finance and financial management

In general terms, finance refers to sources and management of money – both are critical to a firm's survival and success. No business can function without finance, whether to purchase equipment, stock, buildings, vehicles (capital investments) or simply to get by on a day-to-day basis (e.g., its working capital). As Down (2010:132) notes, 'Running a business is dependent on having and generating sufficient cash, and understanding – both knowing and practising – how to use limited resources efficiently is crucial to business survival.' Financial resources are needed to start a venture, for ongoing operations, and also to grow. Unsurprisingly then, lack of access to finance is a key inhibitor of business start-up and growth. Jarvis and Schizas (2012) write of a 'finance gap' that exists when a firm identifies lucrative opportunities but does not have sufficient funds, either for internal or external sources, to exploit those opportunities. The causes of finance gaps for small and start-up firms may differ from those of large counterparts. This section will review sources of finance available to the small firm, whether already established, in the process of being established, or wanting to grow.

In its 2015 report on financing SMEs and entrepreneurs, the OECD (2015) recognised that SMEs may have greater difficulty in obtaining funding than large firms because they are seen as more risky, and more likely to default than large firms, a point confirmed by O'Rourke (2009) with regard to tourism firms in transition economies. There is evidence that the rate of non-performing loans, i.e., loans where the debtor has missed a scheduled payment for at least 90 days, is higher for SMEs than for large firms. The financial crisis that triggered in 2007/2008 has also negatively affected SMEs' ability to obtain funding, as banks tried to shore up their balance sheets in the aftermath (weak bank balance sheets translate into a reduction in the availability of credit, at higher interest rates and more stringent conditions).

Jarvis and Schizas (2012) have pointed to the important role industry and firm characteristics play when assessing risk for small firms (they also argue that assessing risk at the level of the small firm is extraordinarily difficult). Risk is generally understood as relating to variability in returns. It is recognised that demand for tourism services and products is susceptible to fluctuations, often unpredictable, so a case can be made that lending to tourism firms carries an element of structural (as opposed to firm-specific) risk. However, publicly available data on small firm finance is sparse because they are not subject to the same reporting requirements as large or even listed firms.

It is often assumed that the first port of call for financing small firms comes from banks. However, in a tongue-in-cheek remark that nonetheless contains more than a grain of truth Austin et al. (2006:11) quip: 'Traditionally, start-ups rely on the three "F"s (friends, family, and fools) for most of their funding.' There is some evidence to support the reliance on family and friends at least as a source of start-up finance. With reference to Turkey, for example, based on a sample of small hotels, Özer (1996) found that personal funds were the main source of initial investment. As we have seen, the new venture creation process is rarely linear and neat. The notion that an entrepreneur has an idea, draws up a business plan and then goes to the bank to obtain funding is probably less accurate than many would believe. This has been reinforced by developments in ICT that permit businesses to start up 'on a shoestring' and only when they grow seek traditional means of funding such as bank loans.

Furthermore, contextual factors will also determine the extent to which family and friends (let's just forget about fools for now) are able to support a new venture. Lingelbach et al. (2005) suggest, for example, that limited personal and family savings and an absence of financial innovation severely limit the growth prospects of promising start-ups in developing countries specifically. By the same token, in the United Arab Emirates, Ahmad (2015) identified that small and medium-sized hotel owners were able to draw on family and friends' savings to a large extent, which he puts down to general levels of personal wealth in the area. We will have a look at financial innovations below but it is to be noted that alongside levels of wealth, attitudes to risk, borrowing and saving, which are at least in part culturally determined, will all affect the ability and willingness to lend to a family member or a friend.

Case study 4.1: Understanding context – what drives private savings rates?

Individual savings rates play an important role in economics and entrepreneurship. One person's savings are another person's investment. Savings and investments are two sides of the same coin (the assumption here is that our savings are in some way – for example, via bank deposits or as shares in a company – introduced to the financial markets; it is no good if the money is tucked away under the mattress!). Unsurprisingly, governments and policy-makers are therefore interested in understanding what drives individual savings rates. The OECD (2017): Household Savings Forecast for 2018 covers data on 23 developed countries (the saving rate is defined as the share of household net disposable income that is saved). Here is a sample of savings rates from the highest to lowest (%):

- Switzerland: 17.466
- Luxembourg: 16.648
- Sweden: 15.713
- USA: 5.597
- Australia: 4.754
- Finland: –4.944
- Latvia: –5.479
- Lithuania: –5.872

Based on these data alone, it is evident that even in developed economies individual savings rates can vary considerably, and thinking about the role of culture one could tentatively see some evidence of its influence in those countries with the lowest savings rates (Finland, Latvia and Lithuania). However, we cannot conclude that because one individual's savings rate is higher than that of another, one individual is necessarily more inclined to save. Savings rates also increase with income growth and levels (Loayza et al., 2000) and many individuals are simply not able to save because meeting their daily needs presents such a challenge (hence why the measurement relates proportion of disposable income; if one's entire income is used up on day-to-day necessities, there is no disposable income). Unsurprisingly perhaps then, the influence of income growth is larger in developing than in developed countries. In developing countries, a doubling of income per capita is estimated, other things equal, to raise the long-run private saving rate by some ten percentage points of disposable income (Loayza et al., 2000).

Cash is king: cash flow and the untimely demise of the successful firm

Sadly, it is the case that many otherwise successful tourism firms, those with a successful business model at least, fail. Frequently the reason is a failure of managing working capital – the money that is required on a day-to-day basis to manage the firm's operations. Sometimes small and rapidly growing firms fall victim to their own success. In this regard Churchill and Lewis (1983) point to the so-called omnipotence syndrome where a growing business grows too fast. A cash flow short-fall occurs when a company is owed more in the short term than it owes in the short term but a debtor delays payment leaving the company short of cash. If there are insufficient funds to cover the day-to-day running of the business it will ultimately fold. Here is a hypothetical example, simplified to illustrate the point:

A family-owned and family-run hotel in the Greek resort of Kefalonia receives a block booking to the value of €20,000 from a specialist French-based tour opera-tor for next year's peak season. Payment terms are 15% upfront (September) with the remainder to be paid by March the following year. As promised, the operator pays €3,000 in September but fails to pay the outstanding amount of €17,000 in March. The French tour operator is itself facing financial difficulties following ter-rorist attacks in Egypt, one of its key markets, and assures the hotel it will be able to cover the outstanding debt by the end of May. Unfortunately for the Greek hotel, it was relying on the funds from the tour operator to undertake essential maintenance to the hotel's swimming pool and dining facilities. Because of its already precarious financial situation, it is unable to source funding elsewhere and so has to delay the maintenance plans, which result in the temporary closure of the pool and a less than inviting ambience in the dining room. This results in customer complaints, negative online reviews and cancelled bookings. The company's financial situation goes from bad to worse (despite the French tour operator eventually paying the outstanding amount, the negative publicity has taken its toll). Unable to meet its own financial commitments and pursued by its creditors and suppliers via the courts for payment, the hotel has to close.

This serves as an example of a number of characteristics of the management of tourism firms:

- A lack of financial acumen on the part of owner/managers
- Greater difficulty of small firms to obtain funding and lack of cash reserves
- Power of large suppliers to dictate favourable financial terms
- Overreliance on key source markets with attendant risk (the 'all eggs in one bas-ket' scenario)
- Related to the previous point, tourism's susceptibility to crises
- The power of online review sites.

Case study 4.2: Foot and mouth disease and the Lake District, UK

Foot and mouth disease (FMD) is a highly contagious disease that affects cattle, swine and other cloven-hooved animals. The UK had witnessed outbreaks of FMD previously, prior to the 2001 outbreak, most recently in 1967. However, when the disease struck again in 2001 the UK government was accused of hav-ing been ill-prepared. Much had changed, however, in the English countryside since 1967. As Miller and Ritchie (2003) explain in their review of the impact of FMD on the Cheltenham Festival, in part at least any lack of preparation could be explained by the ascendancy of tourism in rural economies. Indeed, while the government was keen to contain the disease (more than 2,000 cases were reported and more than 4 million animals culled) for a fear of its impact on agriculture, accusations were levied against the government that it underestimated, in fact initially ignored, the impact on the visitor economy. Although the disease is not serious in humans, and no single case of transmission to humans was noted in the 2001 outbreak, images of a landscape covered in palls of smoke from burning animal carcasses suggested to many that the countryside was off-limits. In many instances the government did restrict access to disease-affected areas to reduce contagion. The toll on the tourism industry was extensive (calculated in the billions of pounds; Miller and Ritchie, 2003).

In the Lake District tourism employs a quarter of the workforce (Cowell, 2001); it is vital to the region's economy. The impact of FMD on tourism in this region was severe. Results from the United Kingdom Tourism Survey show that in the months from January to June 2001 there were 23% fewer trips to Cumbria (the county containing the Lake District) than in the corresponding period in 2000, resulting in 22% fewer overnight stops and a 16% reduction in visitor spending (equivalent to £266 million) (Bennett et al., 2002). The impacts extended to tourism-dependent businesses also: 'This outbreak is not just affecting farmers,' Robert Perkins, who runs a company that makes walkers' boots and other gear, was quoted as saying. 'It's affecting the whole rural infrastructure. It's only a matter of weeks before some small retailers go bust' (Cowell, 2001).

A Business Recovery Fund (£80 million) was introduced to provide targeted help for small businesses. It was designed to cover measures that would allow viable businesses to improve their prospects after FMD was over, but it specifically excluded payments to assist with cash flow shortfalls. Grants under the scheme were limited to £15,000, of which up to £7,500 could be used to help meet interest on bank loans (Cumbria County Council, 2002).

Non-bank finance

O'Rourke (2009) argues that for the tourism SME, the traditional bank loan is not necessarily the most fitting source of funding because of the reliance on regular payments that do not align with income generation patterns (this relates to Jarvis and Schizas', 2012, point that small firms are riskier because returns are more variable than in large companies). However, today there are far more sources of finance available to tourism SMEs than used to be the case. The budding entrepreneur is faced with more options than going to his/her bank or relying on friends and family. The financial services sector has itself undergone rapid changes and innovation in the sector is rife. Alternative financial instruments, which include venture and growth capital, business angel investment, asset-based finance instruments such as leasing and factoring, mezzanine finance and crowdfunding, are garnering increasing attention by policy makers (OECD, 2015). The sources of funding available will depend on the sophistication of the financial markets in a given country.

- **Venture capital (VC) and angel investors**: VC is provided by an investor or group of investors who pool together and invest in what they believe is a start-up with potential to generate substantial returns on their investment. Often venture capital comes from so-called angel investors, usually high net worth individuals. The ventures supported are likely to be more risky than those banks would lend to, but also offer the potential for greater returns. Rather than charging interest on a loan as banks would do, angel investors seek equity (a share in the company) in return for their investment. As the value of the company increases, so does the return on their initial investment. While crucial for firms that are otherwise not able to access more traditional sources of finance, a possible downside is that the investors may want a say in the company. Creating a compelling business plan is critical to obtaining VC and the process has been popularised globally in television programmes such as *Dragons' Den* in the UK, *Die Höhle der Löwen* (*Lion's Den*) in Germany, *Tu Oportunidad* (*Your Chance*) in Spain, or the original *Money Tigers* in Japan (Nisen, 2013).
- **Crowdfunding**: In straightforward terms, crowdfunding involves raising capital from a large number of people. Hornuf and Schwienbacher (2017:579) provide a more academic definition: 'equity crowdfunding (also referred to as investment-based crowdfunding, securities crowdfunding, or crowdinvesting). . . describes a financial innovation in securities issuance that gives small entrepreneurs access to the general public'. Crowdfunding occurs in different forms, the two most prominent being equity crowdfunding and the reward-based crowdfunding. Reward-based crowdfunding occurs when, for a small amount of money (usually less than US$1,000), the funder receives a reward, often the product or service that the start-up is seeking funding for. One of the benefits of crowdfunding is that start-ups are able to keep their equity and therefore maintain control of their business. They also gain a committed community of backers/early adopters. Equity crowdfunding, on the other hand, usually involves the funder providing larger amounts of money (greater than US$1,000) and where the funder gains a stake (equity) in the venture. Whereas venture capital and angel investors are professional investors, most individuals who invest via crowdfunding will not be professionals. Because of this, however, certain forms of crowdfunding (e.g., equity crowdfunding) are more heavily regulated in certain countries.
- **Asset-based financing (ABF)**: This is also known as commercial financing and occurs when a loan is provided against collateral, normally a balance sheet asset such as inventory or accounts receivable. It is usually used when traditional bank financing is hard to find. As was noted above, small and medium-sized firms tend to be riskier in terms of non-performing loans and therefore lending is often asset-based, a form of guarantee for the lender that they will be able to recoup their funds should the borrower default on the loan. Asset-based lending will also become more prevalent in an environment of tightening lending conditions, such as many financial markets have encountered since the global financial crisis in 2007/2008. Different types of ABF exist, such as factoring (using a company's accounts receivable to secure funding) or invoice discounting (similar to factoring, it uses cash tied up in a company's assets, here outstanding invoices). Invoice discounting differs from factoring in that the sales ledger (the record

of sales) is not taken over by the invoice discounter as happens with factoring, which means charges tend to be lower. ABF offers a number of advantages but also risks: funds can be generated quickly, the level of borrowing possible is usually higher than via a bank loan or overdraft facility and factoring offers a range of services such as accounts receivable invoicing, processing and collection. The downside is they can be more expensive than traditional loans, and they may affect the customer relationship.

- **Mezzanine finance**: This form of finance offers the lender equity in case of default on a loan. In simplified terms, it sits between traditional forms of loan finance (senior debt) and the owner's own equity and is therefore termed 'mezzanine' (it is often described as a hybrid form of finance). There are many different forms of mezzanine finance but the most common is where the lender has the right to turn a portion of the money into equity. It should be noted that mezzanine finance is very expensive and is not a source of start-up finance.

The number and variety of fundraising sites for entrepreneurs continues to grow. Examples of such fundraising sources include:

- Kickstarter (New York City), www.kickstarter.com
  Kickstarter was originally founded to support creative projects but now tends to finance technology start-ups. Individuals wishing to raise funds establish a funding target to which others can then pledge. If a project fails to reach its target (54% in 2011; Greenwald, 2012) supporters pay nothing.
- Indiegogo (San Francisco), www.indiegogo.com
  Similar to Kickstarter, Indiegogo, which was founded in 2008, is a form of reward-based crowdfunding. It describes itself as a launchpad for entrepreneurial ideas and promises support from concept to market. It tries to portray a community-orientated approach. Its website claims: 'With the help of our Indiegogo community, we're redefining entrepreneurship – shifting it from being a privilege to a right. Because every inventive idea should have its shot, and every creative entrepreneur should have their moment. Together we can do anything' (Indiegogo, 2017).
- Crowdcube (Exeter, UK), www.crowdcube.com
  Crowdcube, an equity-based crowdfunding platform, was established in 2011. In 2017 it claimed to have a 48% share of the crowdfunding market in the UK, and more than 400,000 registered users. In its own words, and with reference to the angel investor programme *Dragons' Den* it offers investors the opportunity to become armchair dragons (Crowdcube, 2017).
- RocketHub, www.rockethub.com
  Similar to Indiegogo, RocketHub.com prides itself on being more than 'just' a source of funding: 'At RocketHub.com it is our mission to offer the achievers of the world networking, funding and growth opportunities' (RocketHub, 2017). It also boasts of being the world's leading social network for entrepreneurs. It is evident that these platforms are more than just sources of raising capital. RocketHub has partnered with Bankroll Ventures to create the ELEQUITY Funding™ platform. If you are thinking of starting a business you need to provide details which a team of individuals at ELEQUITY Funding™ will review before getting back in touch to discuss the best way of raising finance for the business idea.

- GrowVC (Hong Kong)

  GrowVC explains what it does as follows: 'GrowVC Group is the global leader of fintech innovations, digital and distributed finance services, and digital infrastructures.' This is admittedly quite a mouthful and no less confusing for those not familiar with the jargon. In essence, however, as its website goes on to explain: 'Our mission is to make the finance services more effective, transparent and democratic' (GrowVC Group, 2017), which is easier to digest. It claims it started the world's first equity crowdfunding service.

As we can see from the above examples, crowdfunding takes many forms and there are now a plethora of avenues open to those seeking funding for their start-ups. Importantly for the tourism entrepreneur, these platforms often provide a networking platform that can offer advice and product testing. None of these forms of finance are tourism-specific, but they are open to firms of all sectors including tourism.

Bootstrapping

In contrast to conventional wisdom, many firms are started without the need for substantial financial resources. Some entrepreneurs start their businesses on the proverbial shoestring, with very little finance at all. In fact the term 'bootstrapping' means to start a business with very limited financial means. Money can be saved for example by: setting a business up from home (think not only Microsoft or Apple but the majority of B&Bs operate out of someone's home, as well as tourism intermediaries, such as holiday cottage marketing companies, specialist travel agents, etc.), minimising your salary until the business has grown sufficiently, seeking discounts from suppliers, calling in favours from your network and so forth.

Financial support for tourism firms

Tourism, as we shall discuss in more detail in Chapter 10, is promoted in many instances as a means of reversing economic decline in poor-performing regions. Consequently, numerous initiatives can be found that seek to support tourism firms. The Australian territory of Queensland for example offers a range of grants (one-off funding) and programmes (ongoing funding) to tourism firms. These grants and programmes are made available in an attempt to develop 'the capability and capacity of businesses to grow, become resilient, and achieve the 2020 expenditure growth target' (Queensland Government, 2017). By publishing *The Grants Guide* in 2015 the government of Queensland recognises the challenges many small tourism firms, including start-ups, face in identifying appropriate grants and then successfully applying for them (most grants come with extensive documentation that the small business owner/manager may simply not have the time to digest). Grants will vary in size, from a couple of thousand US dollars equivalent to over a million US dollars. Some grants require match funding by the firm, others do not. Grants are sometimes paid up front, others when the business has made the initial outlay.

Frequently funding for the tourism sector will be indirect. Thus, many tourism firms rely on the participation of the local community or indigenous population. Funding schemes to support indigenous businesses may thereby indirectly equate to funding for tourism firms. The same logic applies to non-sector-specific funding that nonetheless targets particular locations that may be heavily tourism-dependent. The important thing the tourism entrepreneur should be aware of is the likelihood of the existence of financial assistance, or assistance in kind (e.g., free training).

Networks and social capital

Networks, which can be both formal (between official public sector bodies and businesses) and informal (social, such as family and friends), are crucial in most entrepreneurs' start-up stories, including in tourism. Entrepreneurship has been considered for some time now to be embedded within social networks (Aldrich, 1987; Johannison, 1988; Anderson and Miller, 2002) and it is clear to see from Gartner's (1985) framework of new venture creation (Figure 2.1) that entrepreneurship is a culturally and historically embedded phenomenon. Copp and Ivy (2001:346) within the context of tourism start-ups claim: 'The survival of a business venture, particularly a small one, can be greatly aided by interaction with and the support of other entities (networking).' Zhou et al. (2017:340) go so far as to conclude: 'social capital is linked to the success and sustainability of tourism entrepreneurship', and this is by no means an overstatement. It affects start-up rates, start-up survival and success, with the literature generally showing a positive relationship between social capital and these variables (Audretsch et al., 2011).

Social capital has been defined in numerous ways and in fact social networks and social capital are often used interchangeably (Casson and Della Giusta, 2007). Putnam (2000), for example, has defined social capital as involving the building and maintaining of networks and the norms of behaviour that underpin them, and along similar lines Bourdieu and Wacquant (1992) suggest social capital is the sum of the resources that accrue to an individual or group, by virtue of possessing networks. Field (2003) explains how a network becomes a resource underpinned by social capital, which then constitutes an intangible asset. This is a useful bringing together of the two concepts.

Casson and Della Giusta (2007) provide examples of how social capital, and associated social networks, can help the entrepreneur, from the obvious to the less considered: an individual may benefit from a strong extended family to draw on intergenerational finance, as well as from childcare support. Gaining access to information is one of the key benefits of social networks and frequently it involves exploration of opportunities. An individual who belongs to a local club or society may find out about a development opportunity; for example, a brownfield site that could be converted to residential use, or, to use a tourism example, a local B&B that the current owner wants to put up for sale. Using Sorensen's (2007:26) words, 'destination-specific know-how and specialist tacit knowledge provide the means to exploit new opportunities and develop new products'. This was also evident in Novelli et al.'s (2006) investigation of a Healthy Lifestyle Tourism Cluster in the south of England, where newly established businesses that were part of this cluster were able to share market and environmental knowledge.

Sorensen (2007) also discusses vertical and horizontal networks in tourism. Vertical distribution networks are those between tourism firms at destinations and their distributors; vertical input relations are those between tourism firms and their suppliers; horizontal competitive or chain relations are those between similar tourism firms, such as hotels; and horizontal complementary networks between different types of tourism firms, such as hotels and attractions. As the tourism product is an amalgamation of different components, with these elements provided by different suppliers, the importance of networks to strengthen and sustain these activities becomes apparent.

In a business context, networks consist of nodes (e.g., businesses and support agencies) and the links between them. However, taking a step back we can identify networks within networks, and links between networks. In this regard Morrison and Teixeira (2004:201) write about learning communities, which are concerned with the concept of networks of networks, 'meshing and interconnecting diagonal, horizontal and vertical organisational types and configurations as appropriate'. For the tourism entrepreneur it is vital that s/he is part of these networks, which can provide access to resources, information and even a voice in destination management, ensuring s/he is part of decision-making.

Many studies of social networks in tourism exist that provide some useful examples of the value of these networks to entrepreneurship. Viren et al. (2014) reflect on the use of social networks in the Roanoke River Valley, North Carolina, USA. Businesses in rural communities often lack financial and technical support, but by joining business associations may be able to overcome some of these challenges. Viren et al. (2014:486) conclude: 'As rural communities embrace tourism as means to diversify the economy, harnessing the power of social networks is essential to their success.' Their study also mentions trust, and the increase in trust that social networks provide.

Despite the importance of social capital to the entrepreneurial process, not all nascent entrepreneurs feel inclined to draw on or create social networks to support their new ventures. In some of his own research (Nabi et al., 2010), the author explored the transition into graduate entrepreneurship in the UK. Findings suggested a distinction between entrepreneurially mature and immature graduate entrepreneurs. We do not place a value judgement on the term 'mature' here, the entrepreneurial mature individual is simply described as an individual who displays a more reflective sense of self, where a career in self-employment has been explored and thought through realistically (Nabi et al., 2010). This includes an openness to support from others, thinking one does not have to 'go it alone' (this can be difficult for some entrepreneurs, as independence is often a key motivator). The study (Nabi et al., 2010) provided examples of 'immature' entrepreneurs who struggled because they ignored the advice and support available from public sector support agencies.

Case Study 4.3: Guanxi in China

'In China, Guanxi is everything' (Fox, 1987:12). Guanxi is a Chinese term and literally means relations or connections. Much has been written about *La Guanxi* or 'entering relationships' but Guanxi continues to confuse non-Chinese as a culturally embedded institution. Rather than being based on contractual law, Guanxi is based on good faith and personal feelings, something that is evidently less clear to someone not conversant with 'the Chinese way'.

Su and Littlefield (2001) distinguish between two types of Guanxi: a) favour-seeking Guanxi and b) rent-seeking Guanxi. Favour-seeking Guanxi relies on friendship or intimacy oriented towards continued exchange of favours. It is deeply rooted in Chinese feudal ethics where social bonds are based on genealogical or cliquish relations. Rent-seeking Guanxi is described by Su and Littlefield (2001) as relating to corruption or 'crooked winds' associated with a socialist market economy. The term *hou-men guanxi* stands for back-door deals. Su and Littlefield (2001) explain the emergence of rent-seeking Guanxi as a form of bureaucracy that capitalises on monopoly power and common people's favour-seeking behaviour.

The role of Guanxi was recognised in Zhou et al.'s (2017) study of entrepreneurial mobility in early-stage tourism development in rural China. Here the handling of Guanxi networks proved a challenge to entrepreneurial mobility, and certainly featured as an important part of the entrepreneurs' experience. Specifically when dealing with local government officials Guanxi raised challenges, although the difficulties encountered depended on what level of local government the entrepreneur was dealing with. Zhou et al. (2017) explain how not having *Shouren Guanxi* (acquaintances Guanxi) prevented many tourism entrepreneurs from applying for funding, or a reluctance to seek and maintain *Shouren Guanxi* through gift-giving and social dining. As Zhou et al. (2017) conclude: 'Shouren guanxi is obtained through acquaintances and friends, and seeking and maintaining it was possible, although doing so involved exerting extensive effort and many social courtesies, and also induced mental stress.' Hsu et al. (2012) likewise looked at the role of Guanxi in 'economy hotels' in China. Their study demonstrated how different types of ownership types resulted in the reliance on different types of Guanxi (network relations) in the entrepreneurial process. Crucially, Guanxi can be seen to oil the wheels of business, but unfortunately, for tourism entrepreneurs who lack the required Guanxi, setting up a firm can be nigh on impossible.

Trust and social capital

Trust is an elusive concept (Welter, 2011) and yet of fundamental importance to social networks and therefore to entrepreneurship. Trust is both the glue that holds social networks together, as well as the lubricant that facilitates their operation (Anderson and Jack, 2002). Trust is something that comes with time, that is learned when interacting with another individual, and can be considered 'a cumulative process of increasing vulnerability to each other's opportunism' (Bowey and Easton, 2007:273). Trust entails a preparedness to offer oneself up to another's opportunism; there is always an element of 'calculated risk' (Williamson, 1993).

As Welter (2011) has indicated (see Table 4.4), trust resides not solely at an individual level but can focus at meso and macro levels also. Trust may be enhanced between members of a group, sector or institution even. Thus, shared knowledge or experiences may create a degree of empathy and subsequently trust, say between attraction providers who have witnessed a difficult season.

Table 4.4 Form, levels, objects and sources of trust

Forms	Level	Object	Source
Personal trust	Micro	Relationship, person	Emotions, intentions, goodwill, benevolence, characteristics of persons
Collective trust	Meso	Community (e.g., ethnic group, profession), organisation (e.g., industry, sector)	Information, reputation, certification, professional standards
Institutional trust	Macro	Cultural rules (e.g., norms, codes of conduct), regulations (e.g., laws, licences), economic infrastructure (e.g., capital markets, competition authorities)	

Source: Welter (2011:196)

Putnam (1995) suggests social capital increases rather than decreases with use. Just as social capital can be created, it can also be destroyed by behaving in a way that reduces trust. The tourism entrepreneur who misleads a community with false promises (for example, of jobs, income, conservation of the natural environment) is likely to result in the removal of trust and goodwill on the part of the host community towards his/her venture. This lack of trust, and associated animosity can then spill over to those associated with the venture, i.e., the tourists. A community that feels disenfranchised and lied to about tourism's benefits may well turn against the operators and the tourists.

There is also a 'dark side' to trust. As Cope et al. (2007:215) point out: 'Access to social networks is based upon mutual trust and shared understanding, which means that many are exclusive rather than inclusive.' We have seen elements of this in the discussion of Guanxi above. Accessing social networks is not always a straightforward affair, especially considering the power relations inherent in tourist destinations (Hall, 2007). In certain cultures and contexts, who has, and crucially who does not have, access to social networks is determined based on an individual's social standing in the community, class or religious background. Paradoxically, while not being able to access certain social networks can stymie entrepreneurship, at the same time bias can facilitate it. This is where access to some professions is more difficult, impossible even in some societies, for some individuals who then see entrepreneurship as an option (possibly the only option) for social and economic advancement.

Summary

After a review of key concepts in entrepreneurship in Chapters 2 and 3, Chapter 4 moved to more practical aspects of entrepreneurship. It reviewed the entrepreneurial process, offering an overview of different tasks associated with start-up. The role of business plans was discussed, whereby it was recognised that their value as a static document has been queried, but that the process of compiling a business plan is itself a very valuable part of setting up a successful venture. For the purposes of obtaining funding, a business plan is indispensable. Managing cash flow was discussed in some detail with an example of the impact of foot and mouth disease being offered to demonstrate how things can quickly go wrong for tourism firms that fail to keep an eye on their cash flow (or liquidity). This chapter also recognised that the market for finance is becoming more sophisticated with new products being offered to the entrepreneur. It is likely that these financial innovations will continue to develop. Not all businesses require much capital to start up though – bootstrapping can assist those tourism entrepreneurs that cannot readily draw on standard forms of finance (e.g., bank loans). The final part of this chapter looked at the role of networks and social capital in setting up a successful venture. Even though entrepreneurs are sometimes viewed as independence-loving, singular-minded mavericks, the literature quite readily accepts that social networks and social capital are key ingredients to the venture creation process. Trust as a key ingredient to oiling the wheels of business, including business start-up, was also reviewed.

Review questions/discussion points

1 Bygrave and Hofer (1991:17) with regard to the venture creation process claim 'its outcomes are extremely sensitive to the initial conditions of these variables'. Consider what variables these might be and how they might affect the venture creation process.
2 Do you think the entrepreneurial process as depicted in Figure 4.1 is indicative of a causation or an effectuation logic? Explain your response.
3 List reasons why you might create a business plan as well as some of the dangers in an overreliance on business plans.
4 How is it possible that a profitable business can fail?
5 What are the potential sources of finance available to a tourism start-up? Why might it be more difficult for a recently established tourism firm to gain access to finance than an established firm?

Notes

1 The WTO (2005) have argued that it is often very difficult for tourism SMEs and micro-enterprises to estimate income because of the difficulties in estimating tourism demand. Especially in developing countries micro-entrepreneurs can find it difficult to conduct market research and so estimates of demand and income are rough approximations.
2 www.princes-trust.org.uk/help-for-young-people/tools-resources/business-tools/business-plans
3 The gearing ratio is defined as: $gearing\ ratio = \dfrac{Non\text{-}Current\ liabilities}{Share\ capital + reserves + non\text{-}current\ liabilities}$

References

Ahmad, S. Z. 2015. Entrepreneurship in the small and medium-sized hotel sector. *Current Issues in Tourism*, 18, 328–349.

Aldrich, H. E. 1987. The impact of social networks on business founding and profit: a longitudinal approach. *Frontiers of Entrepreneurship Research*. Wellesley, MA: Babson College.

Anderson, A. and Jack, S. 2002. The articulation of social capital in entrepreneurial networks: a glue or a lubricant? *Entrepreneurship & Regional Development*, 14, 193–210.

Anderson, A. and Miller, C. 2002. 'Class matters': human and social capital in the entrepreneurial process. *Journal of Socio-Economics*, 32, 17–36.

Audretsch, D., Aldridge, T. T. and Sanders, M. 2011. Social capital building and new business formation: a case study in Silicon Valley. *International Small Business Journal*, 29, 152–169.

Austin, J., Stevenson, H. and Wei-Silkern, J. 2006. Social and commercial entrepreneurship: same, different or both? *Entrepreneurship Theory and Practice*, 30, 1–22.

Barrow, C., Barrow, P. and Brown, R. 2001. *The Business Plan Workbook*, 4th edn. London, Kogan Page.

Bennett, K., Carroll, T., Lowe, P. and Phillipson, J. 2002. *Coping with Crisis in Cumbria: Consequences of Foot and Mouth Disease*. Newcastle Upon Tyne: Centre for Rural Economy, University of Newcastle Upon Tyne.

Bird, B. 1988. Implementing entrepreneurial ideas: the case of intention. *Academy of Management Review*, 13, 442–453.

Bourdieu, P. and Wacquant, L. 1992. *An Invitation to Reflexive Sociology*. Cambridge: Polity Press.

Bowey, J. L. and Easton, G. 2007. Entrepreneurial social capital unplugged. *International Small Business Journal*, 25, 273–306.

Bridge, S., O'Neill, K. and Cromie, S. 2003. *Understanding Enterprise, Entrepreneurship and Small Business*. Basingstoke: Palgrave Macmillan.

Bygrave, W. 1989. The entrepreneurship paradigm (I): a philosophical look its research methodologies. *Entrepreneurship Theory and Practice*, 14, 7–26.

Bygrave, W. and Hofer, C. 1991. Theorizing about entrepreneurship. *Entrepreneurship Theory and Practice*, 16, 13–22.

Casson, M. and Della Giusta, M. 2007. Entrepreneurship and social capital: analysing the impact of social networks on entrepreneurial activity from a rational action perspective. *International Small Business Journal*, 25, 220–244.

Cheung, K. and Norton, M. 2016. Food waste meets food poverty: closing the loop. *In:* Banks, K. (ed.) *Social Entrepreneurship and Innovation: International Cast Studies and Practice*. London: Kogan Page.

Churchill, N. and Lewis, V. 1983. The five stages of small business growth. *Harvard Business Review*, 83, 30–50.

Cope, J., Jack, S. and Rose, M. 2007. Social capital and entrepreneurship: an introduction. *International Small Business Journal*, 25, 213–219.

Copp, C. and Ivy, R. 2001. Networking trends of small tourism businesses in post-socialist Slovakia. *Journal of Small Business Management*, 39, 345–353.

Cowell, A. 2001. Foot-and-mouth damages English tourism, too. *New York Times*, 16 March 2001.

Crowdcube. 2017. *About us* [Online]. Crowdcube. Available: www.crowdcube.com/pg/crowdcube-inc-about-us-1 [Accessed 12 September 2017].

Cumbria County Council. 2002. *Cumbria Foot and Mouth Disease Inquiry Report*. Cumbria: Cumbria County Council.

Down, S. 2010. *Enterprise, Entrepreneurship and Small Business*. London: Sage.

Field, J. 2003. *Social Capital*. London: Routledge.

Fox, M. 1987. Marketing/advertising research in China: Guanxi is everything. *Advertising Age*, 58, 12–14.

Friend, G. and Zehle, S. 2004. *Guide to Business Planning*. New York: Economist Intelligence Unit.

Gartner, W. B. 1985. A conceptual framework for describing the phenomenon of new venture creation. *Academy of Management Review*, 10, 696–706.

Gemmel, R., Boland, R. and Kolb, D. 2012. The socio-cognitive dynamics of entrepreneurial ideation. *Entrepreneurship Theory and Practice*, 36, 1053–1073.

Greenwald, T. 2012. Crowdfunding: Kickstarter is funding the commercialization of new technologies. *Technology Review*. Massachusetts: Massachusetts Institue of Technology.

GrowVC Group. 2017. *Enabling Digital Finance* [Online]. GrowVC Group. Available: http://group.growvc.com/ [Accessed 12 September 2017].

Hall, M. 2007. Tourism, governance and power. *In:* Church, A. and Coles, T. (eds.), *Tourism, Power and Space*. London: Routledge.

Hannon, P. and Atherton, A. 1998. Small firm success and the art of orienteering: the value of plans, planning, and strategic awareness in the competitive small firm. *Journal of Small Business and Enterprise Development*, 5, 102–119.

Hornuf, L. and Schwienbacher, A. 2017. Should securities regulation promote equity crowdfunding? *Small Business Economics*, 49, 579–593.

Hsu, C., Liu, Z. and Huang, S. 2012. Managerial ties in economy hotel chains in China: comparison of different ownership types during entrepreneurial processes. *International Journal of Contemporary Hospitality Management*, 24, 477–495.

Indiegogo. 2017. *About us* [Online]. Available: www.indiegogo.com/about/our-story [Accessed 12 September 2017].

Jarvis, R. and Schizas, E. 2012. Finance and the small business. *In:* Carter, S. and Jones-Evans, D. (eds.), *Enterprise and Small Business: Principles, Practice and Policy*, 3rd edn. Harlow: Pearson.

Johannison, B. 1988. Business formation: a network approach. *Scandinavian Journal of Management*, 4, 83–99.

Lee-Ross, D. and Lashley, C. 2009. *Entrepreneurship & Small Business Management in the Hospitality Industry*. Oxford: Butterworth-Heinemann.

Lingelbach, D., de la Vina, L. and Asel, P. 2005. *What's Distinctive about Growth-Oriented Entrepreneurship in Developing Countries?* UTSA College of Business Center for Global Entrepreneurship Working Paper No. 1.

Loayza, N., Schmidt-Hebbel, K. and Serven, L. 2000. What drives private savings across the world? *Reveiw of Economics & Statistics*, 82, 165–181.

Mason, C. and Stark, M. 2004. What do investors look for in a business plan? A comparison of the investment criteria of bankers, venture capitalists and business angels. *International Small Business Journal*, 22, 227–248.

McLaney, E. 2011. *Business Finance Theory and Practice*. Harlow: Financial Times/Prentice Hall.

Miller, G. and Ritchie, B. W. 2003. A farming crises or a tourism disaster? *Current Issues in Tourism*, 6.

Mintzberg, H. and Waters, J. 1985. Of strategies, deliberate and emergent. *Strategic Management Journal*, 6, 257–272.

Moroz, P. and Hindle, K. 2012. Entrepreneurship as a process: toward harmonizing multiple perspectives. *Entrepreneurship Theory and Practice*, 36.

Morrison, A. and Teixeira, R. 2004. Small business performance: a tourism sector focus. *Journal of Small Business and Enterprise Development*, 11, 166–173.

Nabi, G., Holden, R. and Walmsley, A. 2010. From student to entrepreneur: towards a model of graduate entrepreneurial career-making. *Journal of Education and Work*, 23, 389–415.

Nabi, G., Walmsley, A. and Holden, R. 2013. Pushed or pulled? Exploring the factors underpinning graduate start-ups and non-start-ups. *Journal of Education and Work*, 10, 1–26.

Nisen, M. 2013. Here's what 'Shark Tank' looks like in 9 different countries [Online]. *Business Insider*. Available: www.businessinsider.com/shark-tank-international-versions-2013-11?IR=T [Accessed 30 August 2017].

Novelli, M., Schmitz, B. and Spencer, T. 2006. Networks, clusters and innovation in tourism: a UK perspective. *Tourism Management*, 27, 1141–1152.

O'Rourke, T. 2009. Access to finance: delivery structures and the problems faced by micro and small tourism entrepreneurs. *In:* Ateljevic, J. and Page, S. (eds.), *Tourism and Entrepreneurship: International Perspectives*. London: Routledge.

OECD. 2015. *Financing SMEs and Entrepreneurs 2015: An OECD Scoreboard*. Organization for Economic Co-operation and Development.

OECD. 2017. *Household Savings Forecast (Indicator)* [Online]. OECD. Available: https://data.oecd.org/hha/household-savings-forecast.htm [Accessed 26 August 2017].

Özer, B. 1996. An investment analysis model for small hospitality operations. *International Journal of Contemporary Hospitality Management*, 8, 20–24.

Peters, M. 2005. Entrepreneurial skills in leadership and human resource management evaluated by apprentices in small tourism businesses. *Education & Training*, 47, 575–591.

Putnam, R. D. 1995. Bowling alone: America's declining social capital. *Journal of Democracy*, 6, 65–78.

Putnam, R. D. 2000. *Bowling Alone*. New York: Simon and Schuster.

Queensland Government. 2017. *Grants and Funding for Tourism Businesses* [Online]. Available: www.business.qld.gov.au/industries/hospitality-tourism-sport/tourism/funding-support/grants [Accessed 12 September 2017].

RocketHub. 2017. *ELEQT Group* [Online]. Available: www.eleqtgroup.com/about#rockethub [Accessed 12 September 2017].

Sarasvathy, S. 2001. Causation and effectuation: toward a theoretical shift from economic inevitability to entrepreneurial contingency. *Entrepreneurship Theory and Practice*, 26, 243–263.

Shane, S. 2003. *A General Theory of Entrepreneurship: The Individual-Opportunity Nexus*. Cheltenham: Edward Elgar.

Sorensen, F. 2007. The geographies of social networks and innovation in tourism. *Tourism Geographies*, 9, 22–48.

Su, C. and Littlefield, J. 2001. Entering Guanxi: a business ethical dilemma in Mainland China? *Journal of Business Ethics*, 33, 199–210.

Szycher, M. 2015. *The Guide to Entrepreneurship: How to Create Wealth for Your Company and Stakeholders*. Boca Raton: CRC Press.

Viren, P., Kline, C. and Tsao, J. 2014. Social networks and tourism in the Roanoke River Valley. *Anatolia*, 25, 483–486.

Welter, F. 2011. All you need is trust? A critical review of the trust and entrepreneurship literature. *International Small Business Journal*, 30, 193–212.

Williamson, O. E. 1993. Calculativeness, trust, and economic organization. *The Journal of Law and Economics*, 36, 453–486.

WTO. 2005. *Tourism, Microfinance and Poverty Alleviation*. Madrid: World Tourism Organization.

Zhou, L., Chan, E. and Song, H. 2017. Social capital and entrepreneurial mobility in early-stage tourism development: a case from rural China. *Tourism Management*, 63, 338–350.

Chapter 5

Marketing

In small businesses it is impossible and not fruitful to seek to differentiate between marketing, innovation, entrepreneurship and customer engagement.

(Jones and Rowley, 2011:30)

Introduction

Although a section on marketing could be included in a discussion of the business plan, it is such a fundamental part of any new venture that it merits its own chapter. The term marketing here is used in its wider sense to include not just the promotion of the tourism product/service but also aspects relating to product design, market positioning, pricing, people (e.g., extended marketing mix). Issues this chapter will cover include:

- Marketing within the context of the small and newly established tourism firm
- Entrepreneurial marketing
- The marketing management process
- Direct marketing, digital marketing and 'big data'.

Learning outcomes

At the end of this chapter the reader should be able to:

- Discuss the notion of entrepreneurial marketing.
- Describe how ICT has transformed marketing opportunities for small tourism firms.
- Identify the role big data plays for tourism firms.

Marketing and tourism

Marketing is one of the key business functions along with others such as human resources, finance and accounting, purchasing, and production/operations. The

Chartered Institute of Marketing defines it as 'the management process responsible for identifying, anticipating and satisfying customer requirements profitably' (Chartered Institute of Marketing, 2015). While the importance of marketing is a given, for marketers, unsurprisingly, it can even adopt the status of a philosophy that underpins the entire organisation, sometimes referred to as a market orientation (e.g., Jones and Rowley, 2011) or marketing concept (e.g., Hatten, 2016). Without marketing, thus understood as recognising and satisfying customer needs, there would indeed be no viable business. It has been argued that many SMEs lack a market orientation, which impedes their performance (e.g., Brooksbank et al., 2004; Alpkan et al., 2007).

Marketing in SMEs is, as so many things relating to small firms, often tied to the characteristics and knowledge of the entrepreneur. Often it is spontaneous, unstructured and haphazard responding to a dynamic environment (O'Dwyer et al., 2009). At the same time, Hatten (2016) claims that a refocus on small firms towards the end of the 1970s and early 1980s is the result of the emergence of the marketing concept, a general move towards a more consumer-focused approach to business (there are leanings here to post-Fordism in tourism (non-standardisation), see Mowforth and Munt (1998). Rather than producing a standardised product and then seeking a market, the marketing concept puts the consumer first, and from the outset puts their needs at the heart of product development. As we discuss later in the chapter, there are grounds to believe small firms are better at meeting individual customer needs than their large counterparts.

In a competitive environment, marketing assumes a fundamental role in all businesses whether large or small. That said, large-scale service operations dominate travel and tourism marketing according to Middleton et al. (2009), and marketing in tourism often focuses on large-scale, widely distributed, quality-controlled products and services. This should not be interpreted as referring necessarily to product homogeneity, as the increasing interaction of consumer and businesses permits a tailoring of the product to the individual consumer's requirements. The shift towards a more consumer-centric approach continues apace (see also below).

As part of the service sector, marketing for tourism distinguishes itself in a number of key aspects from marketing for products or goods. Whether marketing in tourism itself is distinct again from marketing for services more generally is a moot point, although Middleton et al. (2009) make a strong case that it is not any specific aspect on its own that shapes marketing for tourism, but a combination of five characteristics of supply and demand that makes tourism marketing distinct. These are outlined in Table 5.1 and their implications will be discussed later.

Ateljevic and Li (2009) underline the importance of tourists' curiosity in their case for the specificity of the tourism product, thereby making a connection also to entrepreneurship:

> Understanding human curiosity is, in fact, an essential precondition to understanding tourism entrepreneurship as manipulation of human curiosity for commercial purposes is at the very heart of the entrepreneurial ability.
>
> (Ateljevic and Li, 2009:15)

As opposed to many other more tangible products, with more clearly defined utility (Ateljevic and Li, 2009), in tourism the utility is tied to perceptions and curiosity. It appears the connection here is being made to tourist motivation where again we

Table 5.1 Characteristics of marketing for tourism

Inseparability	Provision of a service and consumption of that service are simultaneous. As a result both provider and consumer must be present at the moment of consumption, and this consumption happens away from the consumer's home environment.
Perishability	Perishability follows from inseparability of consumption. Consumption must take place in a specified location, and at a given time. If consumption does not take place a sales opportunity is irretrievably lost, in other words we cannot store tourism consumption. Every hotel room not booked or aircraft seat not taken is a missed opportunity.
Seasonality	Seasonality is endemic to much tourism. Demand can fluctuate considerably depending on time of year, and with some regularity (although tourism demand is notoriously fickle too, susceptible to environmental changes, such as political turmoil, terrorism, economic uncertainty, etc.). The element of perishability aggravates the impact of seasonality.
High fixed costs	For many providers of tourism services (transport, accommodation, attractions) initial capital investments are high. As a consequence profits and losses fluctuate greatly around the break-even point. In other words, once the break-even point is reached each additional unit sold (airline seat, hotel room) can contribute greatly to profits because of the high fixed costs and low variable costs.
Interdependence	The total tourist experience usually relies on products and services provided by a number of businesses (and the public sector). Even if the tourist purchases a package, sold by a tour operator, the individual components of that package are likely to be delivered by different organisations. Tourism is very much therefore characterised by interdependence.

can see links to the more general nature of the tourism product, specifically intangibility and inseparability. An example of a curiosity-driven innovation in tourism is provided by Sweden's Icehotel in Swedish Lapland, which has led to further innovations such as an Ice Church and Ice Theatre, and of course, imitation ice-hotels in other Nordic countries.

Although curiosity itself may not be the driving force for all forms of tourism, we need only look at early models of tourist motivation to understand that tourists are driven by different things (e.g., Plog's, 1994, psychocentrics and allocentrics, or Gray's, 1970, sunlust and wanderlust types), discovery, the search for 'the other' certainly plays an important role in many tourists' motivation, and therefore offers the tourism entrepreneur a marketing opportunity.

Entrepreneurial marketing

Storey's (1994) dictum that small firms are not simply scaled-down versions of large firms is often referred to when analysing SMEs and this principle has been picked up by Thomas (2000; Thomas et al., 2011) with regard to tourism SMEs. The issue of firm size can certainly be considered within the context of marketing. Here Shaw (2012) argues that entrepreneurial marketing is not just a stage of marketing in the latter stages of a firm's evolution (Kotler, 2003), but that it is distinct because of Storey's (1994) small-firm argument, and also because of similarities between entrepreneurship and marketing. We will explore both issues in more detail now.

Jones and Rowley (2011; see also quote at the start of the chapter) point to the significance of the interaction between entrepreneurship and marketing that has led to the concept of entrepreneurial marketing. It is commonly acknowledged that firms that have a marketing and entrepreneurial orientation are often more successful than those without this orientation (e.g., Miles and Arnold, 1991; Wiklund, 1999).

Staying with the distinctiveness of small firm argument, it is acknowledged that the owner/managers of small firms typically tend not to demonstrate a marketing orientation as they are usually generalists rather than marketing specialists. However, there is also a view that entrepreneurs in small firms are frequently closer to their customers than large organisations (Hatten, 2016) and are able to embed a customer orientation into the organisational culture (Zontanos and Anderson, 2004).

Collinson and Shaw (2001) describe three aspects of the entrepreneurship and marketing interface to support the contention that entrepreneurial marketing is more than just a stage of marketing in the lifecycle of the firm. They do this with a focus on the entrepreneur who is change-focused, opportunistic in nature, and innovative in their approach to management. These points align very clearly with Kuratko's (2014:23) definition of the entrepreneur as:

> an innovator or developer who recognizes and seizes opportunities, converts those opportunities into workable/marketable ideas, adds value through time, effort, money or skills, assumes the risks of the competitive marketplace to implement these ideas and realizes the rewards from these efforts.

Innovation in marketing is furthermore seen as a key way SMEs can compete with larger organisations: 'Innovation is the most significant factor that can be used by SMEs to compensate for disadvantages experienced because of firm size' (O'Dwyer et al., 2009:55).

Jones and Rowley (2011) provide a conceptualisation of entrepreneurial marketing. They suggest an entrepreneurial marketing orientation (EMO) should consist of the four scales of:

- entrepreneurial orientation
- customer orientation
- marketing orientation
- innovation orientation.

As the brief discussion above has shown, and as Jones and Rowley (2011:30) argue more fully in their paper, 'in small businesses it is impossible and not fruitful to seek to differentiate between marketing, innovation, entrepreneurship and customer engagement'. Certainly, small tourism firms may seek differentiation through an entrepreneurial marketing orientation. Examples of how social media can be used in innovative ways to market the tourism product are provided below.

The marketing management process

Shaw (2012) describes the traditional marketing management process as consisting of identifying a target market, developing a marketing strategy (see Table 5.2), developing marketing objectives, devising marketing tactics and plans and finally implementation and evaluation. In many respects, this approach is analogous to the (prescriptive) strategy process in that objectives need to be set, actions need to be identified, these need to be implemented and evaluated feeding back into the strategy process (e.g., Lynch, 2009:491). However, as was discussed above, entrepreneurial marketing is distinct from traditional marketing in that the owner/manager of an SME does not usually have the resources or expertise to develop a full-blown marketing strategy. In theory, the marketing management process makes sense, but it may not fit the real world of the small business owner.

Nonetheless, this does not mean that the tourism entrepreneur should neglect marketing or take a haphazard approach to it. A clear distinction is to be made between normative theory, what is recommended or should happen, and a description of practice (what tends to happen). In particular the nascent entrepreneur should consider the relationship between product/service and the market which Ansoff's (1957) model, despite its age and focus on firm growth, is still very useful in assisting with (Table 5.2).

- **Market penetration:** This applies to an existing firm whose growth strategy is based on an existing product-market strategy. It can do this by either selling more to existing customers, or selling to new customers within an existing market.
- **Market development:** This takes a given product or service and tries to find new markets for it (e.g., the tourism entrepreneur might identify how a potential competitor is offering package holidays to Thailand to the Chinese market, and decide to offer similar packages but to Malaysian tourists).
- **Product development:** This entails developing an existing product to more closely fit the needs of an existing market (e.g., in the previous example, the tourism entrepreneur might put together an enhanced package, or perhaps offer different payment terms, insurance benefits, etc. to Thailand for the same Chinese market).
- **Diversification:** This comprises a simultaneous departure from an existing product and an existing market. Extending the above example, the tourism entrepreneur might decide to offer a luxury package holiday to Thailand to Australian tourists.

Table 5.2 Ansoff's product market matrix

		Market development	
		Existing	New
Product development	Existing	Penetration	Product development
	New	Market development	Diversification

Source: Adapted from Ansoff (1957:114).

In considering these product-market scenarios we need to also consider, inevitably, the so-called marketing mix. The layperson, when he or she hears the term marketing, frequently thinks just of advertising or promotion (indeed, marketing and advertising are often used synonymously). A consideration of the concept of the marketing mix as applied to services (sometimes called the extended marketing mix) demonstrates that marketing is far more than advertising and promotion.

McCarthy first wrote about the '4 Ps' that constitute the marketing mix. These are product, price, promotion and place. Crucially, they recognised that the entrepreneur, or businessperson, needs to focus on more than just product characteristics if they are to be successful, frequently against strong competition. It is the way these four aspects are combined that can provide for a competitive advantage, albeit not necessarily a sustained one. In 1996, Kotler and Armstrong developed, based on the 4 Ps, the '4 Cs', which they argued were more aligned with the customer orientation required in services marketing (Middleton et al., 2009). The four Cs are customer value, cost, communication and convenience. They each correspond to the original 4 Ps but also differ in important ways (important to the delivery of a service).

- Customer value relates to the perceived and experienced benefits of the service provided, including service quality.
- Cost is the equivalent of price but seen from the perspective of the consumer (i.e., what is the cost to the customer, value for money considerations in combination with customer value are important here).
- Communication is about promotion, how do you 'get the message out there' – but also about listening to customer feedback. Communication is two-way.
- Convenience is likewise of paramount importance to the marketing mix. Being able to sell online is today no longer a 'whether' but a 'how' issue.

With the increasing importance of services to the economy came calls to extend the 4 Ps to make them more applicable to services. The extended marketing mix includes people, process and physical evidence. The people element recognises the importance of human interaction in the service encounter and the skills, attitudes and attributes of those delivering a service. A small tourism firm can create competitive advantage by providing a more bespoke, personalised service. Process relates to the different steps of service delivery, from initial awareness-raising to the purchase decision and post-purchase evaluation. The tourism entrepreneur needs to ensure the process of service delivery is as smooth as possible and meets, or in fact exceeds, customer expectations. Physical evidence literally relates to the physical attributes surrounding the service delivery, such as the design of a reception area in a hotel, the condition of the tour bus, the cleanliness of the campsite facilities.

Direct and digital marketing

Today, a three-bedroom guesthouse in New Zealand is able to reach out to a prospective tourist in, say, Fairbanks, Alaska, just as easily as it would be for that guesthouse owner to make themselves a cup of instant coffee. Anyone born after 2000,

Generation Z or 'Linksters' (the first generation who are linked into technology), will at this stage probably be wondering what all the fuss is about, but it is salutary to step back and just consider for an instant how developments in ICT that seem unremarkable today have changed the way many of us work, and live, in less than a generation.

The internet has changed the way a majority of prospective tourists consider, select and evaluate the holidays and trips they undertake (Buhalis and Law, 2008; Xiang and Gretzel, 2010). Tourism is an information-intensive sector where traditionally the tourist sought information from a high street travel agent, or from brochures picked up at a high street travel agent, subsequently booking the holiday through said travel agent. Getting the right advice and information on your prospective holiday purchase was, and still is, key; this has not changed. Not only are holidays usually big ticket items, i.e., relatively expensive compared to the purchase of everyday items, they use up highly valued annual leave entitlements: get it wrong, and it is not just a case of losing money, in other words. Today, however, information is ubiquitous (we live after all in the so-called 'information age') and online sales of holidays and other items continue to rise (data provided by Statista (2018) suggest the value of online travel sales worldwide is set to almost double between 2014 and 2020, from US$470.97 billion to US$817.54 billion).

Unsurprisingly, advances in ICT, have changed the nature of marketing too and opened up opportunities for tourism entrepreneurs, as well as destination management organisations (Hays et al., 2013). Today, travel planning, review and price comparison websites are just some of the digital tools at the disposal of the prospective tourist. We can also consider, for example, the emergence and rapid rise of travel apps, which are some of the most popular in the app market. The increased and ongoing embedding of ICT in the marketing of tourism products presents challenges but also opportunities for the nascent or small tourism firm. By lowering some marketing costs and providing easier access to markets, the dawn of the internet age can be associated with a democratisation of business, creating a playing field that if not level, is at least not skewed as steeply against the small firm.

Direct marketing

Kotler et al. (2014:498) define direct marketing as 'connecting directly with carefully targeted individual consumers to both obtain an immediate response and cultivate lasting customer relationships'. Direct marketing meets the needs of individual consumers far better than mass marketing approaches for obvious reasons. The move towards direct marketing reflects a move of consumer preferences towards more unique, individually tailored holidays and experiences, and is also fostered by companies' ability to offer more flexible products and services. Tourism firms are able today to take advantage of software that permits the collection and manipulation of 'big data'. The way we interact with adverts and social media (see below), use store cards and more generally leave digital footprints is captured so that companies build up (what they believe) is a clear picture of our individual preferences. This allows them to target the consumer more directly, with products and services that are more likely to appeal to their preferences.

Case study 5.1: 'Big data'

Big data has become something of a buzzword. Tim Harford writing in the *Financial Times* suggests: 'Big data is a vague term for a massive phenomenon that has rapidly become an obsession with entrepreneurs, scientists, governments and the media' (Harford, 2014). In his opinion piece, Harford cogently argues why we need to be careful of drawing causal conclusions based on correlations found in big data sets. Nonetheless, companies with access to large data sets are via an analysis of these data able to draw largely accurate conclusions about individual and collective preferences.

Press (2014), writing for *Forbes*, suggests that the Oxford English Dictionary's definition of 'big data' takes its lead from Wikipedia, which defined it as: 'an all-encompassing term for any collection of data sets so large and complex that it becomes difficult to process using on-hand data management tools or traditional data processing applications.'[1] Press (2014) offers others' definitions including the following, which capture the essence and potential of big data as they relate to the firm:

- The shift (for enterprises) from processing internal data to mining external data.
- A new attitude by businesses, non-profits, government agencies, and individuals that combining data from multiple sources could lead to better decisions.
- The convergence of enterprise and consumer IT.

The amount of information produced/created today vastly exceeds that produced by previous generations. Along with big data comes big data analytics, the use of advanced analytic techniques against very large, diverse data sets that include structured, semi-structured and unstructured data, from different sources, and in different sizes (IBM, 2018). Techniques for analysing big data include text analytics, machine learning, predictive analytics, data mining and natural language processing.

The use of big data in tourism research is picking up pace. A paper by Salas-Olmedo et al. (2018), for example, explores the digital footprint of tourists in a city environment (Madrid) using three separate data sources: Panoramio, which allows the geolocating of photographs; Foursquare, a social network which enables users to inform their friends of check-ins and rate venues visited; and Twitter, where geolocated tweets leave a digital footprint of the place and the time they were sent. Salas-Olmedo et al.'s (2018) study highlighted some of the dangers already identified by Harford (2014) when making assumptions about the generalisability of large data sets simply because they are large. Specifically, if sampling is systematically skewed, then increasing the sample size will not overcome inherent bias. With reference to Salas-Olmedo et al.'s (2018:38) study this is evidenced clearly:

> As in other papers that use Big Data, there is also an underlying problem of bias. Most tourists do not upload their photos to photosharing communities

like Panoramio, and some do not even take photographs. Photographs do not always properly reflect all the monuments in the city, due to the prohibition against taking photographs in some monuments, and particularly in museums. Many tourists do not use social networks like Twitter or Foursquare and only a small proportion of Twitter users send geolocated tweets. The source bias is unquestionably difficult to identify and correct.

In 2013 the then Direct Marketing Association (now Data Driven Marketing Association) in the USA commissioned a report into the 'data driven marketing economy' (DDME). The DDME is defined as 'the ecosystem of supplier firms that help marketers use individual-level customer data (ILCD) to efficiently select, contact, and transact with end customers (whether individual consumers or business buyers) via individually interactive media and non-media touchpoints'. In 2015 the report was updated and indicated the following:

- The use of data-driven marketing added $202 billion in revenue to the US economy in 2014, up from $150 billion in 2012 and representing growth of 35% in just two years.
- The growth in total employment (direct and indirect, data from first and third parties) relating to DDME from 2012 to 2014 is 49%.

It is possible to argue that the move towards individual-level customer data marketing (or direct marketing) eats into small firms' competitive edge where these are traditionally associated with more direct customer contact, a fuller understanding of individual customers' needs (because of the more direct contact) tied in with a greater flexibility to respond to customer needs. Marketing departments of many large firms are moving away from being behemoths, the firm equivalent of supertankers, slow to change direction and difficult to manoeuvre. However, the other side of the coin points to an advantage for SMEs as the cost structure of data-driven marketing services is much more favourable for smaller firms (Deighton and Johnson, 2015). Whereas placing an advert on television (traditional broadcasting advertising) is prohibitively expensive for most small firms, search engine advertising (see also below) is accessible to smaller budgets. With regard to the prohibitive costs of traditional media marketing channels, a further distinction from mainstream marketing as it applies to tourism SMEs is the importance of networking (this can be said to apply to SMEs more generally too, e.g., Gilmore and Carson, 1999). Collaboration between tourism SMEs may help overcome some of the disadvantages of newness and limited budgets.

It is necessary to refer to the idea of customer relationship management (CRM; sometimes also equated with customer relationship marketing) within the context of direct marketing as the two are inextricably linked. In practice, firms have different understandings of what CRM means, from direct mail, a loyalty card scheme, a help desk, a call centre, a data warehouse or an e-commerce solution (Payne and Frow, 2005:167). There is no one accepted definition of CRM, although Payne and Frow (2005) offer a continuum upon which existing definitions can be placed. On one side of this continuum we find a very narrow technology-oriented definition, on the other CRM is regarded as a holistic approach to managing customer relationships to create shareholder value (Payne and Frow, 2005:168). We would advocate that the small tourism start-up use a deliberate approach to CRM, making the management of its customer relationships a core mission. Initially, the small firm or nascent firm may be able to manage customers in an ad hoc, unplanned way, but as the firm grows it will not be possible for the owner/manager on his/her own, to maintain and foster the multiple relationships that are required.

What is clear is that direct marketing permits firms to build stronger relationships with customers but we have thus far taken for granted that these relationships are important. This may seem a peculiar consideration but we know from Porter's Five Forces that one of those forces is 'buyer power' and that, depending on the type of product/service and the competitive conditions surrounding the firm, buyer power will vary.

Not all businesses rely to the same extent on repeat custom; there are certain products and services where brand loyalty is not particularly strong. A hotel in a honeypot location may not suffer as much from poor customer service as a hotel in a resort, for instance. Nonetheless, the typical holiday is a high involvement purchase; getting it wrong has significant negative emotional impact, getting it right not only increases the likelihood of repeat purchase but also serves to attract new customers via word of mouth (electronic or direct). In this sense, buyer power has been strengthened since the advent of the internet and yet it still holds true that a lot of effort, time and resources are usually required to attract new customers. Once these customers have been attracted it therefore makes sense to retain them; witness the proliferation of airline or hotel loyalty programmes. This is not something that is relevant only to large firms, but that the small start-up can equally consider. The 'switched-on' tourism entrepreneur will follow up a sale with a request for feedback, gaining insights into how their offer may be improved, but also demonstrating to the customer that they care, further strengthening the relationship between firm and customer. More generally, CRM reflects a move from traditional marketing with its short-term horizon (e.g., focus on individual sales, one-off perspective of customer contact) to relationship marketing where customer contact is ongoing and where the whole organisation is geared towards satisfying the customer (there are parallels here to a marketing orientation – admittedly, sometimes the concepts used in marketing and management overlap!).

At the heart of direct marketing lies a solid customer database. This would cover 'hard' data such as name, gender, marital status and age but also preferences/psychographic and behavioural data. The tourism firm is then able to match product/service characteristics with individual customers, and in fact tailor their product/service offering to better meet the needs of individual customers. As one marketing expert quoted in Kotler et al. (2014:502) claims: 'A company is no better than what it knows about its customers.' The implication for the tourism entrepreneur is that right from the outset s/he needs to consider creating a customer database – this should not be an afterthought. This is also important when a company expands and the knowledge contained within the mind of the firm's founder needs to be shared. The personal relationships the founder has built up with their clients, the social capital that has been created, cannot be passed on in its entirety. A solid database is, however, crucial in ensuring customers are not lost to the competition.

A final, yet critical consideration is the role and scope of data protection legislation that continues to change (an example of the impact of the legislative environment on entrepreneurship). At the time of writing (December 2017), companies were gearing up for the introduction of the EU General Data Protection Regulations (GDPR), which aim to harmonise data privacy laws across Europe. These regulations are likely to have significant implications for the travel industry as reported on the Direct Marketing Association's website (Barbuti, 2017). During the holiday booking process the customer provides a great deal of information including sensitive data on health and medical circumstances. The travel agent then frequently shares this information with overseas accommodation and excursion providers. Although the more stringent regulations and higher penalties for their breach can be seen to disproportionately affect the smaller firm that may not have their own legal departments to deal with this, this is recognised by the legislators. There is scope for certain relaxations in respect of SMEs (in relation to record-keeping, for example).

Social media

Social media may have been defined in various ways, but its impact on business is unequivocal. For our purposes social media simply refers to web-based platforms that facilitate the creation and sharing of user-generated content, which includes blogs, chat rooms, discussion boards, email, forums, 'moblogs' (where content is generated through mobile devices), service ratings websites and social networks (Mangold and Faulds, 2009).

Social media is now widely and increasingly used as a platform to advertise destinations and tourism products/services. The advantages of using social media for promotion purposes are many. Social media offers a relatively inexpensive (usually the highest cost is time, which should nonetheless be considered) means of creating a 'captive audience', i.e. one that is already interested in your offer and that needs less of a push to make the purchasing decision. It features increasingly in SMEs' marketing strategies as it provides a relatively inexpensive means to reach a global audience (Mitas et al., 2015).

Social media is a double-edged sword, however. Negative publicity can go viral; one thinks here about the negative publicity generated for United Airlines in 2008 when they broke musician Dave Carroll's beloved $3,500 Taylor guitar. Not getting any redress from United he subsequently wrote a song, 'United Breaks Guitars', which he posted on YouTube. The song has now been viewed over 17 million times. In the short term at least, it is said this cost the airline $180 million as United Airlines' share price fell 10%.

Many consumers today receive but also share information digitally on the products and services they use; the tourist co-creates information with the tourism firm and other consumers. The sharing of digital information including videos and photos is also known as user-generated content (UGC). The importance of online consumer reviews, a form of UGC also referred to as e-WOM (electronic word of mouth), should not be underestimated in terms of its impact on sales. For example, according to a UK industry report (Insights, 2015) 15% of consumers would not book a holiday without first checking reviews while only 28% paid 'little' or 'no attention' to reviews. Twelve percent said they would 'drop plans to book and look for an alternative' as a result of reading a negative review of a hotel of travel company.

E-WOM has gained much traction where touristic experiences are concerned; because they are intangible, consumers may place much emphasis on e-WOM (Ye et al., 2011). One of the dangers lurking behind UGC is its authenticity. Negative online consumer reviews are potentially extremely damaging. While there is some evidence that trust in consumer reviews is high, in part because it is believed consumers are more trusting of these reviews as opposed to content offered by marketing and/or advertising agencies (Gretzel and Yoo, 2008), it is recognised that individual companies have an interest in stimulating positive reviews and preventing negative evaluations (Mitas et al., 2015). Similarly, unscrupulous businesses may provide false negative reviews about competitors.

Case study 5.2: The use of social media by destination management organisations in Italy

The use of social media for promotion purposes is not restricted to tourism firms but is being used by local, regional and national destination management/marketing organisations. For example, Mariani et al. (2016) compared the online activities of regional destination management organisations (DMOs) in Italy, specifically looking at how they engaged with Facebook. The study showed a great deal of variation in how Facebook was being deliberately used to promote destinations. Factors such as frequency of posts, length of posts, type of posts and time of posts were analysed to ascertain efficacy in terms of user engagement. With regard to user-generated content, the study also found that most DMOs took a top-down approach, allowing for only limited spontaneous interaction with consumers.

The region of Tuscany was provided as an example of how DMOs can engage and also increase their appeal to consumers. Tuscany had decided it was time to update its photo for its webpage. Instead of simply choosing a preferred image, Tuscany's DMO uploaded four photos it felt represented the region but then put out to popular vote, via Facebook, which of these four should be used. It was, however, not alone in this endeavour, with other regions (e.g., Sicily and Abruzzo) adopting a similar strategy. Overall, Mariani et al.'s (2016) study demonstrated that those regions that used social media more creatively, not just as a means to share promotional material, were also more likely to have greater levels of online engagement (at the end of 2013 Tuscany's official Facebook page had 228,000 fans, mid-July 2017 it was 573,000). The consequences for owner-managers of tourism firms, whether large or small, new or established, are very real. Being able to 'manage' one's online profile across a range of platforms is now a key skill. In this sense, competitive pressures, or the pressures to remain competitive have increased and with it the requirement to be enterprising in tackling these new circumstances.

SEO techniques

SEO, or search engine optimisation, represent a series of tools that the tourism entrepreneur can use to try to establish greater visibility for their business or product/services on the internet. It is about optimising the firm's website for search engines. It does not matter how snazzy a website is, without anyone actually being able to find it, its 'snazziness' is irrelevant.

The difficulty in writing about ICT issues is that by the time words are committed to paper (or screen) things will in all likelihood have already moved on. Some basic SEO rules do exist, however, that the budding tourism entrepreneur should be aware of:

- **The importance of keywords.** Keywords are those words that people who might be searching for your product/service are likely to put into a search engine. Search engines trawl the web and identify pages that contain these keywords (they also identify where in the page the keywords are, how frequently they are used and so forth). In the first instance, the tourism entrepreneur needs to ensure they have an understanding of what their own keywords are. Google AdWords is a service that lets you see which keywords are in your field, and also how many times that particular keyword (or keyword chain) has been searched for on average per month.
- **Keyword placement.** Aside from choosing appropriate keywords that describe your product/service, it is also necessary to consider how and where they are placed in a webpage. Search bots that trawl the web looking for search-relevant webpages identify page titles, headings, the context around a keyword, ALT page tags and meta tags on each page. The algorithms search engines use are sophisticated enough now to identify where someone has simply smattered their webpage with relevant keywords to increase traffic to their site (so-called keyword stuffing).
- **Creating off-site links to your webpage.** Search bots recognise and value external links to your website. As placing links to a site in external content (e.g., blogs, article directories, etc.) can be time-consuming, many companies pay for others to do this. However, it is possible to do this yourself, and will probably appeal to the cash-strapped start-up. Ensuring your business has an online presence should be part of a marketing strategy in any case, and this will include a social media presence as outlined further below. It can also be a good idea to invite people to review your product/service for free in return for writing a review.

Email advertising

Companies have become very effective at gaining customers' email addresses and for good reason. It will allow them to target the customer who has already shown an interest in their product. There is a danger that the email lands in the spam folder and this must also be considered. There are various ways to gain customers'/ potential customers' email addresses but these can be split into two strands: one collects them oneself (e.g., via the enticement of a free newsletter, report, coupon, or when the customer makes a purchase or when a potential customer enquires about the product), or one purchases a list of addresses from market research companies. Software exists that helps the entrepreneur manage their email advertising, such as providing data on email effectiveness, an automatic thank-you upon signing up to a newsletter or purchasing your product, and adding an 'opt-out' function (a legal requirement) at the end of the email.

Internet advertising

It is also possible to pay directly for websites to advertise a product/service. This will take the form of a banner ad on a website where you believe potential customers will already be (e.g., if you are selling car rentals on the Greek island of Rhodes you could pay for a banner on the regional airport's website). A range of factors will affect the price of the advertising from where the advert is placed, what demand is from others to host adverts on that site, to click-through rate. The other main form of internet advertising is 'pay per click' or PPC. Here the advertiser decides where your advert will be placed and you only pay if a potential customer clicks your ad (hence 'pay per click'). PPC rates vary widely, and will depend on conversion rates. It is no use adverts driving traffic to your website if customers do not then purchase. A simple example will illustrate: imagine you are paying $1 every time a potential customer clicks a link that takes them to your website. On average you get 500 clicks a day so the advertising will cost you $500. Imagine now that 5% of those that click through to your website actually make a purchase spending on average $22. This results therefore in revenue of $550. Should you go ahead with the advertising campaign? Probably not as revenue is not equal to profit and unless all your costs are lower than $50 you are still not going to end up making a profit.

We encountered crowdsourcing in Chapter 3 in relation to ideation but crowdsourcing is frequently used for marketing purposes too. In 2013 Marriott Hotels launched its Travel Brilliantly campaign. It set up an online platform and asked consumers to submit their travel-inspired ideas across six different 'passion points': Eat & Drink, Work & Play, Health & Wellness, Style & Design, Technology and Outside the Box. To date, more than 2,500 ideas have been submitted. In 2013 five first prize winners were selected across three rounds resulting in 15 initial prize winners from which a judging panel then selected the grand prize winner. Ideas included room personalisation where customers submit their own photos that are then linked by name and Marriott Rewards number, a concept for an app that enables guests to pre-order groceries to be stocked in their room upon arrival, and the winning idea: a healthy food vending machine that Marriott actually launched in 2014 (Brady, 2014).

Possibly the best-known examples of crowdsourcing in tourism relate to platforms that let users submit their own content and reviews, similar to the DMOs' use of photos and videos, to their own social media platforms. One such example is Brussels-based TagTagCity (www.tagtagcity.com). TagTagCity lets users add their own places and then submit information about those places. The platform is not designed solely for tourists but also for local communities and businesses, although tourists can clearly benefit from obtaining detailed information from previous visitors and locals alike about destinations they would like to visit.

It would be remiss not to mention TripAdvisor when writing of crowdsourcing in tourism. Founded in 2000 it has grown into 'the world's largest travel site'. It features more than 535 million reviews of a variety of accommodation types, food outlets and attractions. According to TripAdvisor's website, it 'provides travellers with the wisdom of the crowds to help them decide where to stay, how to fly, what to do and where to eat' (TripAdvisor, 2017). Despite concerns about things such as fake reviews – one thinks here of the Cove Hotel in Cornwall, which offered guests 10% off a repeat visit and an upgrade for an 'honest but positive' review (*Daily*

Telegraph, 2017) – some firms, such as Hotelied, even deliberately purchase a form of advertising through social media by offering customers with large social networks discounts in exchange for testimonials (Mitas et al., 2015:12). TripAdvisor has done remarkably well, especially considering it was not originally established as a review site for tourists. Initially it was designed as offering a business to business (B2B) service, but when it realised its site was being used by the travel community it decided to refocus (an example of the unexpected success, see sources of innovation, Chapter 3).

Case study 5.3: Meeting millennials' needs

In many advanced economies, certainly in the UK, many millennials (generally considered to be those born between 1980 and 2000) are facing a situation where they are likely to be worse off than their parents. O'Connor (2018) comments that their home ownership rates have collapsed, their wages have stagnated and their degrees are wildly expensive, for example. This breaks with the traditional view that each generation will be better off than its predecessor. Although this may cause concern for some, not least the millennials, the response is being recognised by some tourism firms as an opportunity. Steafel (2017), for example, writes that millennials who are aware they will never be able to afford a house and therefore make no attempt at saving up for a deposit are instead willing to spend money on experiences.

A survey sponsored by Eventbrite (2017) of US citizens born between 1980 and 1996 suggests not only does this generation value experiences highly, they are increasingly likely to spend on experiences. More than three-quarters of millennials (78%) would choose to spend money on a desirable experience or event over buying something desirable. And 69% experience 'fear of missing out' or FOMO. In a world where life experiences are broadcast across social media, the fear of missing out drives millennials to show up, share and engage.

Another survey, conducted by Airbnb in conjunction with GfK (GfK and Aibnb, 2016), of US, UK and Chinese millennials supports the Eventbrite survey's findings of a strong focus on experiences. Millennials, according to the survey, especially in China, value travel over paying off debt or buying a home; they also seek unique and novel travel experiences. Over 70% of millennials surveyed in each country said 'travel is an important part of who I am as a person', and over 65% of millennials said that 'regular travel is an important part of my life'.

Upon this backdrop, Steafel (2017) seeks to understand what kind of travel millennials are after and provides examples of tours that offer 'generation selfie' the opportunity of upping their Instagram game. The tour operator Contiki is highlighted, which offers an 11-day tour in Canada with precisely this goal. Contiki's message is clear: 'At Contiki we have a way of life. It's called #NoRegrets.' Donna Jeavons, sales and marketing director at Contiki, is quoted as suggesting: 'We have found that the three most important factors for millennials when planning a holiday are the food, being able to make Insta-worthy shots to make all their friends jealous, and staying in a variety of different quirky locations.'

Case study 5.4: Myanmar's tourism entrepreneurs

In an article on its website (Long, 2014), the BBC describes how young entrepreneurs in Myanmar are seizing opportunities after the country's opening up and 'discovery' of tourism. In 2011, after decades of military rule, Myanmar held much promise as a new up-and-coming destination. Long (2014) describes a tour operator in Yangon (formerly Rangoon) set up by Min Than Htut, who originally studied chemistry but followed this up with a diploma in tourism. Pro Niti Travel has a very professional-looking website and staff, who are pictured on its 'About Us' webpage wearing branded T-shirts (see Figure 5.1). It is clear from statements there that Min Than Htut has taken his tourism studies seriously, in terms of recognising the potential negative impacts of excessive and unplanned tourism development, as well as in terms of using social media to advertise its services.

As is frequently the case, setting up a tourism firm in a developing economy specifically presented a number of challenges. Licences needed to be obtained, which required much time, and internet access was unreliable. Long writes that Myanmar holds the dubious honour of having one of the lowest rates of internet penetration in the world, with Min Than Htut explaining that sometimes it took him an hour to reply to just one email. He did, however, recognise the importance of the internet in attracting potential customers from around the world, but stresses that word-of-mouth referrals are also critical. In writing about the importance and emergence of online marketing channels, it can be easy to forget important traditional forms of advertising. At the time of writing, the business has diversified into a number of different tour types (e.g., honeymoon, relaxation, road tours, river tours) in a variety of locations across

Figure 5.1 The team at Pro Niti Travel
Credit: Min Than Htut

Myanmar and employs eight people full time. Despite its success as a company, the overall picture for tourism in Myanmar faces numerous challenges, from ongoing ethnic tensions, a strong military influence in politics and consequences of untrammelled tourism development. Tourism arrivals slumped in 2016 and many hotels remained empty (there is also the contention that the government inflated tourism figures in previous years; Heijmans, 2017). Whatever Myanmar's future holds, it is evident that entrepreneurship in developing countries offers both vast opportunities but also numerous challenges.

Summary

This chapter has reviewed a number of marketing issues of relevance to the tourism entrepreneur. The nature of marketing in tourism and marketing services was considered before discussion of the concept of entrepreneurial marketing. The marketing mix was discussed whereby Kotler's '4 Cs' as a service-orientated update to the traditional '4 Ps' was also reviewed. The chapter did not discuss the marketing process in detail as it was recognised that adequate resources to pursue a full-blown marketing strategy are unlikely to be available to the new tourism firm. In fact, this insight led to a fairly 'hands-on' discussion of how direct and online marketing may help the small tourism firm. This included the use of big data and how businesses are in a better position to tailor their offer to specific customers, including how access to and management of data permits small firms to engage more effectively in customer relationship marketing. The chapter also reviewed the notion of SEO, or search engine optimisation, email advertising and different approaches to digital advertising. The chapter concluded with two case studies that serve to demonstrate via the marketing function the pace of change in the sector.

Review questions/discussion points

1   Consider how marketing a service differs from marketing a tangible product. What might the difficulties in marketing a service be, and how might they be overcome?
2   Why is there a commonly held belief that small tourism firms are better able to engage in direct marketing? Do you think this view is justified?
3   Overall, do you think the rise in digital marketing has been good for small tourism firms?
4   Identify a tourism firm and apply Ansoff's product market matrix to its product offering.
5   Come up with three terms that could be used as keywords in an SEO strategy for a tourism firm. Find out how many searches are made for these terms using Google Analytics and identify associated terms.

Note

1 At the time of writing this had not changed much: 'Big data is data sets that are so voluminous and complex that traditional data processing application software are inadequate to deal with them' (20 February 2018).

References

Alpkan, L., Yilmaz, C. and Kaya, N. 2007. Marketing orientation and planning flexibility in SMEs. *International Small Business Journal*, 25, 152–172.
Ansoff, I. 1957. Strategies for diversification. *Harvard Business Review*, 35, 113–124.
Ateljevic, J. and Li, L. 2009. Tourism entrepreneurship – concepts and issues. *In*: Page, S. and Ateljevic, J. (eds.), *Tourism And Entrepreneurship: International Perspectives*. London: Routledge.
Barbuti, L. 2017. How GDPR will impact the travel sector [Online]. *Direct Marketing Association*. Available: https://dma.org.uk/article/how-gdpr-will-impact-the-travel-sector [Accessed 30 August 2018].
Brady, P. 2014. Marriott launches healthy food vending machine, business travelers rejoice [Online]. Available: www.cntraveler.com/stories/2014-09-08/marriott-launches-healthy-food-vending-machine-business-travelers-rejoice [Accessed 14 August 2018].
Brooksbank, R., Kirby, D. and Taylor, D. 2004. Marketing in survivor medium-sized British manufacturing firms: 1987–1997. *European Business Review*, 16, 292–306.
Buhalis, D. and Law, R. 2008. Progress in information technology and tourism management: 20 years on and 10 years after the internet – the state of e-tourism research. *Tourism Management*, 29, 609–623.
Chartered Institute of Marketing. 2015. *A Brief Summary of Marketing and How It Works*. CIM.
Collinson, E. and Shaw, E. 2001. Entrepreneurial marketing – a historical perspective on development and practice. *Management Decision*, 39, 761–766.
Daily Telegraph. 2017. 15 things you didn't know about TripAdvisor [Online]. *The Daily Telegraph*. Available: www.telegraph.co.uk/travel/lists/15-things-you-didnt-know-about-tripadvisor/ [Accessed 14 August 2017].
Deighton, J. and Johnson, P. 2015. *The Value Of Data 2015: Consequences For Insight, Innovation and Efficiency in the US Economy*. New York: Direct Marketing Institute and Data Driven Marketing Agency.
Eventbrite. 2017. *Millennials: Fueling the Experience Economy* [Online]. Available: www.eventbrite.com/blog/academy/millennials-fueling-experience-economy/ [Accessed 9 October 2017].
GFK and Aibnb 2016. *Airbnb and the Rise of Millennial Travel* [Online]. Available: www.airbnbcitizen.com/wp-content/uploads/2016/08/MillennialReport.pdf [Accessed 23 August 2018].
Gilmore, A. and Carson, D. 1999. Entrepreneurial marketing by networking. *New England Journal of Entrepreneurship*, 12, 31–38.
Gray, J. P. 1970. *International Travel – International Trade*. Lexington Heath: Lexington Books.
Gretzel, U. and Yoo, K. 2008. Use and impact of online travel reviews. *In*: O'Connor, P., Höpken, W. and Gretzel, U. (eds.), *Information and Communication Technologies in Tourism*. New York: Springer-Verlag.
Harford, T. 2014. Big data: are we making a big mistake? [Online]. *Financial Times*. Available: www.ft.com/content/21a6e7d8-b479-11e3-a09a-00144feabdc0 [Accessed 20 February 2018].

Hatten, T. S. 2016. *Small Business Management: Entrepreneurship and Beyond*. Boston, MA: Cengage Learning.

Hays, S., Page, S. and Buhalis, D. 2013. Social media as a destination marketing tool: its use by national tourism organisations. *Current Issues in Tourism*, 16, 211–239.

Heijmans, P. 2017. Myanmar's tourism destination dreams fade amid empty hotels. *Bloomberg Business Week* [Online]. Available: www.bloomberg.com/news/features/2017-06-19/myanmar-s-tourism-destination-dreams-fade-amid-empty-hotels [Accessed 26 October 2017].

IBM. 2018. *Big Data Analytics* [Online]. IBM. Available: www.ibm.com/analytics/hadoop/big-data-analytics [Accessed 20 February 2018].

Insights. 2015. *Insight Annual Report 2015*. Travel Weekly in association with Deloitte.

Jones, R. and Rowley, J. 2011. Entrepreneurial marketing in small business: a conceptual exploration. *International Small Business Journal*, 29, 25–36.

Kotler, P. 2003. *Marketing Management*. Saddle River, NJ: Prentice Hall.

Kotler, P. and Armstrong, G. 1996. *Principles of Marketing*. Saddle River, NJ: Prentice Hall.

Kotler, P., Bowen, J. and Makens, J. 2014. *Marketing for Hospitality and Tourism*. Harlow: Pearson.

Kuratko, D. 2014. *Entrepreneurship: Theory, Process, and Practice*. Mason, OH: South Western Cengage Learning.

Long, K. 2014. Myanmar's young tourism entrepreneurs [Online]. *BBC*. Available: www.bbc.co.uk/news/business-28756061 [Accessed 26 October 2017].

Lynch, R. 2009. *Strategic Management*. Harlow: Prentice Hall.

Mangold, W. G. and Faulds, D. J. 2009. Social media: the new hybrid element of the promotion mix. *Business Horizons*, 52, 357–365.

Mariani, M., Di Felice, M. and Mura, M. 2016. Facebook as a destination marketing tool: evidence from Italian regional destination management organizations. *Tourism Management*, 54, 321–343.

Middleton, V., Fyall, A., Morgan, M. and Ranchhod, A. 2009. *Marketing in Travel and Tourism*. New York: Routledge.

Miles, M. P. and Arnold, D. R. 1991. The relationship between market orientation and entrepreneurial orientation. *Entrepreneurship Theory and Practice*, 15, 49–65.

Mitas, O., Van Der Ent, M., Peeters, P. and Weston, R. 2015. *Research For Tran Committee – the Digitisation of Tourism Enterprises*. Brussels: Directorate General For Internal Policies, Policy Department B, European Parliament.

Mowforth, M. and Munt, I. 1998. *Tourism and Sustainability: New Tourism in the Third World*. London: Routledge.

O'Connor, S. 2018. Millennial insecurity is reshaping the UK economy. *Financial Times*, 21 February 2018.

O'Dwyer, M., Gilmore, A. and Carson, D. 2009. Innovative marketing in SMEs. *European Journal of Marketing*, 43, 46–61.

Payne, A. and Frow, P. 2005. A strategic framework for customer relationship management. *Journal of Marketing*, 69, 167–176.

Plog, S. C. 1994. Understanding psychographics in tourism research. *In:* Ritchie, J. and Goeldner, C. R. (eds.), *Travel, Tourism and Hospitality Research: A Handbook for Managers and Researchers*. New York: John Wiley and Sons.

Press, G. 2014. 12 Big data definitions: what's yours? *Forbes* [Online]. Available: www.forbes.com/sites/gilpress/2014/09/03/12-big-data-definitions-whats-yours/#2c10d43a13ae [Accessed 20 February 2018].

Salas-Olmedo, M. H., Moya-Gomez, B., Juan Carlos García-Palomares, J. C. and Gutierrez, J. 2018. Tourists' digital footprint in cities: comparing big data sources. *Tourism Management*, 66, 13–25.

Shaw, E. 2012. Entrepreneurial marketing. *In:* Carter, S. and Jones-Evans, D. (eds.), *Enterprise and Small Business: Principles, Practice and Policy*. Harlow: Pearson.

Statista. 2018. *Digital Travel Sales Worldwide From 2014 to 2020 (in Billion US Dollars)* [Online]. Available: www.statista.com/statistics/499694/forecast-of-online-travel-sales-worldwide/ [Accessed 31 January 2018].

Steafel, E. 2017. Welcome aboard millennial airlines. *The Daily Telegraph Saturday*, 7 October 2017.

Storey, D. J. 1994. *Understanding the Small Business Sector*. London: Routledge.

Thomas, R. 2000. Small firms in the tourism industry: some conceptual issues. *International Journal of Tourism Research*, 2, 345–353.

Thomas, R., Shaw, G. and Page, S. 2011. Understanding small firms in tourism: a perspective on research trends and challenges. *Tourism Management*, 32, 963–976.

TripAdvisor. 2017. *About TripAdvisor* [Online]. Available: https://tripadvisor.mediaroom.com/uk-about-us [Accessed 14 August 2017].

Wiklund, J. 1999. The sustainability of the entrepreneurial orientation–performance relationship. *Entrepreneurship Theory and Practice*, 24, 37–48.

Xiang, Z. and Gretzel, U. 2010. Role of social media in online travel information search. *Tourism Management*, 39, 179–188.

Ye, Q., Law, R., Gu, B. and Chen, W. 2011. The influence of user-generated content on traveller behaviour: an empirical investigation on the effects of e-word-of-mouth to hotel online bookings. *Computers in Human Behaviour*, 27, 634–639.

Zontanos, G. and Anderson, A. R. 2004. Relationships, marketing and small business: an exploration of links in theory and practice. *Qualitative Market Research: An International Journal*, 7, 228–236.

Chapter 6

From birth to growth

Large streams from little fountains flow, Tall oaks from little acorns grow.

(Everett, 1797)

Our founders, J.W. and Alice Marriott started with a small idea, a root beer stand. From there, it grew into a small hotel business, and then another, bigger one.

(Marriott, 2018)

Introduction

The quotations at the start of this chapter provide a glimpse of the potential inherent in any new firm; Everett's quotation metaphorically, and Marriott's manifestly. But growth is a contested concept, it is neither natural for firms to grow, nor is it necessarily valued by the tourism entrepreneur. This chapter explores the theme 'from birth to growth'. It moves beyond initial start-up activities and nascent behaviour to the firm that is poised and ready to grow. It explores challenges the firm and the tourism entrepreneur might face in this regard. It begins, however, by reviewing different stances towards growth, including the view of policy-makers, discussing whether growth is 'natural' or in fact an exception in the overall scheme of tourism firms. Fast-growing firms are reviewed, but set in contrast to the majority of stable firms. The chapter reviews models of firm growth and discusses whether the newly established firm should follow others' examples, or whether it might be better to lead in one's market, or indeed to penetrate new markets. Barriers to growth in small firms are discussed. Non-growth as the prerogative of many small tourism firms is also reviewed.

Learning outcomes

At the end of this chapter the reader should:

- Be able to articulate the concept of firm growth and how it is measured.
- Be familiar with models of firm growth and various challenges the tourism firm faces at different stages of growth.
- Be aware of a strategic approach to firm growth, including distinguishing between different growth strategies.

Firm growth

It is one thing to set up a business; it is another moving it into growth territory. Bridge et al. (2003) argue that the natural state of business, as any other natural system, is inertia and regress. Growth requires energy and purpose. Lacking this, companies will either not grow, or if growth is unexpected (see Drucker's sources of innovation in Chapter 3) it is likely they will fail. This is because they will be unprepared for the challenges growth entails. What could be managed by one individual, the owner, can soon become a wholly unmanageable affair, especially if growth occurs at excessive speed. It is possible for a business to expand too quickly, to over-exert itself, and this does in fact happen more frequently than one might expect. The following excerpt is from a participant in one of the author's studies whose fledgling business expanded rapidly and consequently almost 'went bust':

> Well we nearly went bust pre-Christmas. . . in December. . . because we grew so big quickly. . . we went from no turnover to. . . from five grand a week to 40 grand a week in just. . . we did too much. . . we were just trying to be all things to all people really. . . oh yeah we'll do that we'll do that. . . not looking at profit margins. . . like we were so busy that we were selling things at a loss. . . we ordered too much stock we just made text book mistakes. . . we had so much pressure. . . it was ridiculous . . . you've built yourself up to be this great success and then you're almost losing it.

On the other hand, some businesses, particularly in tourism, never manage to outgrow their micro status; many owners of small firms do not want their firms to grow, especially where we are dealing with lifestyle businesses (Scott et al., 2003) or family firms (Getz et al., 2004). It is even possible to argue, as Leitch et al. (2010) do, that there has been too much focus by policy-makers on growth, given that the vast majority of small firms do not grow and do not want to grow.

At times, policy-makers have moved their attention from business start-up to supporting small firms poised to grow (Gibb and Davies, 1990). Based on US data between 1988 and 1992, Birch and Medoff (1994), for example, estimated that 4% of companies were identified as having high growth, and of these 60% created new jobs. Given limited resources there are perennial debates about where policy-makers should target their support. There are some compelling reasons then to only support small growing firms or small firms that want to grow, rather than small firms generally. It is far better in some minds to support the 'gazelles' or 'fliers', those firms that are growing rapidly, than firms that have no inherent desire to grow.

There are also counter-arguments, however, to the targeted support of small firms. For example, there is the view that a large seedbed of start-ups is needed for high growth potential firms to develop in the first place (at the outset you do not know which are going to be gazelles and which the sloths). There is also the view that start-ups rejuvenate the economy and provide for high levels of competition, whether they grow or not. Furthermore, owner/manager aspirations may develop. While the small tourism business owner may have set up their business for lifestyle reasons, success may breed desire for further success, and while growth was initially not considered, this may change (see Chapter 11 on lifestyle entrepreneurship in tourism).

Gazelles

The term gazelle refers to fast-growing small firms. What constitutes fast-growing is a moot point, but a common measure is to take annual turnover/revenue growth of more than 20% sustained over four years. Because very small firms frequently do initially grow quickly because they start from a small base, these are usually excluded from the gazelle classification (in the US this applies to firms whose turnover is smaller than $10 million, which in fact is likely to exclude the vast majority of tourism firms). Amat and Perramon (2011) review the literature on gazelles and offer a number of contributors to high growth rates:

- Size: small firms are likely to grow more quickly that large firms (from a small base).
- Age: younger firms are likely to grow more quickly than older firms.
- Access to finance: access to finance promotes growth, lack of access hinders it.
- Research and development: R&D spending is positively related to growth in sales.

Amat and Perramon's (2011) own study of gazelles in Spain indicates that they achieve a competitive advantage based on strategic direction, quality, innovation, globalisation, human resources, trade policy and a conservative financial policy.

What is growth?

The meaning of growth has thus far been taken for granted, but alongside the acknowledgement that most tourism firms do not grow, and do not necessarily seek to grow, a further complication is clarifying what is in fact meant by firm growth. Since Penrose's (1959) *The Theory of the Growth of the Firm* it has been established that growth is not just about size (whether measured in number of employees, sales, profits, etc.) but also about a change in processes. In practice, however – i.e., from a policy-maker's preferred perspective – growth is about size rather than a change in processes along the 'bigger is better' theme. It is about quantity rather than quality. The 'more is better' discourse mirrors that of the early stages of tourism development (e.g., Jafari, 2001), but is still witnessed in many tourism development scenarios today (e.g., if we think of overtourism).

When considering amounts (size), often the focus is on number of employees, but growth is not one-dimensional. Growth can be measured in a number of ways; it could be financial growth (e.g., sales, profits) but it could also be physical growth (growth in number of outlets, size of premises), or customer growth (number of customers, geographical location of customers) or product/service-related growth (number of products, product lines, services offered). Within the tourism context we could think of growth in the types of holidays a tour operator offers, or in the number of destinations served, growth in the variety of source markets served, or in the number of contracts with accommodation providers, for example.

It is important to consider carefully how growth is measured, because this will affect the extent to which we witness growth, and, if used as a target in strategic management, the path the growing tourism firm wishes to take (it legitimises goals). Thus, while a reasonable assumption is that where we have growth in one variable, we also witness growth in others, this does not have to be the case. A company whose profits are growing may be reducing the number of people it employs, and may even be shrinking its sales. Growth in market share often comes at the expense, in the short term, of a reduction in profits as prices may need to be reduced, and/or marketing expenses increased.

Growth models

As with many other phenomena (e.g., product life-cycles, destination development, career trajectories), firms too have been assessed as to whether a common pattern or series of stages exist that they typically go through. Within tourism, limited use of the small firm growth/life-cycle literature has been made (Thomas et al., 2011; Altinay and Altinay, 2006), despite the fact that according to Smallbone and Wyer (2012) more has been written about small firm growth in recent years than any other aspect of the development or management of small firms (with the exception of finance). Even though firm growth has received a great deal of scholarly attention, the issue continues to cause debate, with knowledge in this area still fragmented and no integrative theory (Dobbs et al., 2007).

One early model that has received attention in the literature is that presented by Churchill and Lewis (1983), whose model offered five stages (see Table 6.1).

Others have offered similar models such as Hanks et al. (1993), who suggested four stages as applied to technology firms comprising conception and development, commercialisation, growth, and maturity. McMahon (2001), who focused on panel data on manufacturing firms in Australia, discerned three pathways: the first, a low growth pathway (around 70% of the panel); the second, a moderate growth pathway (around 25% of the panel); and the third a high growth pathway leading to what McMahon describes as the entrepreneurial SME configuration (around 5% of the panel). Kuratko and Hodgetts (2001:495) characterise ventures to be either lifestyle, small-profitable or high-growth, whereby growth 'is the phase during which a venture usually reaches major crossroads in the decisions that affect its future'.

Models of firm growth such as those proposed by Churchill and Lewis (1983), Hanks et al. (1993) and McMahon (2001) could, if proven to accurately reflect firm

Table 6.1 Five stages of business growth (Churchill and Lewis, 1983)

Stage	Characteristics/Issues
Existence	Gaining customers/delivering product or service/raising enough capital. Minimal to non-existent formal structures.
Survival	Generate sufficient cash flow to stay in business. Minimal formal structures.
Success	Two types:1: Success-disengagement (managers take over while the owner steps back). Maintaining status quo. Basic formal structures. 2: Success-growth (the owner consolidates the company and marshals resources to grow the firm). Basic formal structures.
Take-off	Focus on how to grow rapidly and how to finance this. Maturing formality.
Resource-maturity	Two key considerations: to consolidate and control the financial gains brought by rapid growth, and to retain the advantages of a small business: flexibility and an entrepreneurial spirit. Extensive formality.

growth trajectories, be of use to policy-makers in deciding which firms to support, how best to support them, and at which point in their development support is required. Unfortunately, in practice things are less obvious than the models suggest. The empirical validation of models such as that proposed by Churchill and Lewis (1983) is difficult; often growth is not linear: firms may grow, decline, and grow again, just like tourist destinations' popularity. The models might be more valuable in a heuristic sense, i.e., in terms of helping us understand an ideal type (Weber, 1949). The fact that for many firms growth does not follow a clear trajectory has been identified among others, by Smallbone and Wyer (2012), who mention growth phases. As these authors point out, it might be more fitting to think of high growth phases that some firms pass through as being of interest to policy-makers. The growth orientation of a firm may change over time; the newly established firm must grow to survive, the rapidly expanding firm may need to cap growth so as not to over-extend itself.

Whether it will ever be possible to come up with a theory that explains firm growth is questionable (Gibb and Davies, 1990), certainly the quest for a comprehensive theoretical model that explains entrepreneurial and business growth has been likened by Leitch et al. (2010:258) to 'tilting at windmills'. The nature or growth, and whether it occurs or not, entails numerous factors both internal to the firm, as well as external to it. From an internal perspective, the firm that wants to grow faces resource challenges, such as financial, IT, HR and control systems, and management expertise. Externally, the organisation's growth trajectory will be influenced by, for example, economic climate, political situation and subsequent economic policies, taxation, interest rates, employment legislation and such like (models such as those frequently referred to in strategic management – for example, Porter's Five Forces or PESTEL – can be used to understand the environment surrounding the firm). In sum, 'the quest for holistic understanding may be unrealistic or at least premature, since growth is a multi-dimensional, heterogeneous, and complex phenomenon, as is each facet of it' (Leitch et al., 2010:250).

Case study 6.1: Tourism growth in Iceland[1]

With regard to the economy, it is frequently claimed that a rising tide lifts all boats. It is certainly easier to grow a company in a booming market such as that witnessed in tourism in recent years in Iceland. Iceland's recent economic history makes for interesting reading, if not a pleasant experience for those involved, that could be summarised thus: from boom to bust to boom within the space of a decade. The 1990s saw major economic reforms in Iceland (reduction of corporation tax from 50% to 18%, trade liberalisation and privatisation of some state-owned businesses). Iceland during this period was sometimes referred to as the Nordic Tiger. In 2008 the economic boom suddenly turned to bust in the wake of the global financial crisis. Iceland's major banks failed and were taken over by the government; the government itself had to be bailed out, the economy fell headlong into a severe economic depression that lasted until 2011. Relative to the size of its economy, the collapse of the banking system was the biggest ever experienced (*The Economist*, 2008).

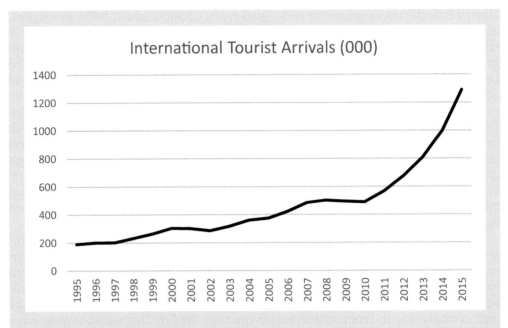

Figure 6.1 International tourist arrivals, Iceland, 1995–2015

Source: Data from World Bank (2017).

As we can see in Figure 6.1, international tourism in Iceland witnessed healthy growth between 1995 and 2007 when it plateaued during the financial crisis (and even declined slightly between 2009 and 2010). However, from 2010 onwards exponential growth occurred, almost trebling between 2010 and 2015. Further statistics from the World Bank indicate that the share of international tourism receipts of total exports grew from just under 12% to 18%. As an article in the *Financial Times* suggests (Moore, 2017) tourists from the US alone now almost outnumber the native population of 340,000. In this kind of environment, one might expect firms that cater to international tourists, and their suppliers, to find growth easier. This kind of environment clearly presents opportunities to the entrepreneur. Some of the growth in demand will be accommodated for by start-ups (followers rather than pioneers of which there certainly are plenty in Iceland; Moore, 2017), but initially, at least until the opportunities become more widely recognised, but in Iceland's dramatic case also beyond, the growth in demand offers ample expansion opportunities for the existing firm.

Notwithstanding the complexity inherent in trying to explain small firm growth, frameworks such as those proposed by Churchill and Lewis (1983) and Storey (1994) can help us consider and subsequently comprehend challenges the growing firm may encounter. Storey's (1994) framework was developed further by Smallbone and Wyer (2012) and comprises three key elements: characteristics of the entrepreneur, the firm and management strategies, and the external environment.

Characteristics of the entrepreneur

One of the defining features of small firms is the close correspondence between management and ownership; in most instances the owner is the manager, the person who runs the business on a day-to-day basis. The consequence of this is that the culture of the firm is intimately tied up to the character of the owner. A firm is evidently more likely to grow if this is desired by the owner, just as the reverse will be true. More generally, any kind of major transformation in an organisation, of whatever size, will require commitment at the highest levels (see for example Kotter's, 1995, widely-cited eight steps of organisational transformation where steps 1 and 2, 'creating a sense of urgency' and 'forming a powerful guiding coalition' respectively, are indicative of this).

The owner/manager's attitudes towards growth may change too, which aligns with the view of growth phases (Smallbone and Wyer, 2012). After an initial period of growth the owner may reach a stage where s/he feels their goals have been achieved and wants no further expansion. Fagenson (1993) has drawn attention to a potential conflict owners face when their firms expand. The growing firm will require a greater focus on the role of management, which may sit at odds with the role of the entrepreneur. Messeghem (2003), reviewing the literature on firm size, formality and entrepreneurial orientation, also draws attention to this potential conflict in arguing that new managerial practices such as quality management may prevent the adoption or maintenance of an entrepreneurial orientation.

Conversely, the owner/manager of what might have been started as a type of artisan firm may then develop into a more business-minded entrepreneur (i.e., the entrepreneur in a traditional sense) as business opportunities present themselves (Smallbone et al., 1995). In fact, this was demonstrated by some surfing lifestyle entrepreneurs in Devon and Cornwall in a more recent study: passion for surfing led to a passion for business (Beaumont et al., 2016).

Characteristics of the firm and management strategies

Age is an organisational characteristic that has been used to explain the nature of firm growth. As briefly alluded to earlier in this chapter, one might expect the younger firm to grow more quickly than the older firm. Smallbone and Wyer (2012) comment that this is due to younger firms having to build up resources to withstand unforeseen external shocks. A further explanation is that small firms tend to be more entrepreneurial, and thus more prone to exploit new market opportunities. Furthermore, firms that have just been set up need to grow just to survive (initially). However, some larger firms may start growing rapidly again after a period of apparent stagnation. Age on its own is insufficient to explain firm growth. Management strategy will also affect the nature and speed of growth, whereby strategic management in small firms is usually tacit rather than explicit. Whether the owner/manager has the requisite managerial skills (e.g., covering finance, marketing, IT, etc.) can be a determining factor of whether a company grows or not. It is furthermore recognised that small firms face greater resource constraints than large firms and that how this is managed will affect growth too (this resource-based view of small firm growth was recognised early on by Penrose, 1959).

The external environment

'Arguably, it is the impact of the external influences and the unpredictable manner in which they emerge, and change over time, that has the greatest influence on the nature and pace of small business growth' (Smallbone and Wyer, 2012:485). We have already referred to this above in our presentation of common frameworks or tools available to the owner/manager to make sense of the environment (e.g., PESTEL, SWOT analysis and Porters' Five Forces[2]) and in the case study on tourism growth in Iceland.

Not only is the environment, whether benign or malign, a determining factor in a firm's growth, it can sometimes present a matter of life or death. In some respects, it can be argued that tourism is a sector that is not as sensitive to environmental change as others, because it is highly labour intensive and is not necessarily as technologically driven. Some tourism firms continue to operate in largely the same way as they did ten, 20 or even 30 years ago. As a sector it offers low entry barriers and is therefore favoured by policy-makers when it comes to providing employment in regions undergoing economic decline. But this view contrasts with the 'accepted' wisdom surrounding change and high levels of competitive rivalry in the sector. Indeed, this is only a partial and therefore not wholly accurate view. Technological developments have transformed the supply and demand side of tourism and as a sector it is dependent on numerous environmental factors that can suddenly change and spell disaster for the nascent tourism firm. These can be man-made crises such as political upheaval, wars and conflicts, or natural disasters such earthquakes, flooding/droughts or disease (Ritchie, 2004). Plenty of examples of all of these and their negative impacts on tourism exist.

One recurring issue that focuses less on causes of firm growth, but how it manifests itself, is the replacement of informality with formality. Put differently, the operations in a growing firm become more complex to the extent that their coordination goes beyond the capabilities and time of just one individual, the owner/manager. To manage the growing, firm systems and procedures need to be introduced and formalised (see also Table 6.1). Staff need to be recruited and developed. The owner/manager needs to delegate and relinquish some control (not always a straightforward undertaking). Overall, some level of bureaucratic control is called for (whereby the danger lies in losing the dynamism and flair that can be characteristic of many small, fast-growing start-ups; e.g., Messeghem, 2003).

Case study 6.2: Growth tips from Y Combinator

In an article on its website (Hariharan, 2017) Y Combinator, a company offering seed funding for start-ups, offers advice from 25 growth experts on what to do and what to avoid when seeking to grow a business. Some examples are provided from tourism firms (e.g., Airbnb and Uber) as well as generally offering sound advice and so selected key points are summarised here.

The starting point in the article is to avoid 'growth hacking', which means taking a haphazard approach to growth, something that has been recognised as applying to tourism firms (Peters, 2005). The idea is to foster a scientific approach to growth, to move away from a functional organisational design and to create growth teams. However, the firm should not rush into growth before it is ready. It needs to fix 'leaky bucket' problems first; that is, ensuring it can retain existing customers.

To check whether you are retaining customers it is important to use the right metrics. Avoid vanity metrics such as 'number of times an App has been downloaded'. Airbnb for example uses a 'rebook' rate – the percentage of users who rebook after first use, and 'nights booked per user' – the number of nights booked per user over time. These are examples of demand-side metrics, but if your business has a supply side too, like Airbnb does, you should also focus on this; for example, 'active hosts' – percentage of hosts that are active, i.e., have a booking. Another metric that could be used is 'bookings per active host'.

It is also important to distinguish between good retention and bad retention. You want to ensure long-term retention is stable (frequently long-term retention dips after an initial period), that it aligns with benchmarks for your sector, and newer cohorts should perform better, i.e., display higher retention rates (this indicates you are improving your product or service).

Once the business has tackled retention it can then focus on growth by creating a growth team. This should be headed by a growth product manager who will lead the establishment of the company's growth culture and experimental framework, and the appointment of 'growth engineers'. Crucially, all of these hires need to be data driven and of an inquisitive mindset.

Once the growth team is in place, targets need to be set. These need to be absolute, rather than relative. For example, instead of suggesting improve conversion rates by 10%, you could stipulate 'achieve 5 million first-time room-night bookings this year' (in Airbnb's case). These goals should then be broken down further into sub-goals. Staying with the Airbnb example, if the overall target was to achieve incremental bookings of 15 million this year, this could be broken down into bookings from new and from existing customers:

[x] Room Nights = [A] Room nights from new users + [B] Room nights from existing users

In accordance with standard goal-setting theory, goals should be challenging but not so challenging that they demotivate because regarded as unachievable/unrealistic.

Once goals and sub-goals have been identified, it is time to explore growth channels as a basis for experimentation. The main source of these is consumer behaviour; for example, how do your best users/customers use your product or service and how can you ensure more customers adopt the same behaviour? Alternatively, how are customers today overcoming some of the challenges associated with the product or service? It is very important to keep track of the experiments one conducts, and to do so centrally; for example, by means of an experiment dashboard that the entire growth team has access to.

Seeking peer feedback is very important, to query results of the experiments and provide alternative explanations. Normally, only 20–30% of experiments have a positive outcome, but this will encourage growth engineers to take risks (i.e., because failed experiments are recognised as part of the process).

It is also important to seek user feedback. Although the quantitative data are key, not all useful insights will come solely via quantitative data. Variation may be found between users in different locations, age, social background, etc. The ultimate goal, according to Hariharan, is that growth becomes embedded in a company's DNA: 'When done right, an amazing growth program will permeate the entire organization, making an evidence-based mindset part of the company's DNA.' It should be noted, however, that the companies Hariharan refers to have access to large data sets, and are high-tech firms (e.g., Facebook, Slack, Uber, Airbnb and Stitch Fix). Many of the recommendations here are aspirational targets for the 'ordinary' tourism firm. That said, the majority of tourism firms do not seek growth, so we are not necessarily describing normal firms in this chapter as outlined previously. Understanding best practice is, however, never a bad idea!

To follow or to lead?

The steps a company needs to take to grow will not necessarily require a great deal of innovation or originality, but can simply take the form of competitive mimicry. The notion of (competitive) mimicry originates in biology and refers to one species mimicking some aspect of another species to gain an evolutionary advantage. Rather than coming up with an entirely new idea, a firm could simply emulate leaders in its field. The danger here, however, is that in competitive markets this may lead to price competition, which in turn drives down profits for all. The only way to overcome this is differentiation (Porter, 1985).

While mimicry can offer low-risk, short-term returns, the danger of price-based competition is very real, which calls for a pioneering or market leadership role. In a study of pioneers and followers, Covin et al. (2000) found that in a hostile environment, pioneering can be a way to break out of price-based competition and grow in spite of charging high prices. Achieving a tight fit with market needs, around a well-defined product/service line, allows the pioneering firm to excel in a hostile environment. Thus, the pioneering firm demonstrates entrepreneurial behaviour in that it enters a new product-market arena that others have either not recognised or sought to exploit. It may then also achieve a first-mover advantage in, for example, being recognised as setting an industry benchmark or standard to which others must strive.

For those firms that do want to follow, the strategy, according to Covin et al.'s (2000) study, needs to focus on achieving cost advantages as the product/service is in essence identical to that of competitors restricting the ability to charge a premium price. On the contrary, in a hostile environment focusing on the cost structure allows followers to pursue a low-price strategy: 'Accordingly, the follower with the most competitive price coupled with a supportive low cost structure will likely be the follower that grows' (Covin et al., 2000:204). This is very similar to Michael Porter's (1985) sources of competitive advantage, which reside in either differentiation or cost leadership (or a combination of both).

What is furthermore recognised in Covin et al.'s (2000) study is that market conditions will inevitably influence a firm's growth and should determine its growth strategy. Hostile environments may call for greater entrepreneurial behaviour, and firms may find growth more difficult to achieve. In a hostile environment, there is a greater need to demonstrate pioneering behaviour; followers have an easier time in benign environments.

What Covin et al.'s (2000) study also points to is the meaninglessness of one-size-fits-all approaches to growth. A firm's growth trajectory, in fact whether it grows at all, is dependent on a number of internal and external factors, not least the level of competition within the sector. The starting point for growth is the desire to grow, or at least its acceptance should one be so fortunate as to stumble upon it, as can happen. We should not presume that the majority of tourism firms desire and therefore seek to grow. This does not detract, however, from the quest to make sense of those that do.

Summary

This chapter has discussed the concept of firm growth as it applies to the small tourism firm specifically. We have recognised that growth itself is a slippery concept. It can be measured in a number of ways that are, crucially, not necessarily mutually supportive. Growth in one area does not mean growth in another. Growth in the short-term may result in slower growth or even decline in the medium-to-long term.

It is frequently assumed that firms will grow, or will seek to grow, but we have recognised that growth can be regarded as the exception rather than as the rule. Growth in other words is not a 'natural process' for firms. The vast majority of tourism firms do not grow beyond Churchill and Lewis' (1983) 'survival' or 'success-disengagement' stages. Although models of firm growth exist, some argue that given the idiosyncrasies of firms and markets the search for 'the' model of firm growth will remain elusive. There are clear parallels to Butler's (1980) lifecycle model of destinations – while the model may only find limited empirical support, as a heuristic device it proves very useful in helping understand the challenges that come with growth. Others such as Smallbone and Wyer (2012) have argued that it is more appropriate to write of growth phases as opposed to growth trajectories from birth to demise (in the lifetime of a company growth can come and go, it can be positive but also negative).

A case study of Airbnb and Uber's growth strategies illustrated how firms that do want to grow should take a strategic, i.e., planned approach to doing so, considering in detail the kind of measures and growth targets that are meaningful to the firm. Following on from this point, the chapter closed with a brief discussion of whether it is better to lead or to follow in terms of pursuing a growth strategy. Although pioneering is more risky than mimicry as the firm is trying something new that has not been tested before, in highly competitive markets there is also a risk associated with simply following others' lead, which may result in coming 'too late to the party'. As will be discussed in greater detail in Chapter 8, first-mover advantages should not be ignored. Certainly, competition based on price alone is extremely risky (Porter, 1985) and so the tourism firm should try to distinguish its offer in some way from that of the competitors, i.e., adopt a differentiation strategy when establishing itself, and when seeking to grow.

Review questions/discussion points

1 Given limited resources, should policy-makers only support high growth firms, or start-ups more generally?
2 Outline the advantages and disadvantages of different measures of firm growth.
3 If in practice very few tourism firms grow, and of those that do, few adhere to the trajectories described by growth models, of what value are the models? (The same question can be applied to Butler's, 1980, Tourism Area Life Cycle model.)
4 Identify and familiarise yourself with a tourism firm of your choice. Then consider what its growth targets could be, as well as what the risks to achieving these growth targets might be.

Notes

1 https://ipfs.io/ipfs/QmXoypizjW3WknFiJnKLwHCnL72vedxjQkDDP1mXWo6uco/wiki/2008%E2%80%932012_Icelandic_financial_crisis.html (accessed 12 October 2017).
2 We have deliberately avoided a discussion of PESTEL and SWOT analyses here as they are discussed in all management and strategic management texts in our experience. There is a danger that students feel these models are being 'done to death'.

References

Altinay, L. and Altinay, E. 2006. Determinants of ethnic minority entrepreneurial growth in the catering sector. *Service Industries Journal*, 26, 203–221.
Amat, O. and Perramon, J. 2011. *Gazelle Companies: Growth Drivers and Evolutionary Analysis*. Economics Working Paper, Department of Economics and Business, Universitat Pompeu Fabra.
Beaumont, E., Walmsley, A., Woodward, E. and Wallis, L. 2016. The freestyle lifestyle entrepreneur: a tale of competing values. *British Academy of Management Conference 2016*. Newcastle: BAM.
Birch, D. and Medoff, J. G. 1994. Gazelles. *In*: Lewis, S. and Levenson, A. R. (eds.), *Labor Markets, Employment Policy and Job Creation*. Michigan: Westview Press.
Bridge, S., O'Neill, K. and Cromie, S. 2003. *Understanding Enterprise, Entrepreneurship and Small Business*. Basingstoke: Palgrave Macmillan.
Butler, D. 1980. The concept of a tourist area cycle of evolution: implications for management of resources. *Canadian Geographer*, 24, 5–12.
Churchill, N. and Lewis, V. 1983. The five stages of small business growth. *Harvard Business Review*, 83, 30–50.
Covin, J., Slevin, D. and Heeley, M. 2000. Pioneers and followers: competitive tactics, environment, and firm growth. *Journal of Business Venturing*, 15.
Dobbs, M., Hamilton, R. T., Matthew Dobbs, R. T. H. 2007. Small business growth: recent evidence and new directions. *International Journal of Entrepreneurial Behavior & Research*, 13, 296–322.
The Economist. 2008. Cracks in the crust. *The Economist* (US edition).

Everett. 1797. Lines spoken at a school exhibition, by a little boy, seven years old. *In:* Blight, D. (ed.) *The Columbian Orator.* New York: New York University Press.

Fagenson, E. 1993. Personal value systems of men and women entrepreneurs versus managers. *Journal of Business Venturing,* 8, 409–430.

Getz, D., Carlsen, J. and Morrison, A. 2004. *The Family Business in Tourism and Hospitality.* Wallingford: CABI Publishing.

Gibb, A. and Davies, L. 1990. In pursuit of frameworks for the development of growth models of the small business. *International Small Business Journal,* 9, 15–31.

Hanks, S., Watson, C., Jansen, E. and Chandler, G. N. 1993. Tightening the life-cycle construct: a taxonomic study of growth stage configurations in high technology organizations. *Entrepreneurship Theory and Practice,* 18, 5–30.

Hariharan, A. 2017. Growth guide: how to set up, staff and scale a growth program [Online]. *blog.Ycombinator.* Available from: https://blog.ycombinator.com/growth-guide2017/ [Accessed 12 June 2018].

Jafari, J. 2001. The scientification of tourism. *In:* Smith, V. L. and Brent, M. (eds.), *Hosts and Guests Revisited: Tourism Issues of the 21st Century.* New York: Cognizant.

Kotter, J. 1995. Leading change: why transformation efforts fail. *Harvard Business Review,* 73, 1–10.

Kuratko, D. and Hodgetts, R. 2001. *Entrepreneurship – A Contemporary Approach.* Orlando: Harcourt College Publishers.

Leitch, C., Hill, F. and Neergaard, H. 2010. Entrepreneurial and business growth and the quest for a 'comprehensive theory': tilting at windmills? *Entrepreneurship Theory and Practice,* 34, 249–260.

Marriott. 2018. *Marriott Careers* [Online]. Available: www.careers.marriott.co.uk/ [Accessed 21 January 2018].

McMahon, R. 2001. Deriving an empirical development taxonomy for manufacturing SMEs using data from Australia's Business Longitudinal Survey. *Small Business Economics,* 17, 197–212.

Messeghem, K. 2003. Strategic entrepreneurship and managerial activities in SMEs. *International Small Business Journal,* 21, 197–212.

Moore, T. 2017. Iceland's tourism boom – and backlash. *Financial Times,* 8 March 2017.

Penrose, E. 1959. *The Theory of the Growth of the Firm.* Oxford: Oxford University Press.

Peters, M. 2005. Entrepreneurial skills in leadership and human resource management evaluated by apprentices in small tourism businesses. *Education & Training,* 47, 575–591.

Porter, M. 1985. *Competitive Advantage.* New York: The Free Press.

Ritchie, B. W. 2004. Chaos, crises and disasters: a strategic approach to crisis management in the tourism industry. *Tourism Management,* 25, 669–683.

Scott, S., Locke, E. and Collins, C. 2003. Entrepreneurial motivation. *Human Resource Management Review,* 13, 257–279.

Smallbone, D. and Wyer, P. 2012. Growth and development in the small firm. *In:* Carter, S. and Jones-Evans, D. (eds.), *Entrepreneurship and Small Business. Principles, Practice and Policy,* 3rd edn. Harlow: Pearson.

Smallbone, D., Leigh, R. and North, D. 1995. The characteristics and strategies of high growth firms. *International Journal of Entrepreneurial Behaviour and Research,* 1, 44–62.

Storey, D. J. 1994. *Understanding the Small Business Sector.* London: Routledge.

Thomas, R., Shaw, G. and Page, S. 2011. Understanding small firms in tourism: a perspective on research trends and challenges. *Tourism Management,* 32, 963–976.

Weber, M. 1949. *The Methodology of the Social Sciences.* New York: Free Press.

World Bank. 2017. *Iceland* [Online]. Available: https://data.worldbank.org/country/iceland [Accessed 12 October 2017].

Chapter 7

Entrepreneurship and employment

The ultimate competitive asset of any organisation is its people.

(Band et al., 1994:22)

Ultimately, those companies that strive for self-renewal will succeed in the long term.

(Markides, 1998:41)

Sweeping global forces are reshaping the workplace, the workforce, and work itself.

(Deloitte, 2016:1)

Introduction

The three quotations provided at the start of this chapter have been included to remind us, first, of the importance of people to organisational success. Whether large or small, established or emergent, enterprises are essentially a collection of resources, primarily human talent, working towards a common purpose. This is true even if the only human resource in the firm is the entrepreneur him/herself. Second, both of the other quotations highlight the dramatic impact broader societal changes are having, and will continue to have, on all firms. Markides (1998) writing more than 20 years ago recognised the need for organisational self-renewal, and therefore implicitly, an entrepreneurial orientation within the firm. Deloitte's (2016) report similarly picks up on the notion of change brought about by 'forces' external to the organisation that will change the nature of work itself. We can suggest therefore that employees play a crucial role in bringing about organisational self-renewal through an entrepreneurial orientation. Employees also need to be more entrepreneurial when it comes to managing their own careers. Picking up on Hagel's (2016) view as mentioned in the foreword to this book: 'we must all become entrepreneurs now'.

It has long been recognised that the small firm is not a mirror of the large firm (e.g., Storey, 1994), a distinction which applies equally to tourism SMEs (Thomas et al., 2011; Page et al., 1999) and which has consequences for the management of human resources within the tourism SME (Lucas, 2004; Walmsley et al., 2012). To illustrate, with regard to differences in human resource management (HRM) in small tourism firms compared to large, Urbano and Yordanova (2008) draw attention to:

- Difficulty recruiting staff compared to large firms (career development opportunities are more limited in small firms)
- Limited financial resources which can result in less training
- Owner/managers' lack of awareness of recent developments in HRM practices
- Small tourism firms will not have HRM departments with the time and know-how to tackle HRM issues

With the exception of the very smallest, micro-firms that have no intention of employing staff, issues surrounding employment are of major and ongoing concern to tourism SMEs. In Chapter 2 we encountered the concept of intrapreneurship; in Chapter 3 the concept of innovation; this chapter continues to work with these concepts within the scope of SME employment. Specifically, while we may take for granted that the individual who has created a new firm has demonstrated entrepreneurial behaviour, it is not a given that individuals subsequently hired will share the entrepreneurial characteristics of the firm's founder. A key question, therefore, for those wishing to either maintain an organisation's entrepreneurial orientation, or to rediscover it, is how may HRM assist in this process? This chapter is primarily involved in addressing this question. In doing so, it will also cover some issues relating to employment in small firms more generally.

The chapter begins by confirming the importance of people (human resources) to the success of the tourism firm. Subsequently the chapter seeks to explore how the small and recently established tourism firm can maintain its entrepreneurial orientation. The chapter then focuses on characteristics of entrepreneurial employees and how entrepreneurial behaviour may be fostered. This will include a review of the concepts of entrepreneurial effectiveness and the entrepreneurial mindset. The chapter then moves on to discuss organisational learning and absorptive capacity, both key concepts and tools to assist the tourism firm in its quest to stay innovative. The chapter then discusses the notion of leadership and its role in fostering entrepreneurship and innovation in the tourism firm. The relationship between the roles of leader and entrepreneur are also discussed, as well as the distinction between managers and leaders. The chapter closes by providing examples of innovation in tourism employment, with a closer look at volunteering as an innovation in tourism employment.

Learning outcomes

At the end of this chapter the reader should be able to:

- Assess methods of fostering an entrepreneurial orientation in the small tourism firm.
- Understand challenges that firm growth can present to managing employees.
- Appreciate the relationship between organisational learning and absorptive capacity and their role in innovation.

- Identify innovations in tourism employment.
- Recognise how developments in artificial intelligence might change the nature of tourism work.

Human resources in tourism

The importance of employees to organisational success in tourism is a given. This is an area where both academia and industry see eye-to-eye. The following quotations from leading tourism organisations serve to illustrate:

- TUI, who offer careers in tourism in 180 countries across 220 brands, claim 'It's our people that make us number one' (TUI Group, 2018).
- Kuoni, a luxury tour operator, proposes: 'Our staff are our biggest asset' and 'We're often voted the UK's Best Luxury Tour Operator and a big part of this is down to our knowledgeable, enthusiastic and friendly team who go the extra-mile for our customers and understand what it takes to deliver the most incredible holiday experience' (Kuoni, 2018).
- Intercontinental Hotels Group who have 12 brands spanning 5,000 hotels in nearly 100 territories and countries acknowledge that their success 'flows from the thousands of people around the world who form part of the IHG team. It's their ideas, inspiration and effort that make us who we are' and explain 'We're a company which passionately believes that it's our people who have brought us to where we are today and our people that will help us grow' (Intercontinental Hotels Group, 2018).

Despite this recognition from industry, working conditions and employee relations in tourism are regularly cause for concern (Baum, 2007, 2018; Walmsley and Partington, 2014; Wood, 1997; Walmsley et al., 2018). Although it is not our intention to explore this issue in any detail here, because this book focuses on entrepreneurship and of necessity therefore on small firms, it is worthwhile noting the ongoing debate about employee relations and the nature of work in small firms more generally as these will affect employee behaviours, including innovation and intrapreneurship. Moreover, given the prominence of small firms generally and in tourism in particular, employment in SMEs shapes the lived experience of the majority of tourism employees.

Employee relations in small firms have often been regarded as weak compared to those in large organisations, with some suggesting they represent a 'bleak house' scenario, or are indeed 'brutal' (Rainnie, 1989:7). This one-sided view contrasts with that of others such as Bacon et al. (1996), Lucas (2004) and Cobble and Merrill (2009) who draw attention to the lack of formality, increased levels of autonomy and a 'family-orientated' approach to employee relations, which can make for a more pleasant working environment. It would therefore be 'a gross oversimplification to lay the blame for tourism's reputation for poor working conditions on the doorstep of small employers' (Walmsley, 2015:50). In fact, because of higher levels of autonomy and less formality generally in small firms, it might be easier for the employee to innovate and be entrepreneurial in a small organisation.

Chang et al. (2011:812) have tried to link the nature of tourism as a service, specifically the intangibility of services, and the success of innovation, to the attitudes and skills of employees. Ottenbacher et al. (2006) expand on this point, confirming the belief that as businesses are increasingly less able to differentiate themselves on the basis of their physical capital, i.e., they will have the same 'hardware', the role of employees as a differentiating factor grows in importance. This is something that has been recognised for some time now in the generic management literature (e.g., Barney, 1986), especially in relation to the concept of core competencies; that is, how organisations use their resources. As the resource-based view of the firm stipulates (Wernerfelt, 1984; Barney, 1991), for a resource to lead to sustained competitive advantage it needs to be both imperfectly imitable and non-substitutable (Barney, 1991). Imperfect imitability and non-substitutability are enhanced where the resource and its use, i.e., the core competence, are in some way tied to the individual firm's situation. This applies to the firm's culture, the way individuals work together and to the knowledge employees have of the firm's individual and unique situation. These are intangibles that a competitor firm cannot simply acquire.

Fostering innovation and entrepreneurship

As the quotations in the introduction to this chapter indicate, to maintain a competitive advantage in today's fast-paced business environment requires nimble, innovative organisations that can move with, even anticipate, changes in the market. Large tourism firms such as Marriott:

> Success is never final. We're always evolving to be even more innovative and relevant.
>
> (Marriott, 2018)

or Accor Hotels:

> Our Group is transforming. We surprise and innovate. We overturn hospitality industry conventions.
>
> (Accor Hotels Group, 2018)

are indicative of this position and also of the fact that being entrepreneurial and innovative is not the prerogative of small tourism firms.

In the very small microbusiness, entrepreneurial drive is often provided by the owner/manager. It is possible that the owner, being more of a craftsman than opportunistic entrepreneur (Smith, 1967), is not all that entrepreneurial and has no desire to grow his/her firm (see also previous chapter). Assuming, however, that the owner/entrepreneur is keen for the organisation to grow, there is a danger that when some organisational functions are separated from the owner, formality sets in; in these circumstances it is all too easy for an organisation to lose its innovative flair and dynamism. The issue is of academic as well as practical interest, regarded as being of such great importance that Stevenson and Jarillo (1991) argue research into the 'entrepreneurial management process' is one of three key research themes in entrepreneurship.

The question then arises as to how an organisation can remain nimble; how can it retain its entrepreneurial orientation (EO)? Before we tackle this, we consider what the term entrepreneurial orientation comprises. Here the literature offers a fair amount of agreement. Thus, the firm displaying a high degree of EO was defined by Miller (1983:777) as 'one that engages in product market innovation, undertakes somewhat risky ventures, and is first to come up with "proactive" innovations, beating competitors to the punch'. Wiklund and Shepherd (2005) pick up on Miller's (1983) work when they argue that firms that display an entrepreneurial orientation are characterised by a combination of innovativeness, proactiveness, and risk. Likewise, Kallmuenzer and Peters (2018) looked specifically at the relationship between EO and business performance of small rural tourism firms in Western Austria with their measure of EO involving Miller's (1983) conceptualisation. We can see then that with regard to EO, Miller's (1983) work has provided a foundation for those of others. It is interesting to note that Kallmuenzer and Peters' (2018) study did not find a link between risk-taking and financial performance of the rural tourism SMEs in their study. This was explained by many family firms' desire to create a business to pass on to the next generation, which precluded any particularly risky undertakings.

From the foregoing, it is proposed that if the individual members of an organisation are entrepreneurial, then the organisation itself should be entrepreneurial. If the same drive, enthusiasm, risk-taking propensity, and innovativeness apply to new organisational members, then the small but growing tourism firm will maintain its entrepreneurial orientation too. However, this is a necessary but not sufficient condition for the creation of an entrepreneurial organisation. Without entrepreneurial members, i.e., innovation happening at the level of the individual employee, it is impossible to have an entrepreneurial organisation, but the context surrounding the employees needs to be conducive to entrepreneurship and innovation too.

It is one of the core insights in HRM that employee performance depends on an employee's skills and competences, but also on the employee's motivation (much has been written on this issue, using a wide range of terminology such as engagement, commitment, employee satisfaction, etc.). Kotler et al. (2014:98), for example, point out: 'The progressive company creates a high level of employee satisfaction, which leads employees to work on continuous improvements as well as breakthrough innovations.' The hypothesis that has been established here is that HRM practices that engender higher levels of employee satisfaction will create a more innovative workforce. This is what Ottenbacher (2007:446) refers to when he states 'hospitality innovation success is strongly related to excellent HRM practices'. The critical idea here is that HRM practices can make a difference. That is, managed or led in a certain way, an organisation can become more entrepreneurial via its people. Put differently, the entrepreneurial tourism organisation needs both entrepreneurial members (employees) and an organisational context that fosters entrepreneurship. This issue, although important, has to date not received much attention in the tourism literature.

HR functions and the entrepreneurial tourism organisation

At an empirical level, limited research exists on the relationship between HRM and corporate entrepreneurship within the context of SMEs (Castrogiovanni et al., 2011). Nonetheless, whether large or small, organisations can use standard HR functions such as recruitment, selection, training, performance management and retention to foster innovation and entrepreneurship. Here are some examples to illustrate:

- Recruitment and selection: seek evidence of innovative behaviour in a candidate's previous work experience, include a test of innovative thinking as part of the selection process.
- Training: provide training that offers experience in different parts of the organisation, which can lead to increased innovation (see also below), offer training in creative thinking, or parallel thinking (De Bono, 2016).
- Performance management: offer a monthly/quarterly prize or bonus for the employee that has come up with the most useful innovation to, for example, improve processes, find new customers, increase repeat visits.
- Retention: retention is related to absorptive capacity (see below) so that by improving retention rates absorptive capacity might be increased. Consider what a 'healthy' level of attrition might be (attrition despite its downsides also offers the opportunity of recruiting 'new blood' into the organisation with new ideas).

Research on HRM's ability to foster an entrepreneurial orientation in tourism is relatively sparse, although it does exist. Returning to Chang et al.'s (2011) study, for example, the focus here was on selection and training, specifically whether there was any relationship between these two HR functions and innovation (incremental innovation and radical innovation). Chang et al.'s (2011) study provides a robust theoretical understanding of how HRM may result in higher levels of innovation within the tourism firm and as such we will review this in more detail.

A distinction frequently encountered in firms' quest to be innovative is that between internal and external sources of innovation. Although it is good practice to invest in a systematic search for innovative opportunities, according to a study cited by Kotler et al. (2014) most innovation ideas come from employees (as opposed to formal R&D activity or customers). Further to this point, Chang et al.'s (2011) explanation for a focus on training as an HR practice likely to increase innovation is based on views that enhanced knowledge are linked to enhanced levels of innovation, as are improved affective states (e.g., commitment and engagement) vis-à-vis the organisation. In a sense this can be argued for enhanced employee performance more generally, i.e., a more knowledgeable and engaged employee is likely to be more productive than the opposite. Chang et al.'s (2011) focus is in particular on front-line – i.e., customer-contact – employees because these are responsible for the screening and testing of new ideas. Based on a review of the literature, Chang et al. (2011) suggest a link therefore between training (which should enhance knowledge and engagement) and both incremental and radical innovation, although at the outset the link to incremental innovation may be deemed more direct.

Turning to employee selection, Mumford (2000) has argued in relation to employees that innovation is more likely to occur when they possess multiple skills across a number of relevant areas. This permits the ability to seek new connections and opportunities in related aspects of a business (e.g., between a customer ordering food and the relaying of that information to the kitchen). Furthermore, Chang et al. (2011) argue two further points why a recruitment and selection strategy focused on innovation could relate to greater levels of incremental and radical innovation. The first focuses on person–organisation fit. An organisation that aspires to be innovative would not harm its endeavours by trying in turn to select innovative employees.

This all sounds fairly obvious, but there is more to this person–organisation fit than initially meets the eye. Individuals that are able to 'fit in' are more likely to be satisfied in their roles, and, following the previous paragraph, more likely to be committed and engaged thereby increasing their ability (and willingness) to innovate. Second, the tourism and hospitality sectors rely heavily on tacit skills that are difficult to learn or train formally (hence a prevalence of on-the-job training in the sector) (Burns, 1997; Baum, 2006). Consequently, the recruitment and selection of employees who already possess these skills is advantageous to the firm.

Chang et al.'s (2011) study confirmed that training core customer employees has a positive impact on innovation (radical and incremental) as does selecting multi-skilled employees. That said, it could be the case that firms that have more stringent recruitment strategies, as well as offering more training, are simply more innovative in the first place. One issue identified here is that establishing causal links between HRM practices and firm performance measures is never a simple undertaking. Measurement issues aside, there are potentially numerous intervening variables making it difficult to establish causality. As with many attempts in related areas to assess the impact of organisational change (e.g., adoption of CSR on firm performance; Margolis and Walsh, 2001), what may be very convincing at a theoretical level is hard to establish empirically (and hence attempts like those offered by Chang et al., 2011, should be welcomed, although read critically).

The issue of whether training employees to be innovative, entrepreneurial and creative can be extended to a consideration of the role of entrepreneurship education (see also Chapter 11) is one of the most researched areas in the field of entrepreneurship. Studies of entrepreneurship education tend to focus on a university context, where entire programmes or individual modules seek to develop students' entrepreneurial intent (Nabi et al., 2017). However, the idea behind entrepreneurship education, broadly speaking, is that it is possible to enhance individuals' entrepreneurial mindsets, or make them more entrepreneurially effective. If it is possible to inculcate an entrepreneurial mindset in university students via entrepreneurship education, by implication this is also something that can be developed within existing organisations. Whether it is called education or training, there is a general understanding that it is possible to make people more enterprising (creative or innovative).

The entrepreneurial mindset and entrepreneurial effectiveness

Before we continue with the review of how HRM policy and practices may create a more enterprising organisation below, we first take a step back and consider two concepts associated with entrepreneurs and entrepreneurship: the entrepreneurial mindset (see also Chapter 2), and entrepreneurial effectiveness. A better understanding of 'the entrepreneur' using these two concepts will lead to a fuller appreciation of the kind of traits an organisation aspiring to be entrepreneurial may seek to inculcate in its employees.

Because enterprise is commonly associated with the application of ideas, we suggest the inculcation of an entrepreneurial mindset must include a proclivity for action. In its guidelines for entrepreneurship education, the Quality Assurance Agency (2018:19) in the UK argues that developing an entrepreneurial mindset involves becoming:

- self-aware of personality and social identity
- motivated to achieve personal ambitions and goals
- self-organised, flexible and resilient
- curious towards new possibilities for creating value
- responsive to problems and opportunities by making new connections
- able to go beyond perceived limitations and achieve results
- tolerant of uncertainty, ambiguity, risk, and failure
- sensitive to personal values, such as ethical, social, diversity and environmental awareness.

This action orientation is thus evident in the Quality Assurance Agency's (2018) review of the entrepreneurial mindset and in many respects mirrors entrepreneurial traits associated with entrepreneurs such as demonstrating resilience and being tolerant of uncertainty (as we would expect). Davis et al. (2016:22) take a more personality-oriented approach to the entrepreneurial mindset defining it as 'the constellation of motives, skills, and thought processes that distinguish entrepreneurs from non-entrepreneurs and that contribute to entrepreneurial success'. Crucially, whereas personality traits may be regarded as being fairly stable and thus less amenable to attempts to change them (e.g., via education or training), it is quite possible to change motives, skills and thought processes. Davis et al.'s (2016) development of what they term the Entrepreneurial Mindset Profile (EMP) distinguishes between personality traits that are more enduring and that attract one to entrepreneurship, and skills that are required to be good at it that are more malleable. The skills Davis et al. (2016) decided to include in their EMP measure, because there was evidence of their malleability, are: creativity, optimism, persistence, self-confidence, execution, future focus and interpersonal skills.

Entrepreneurial effectiveness is the envisaged outcome of enterprise education according to the Quality Assurance Agency (2018). What this means precisely is not outlined (not in any detail) but it is acknowledged that it is only likely to be obtained by students towards the end of their programme, and will assist in the transition into work/self-employment. Cardon et al. (2009) explore the role of passion in entrepreneurship, theorising on its role in the pursuit of entrepreneurial effectiveness. Here entrepreneurial effectiveness may relate to effectiveness in opportunity recognition, in venture creation and in venture growth. More broadly we define entrepreneurial effectiveness therefore as the achievement of a target behaviour requiring entrepreneurship.

Fostering a culture of innovation

A focus on HRM's role in developing the entrepreneurial potential of an organisation's workforce needs to consider not just individual HR functions (recruitment, training, retention, etc.) but the entire organisational culture. The value to tourism firms of fostering an enterprise culture was already recognised by Kaspar (1989) some time ago. Similarly, works such as those by Charles Handy (1978, *Gods of Management*), Peters and Waterman (1982, *In Search of Excellence*) or Deal and Kennedy (1982, *Corporate Cultures: The Rites and Rituals of Corporate Life*) ushered in an era of interest in organisational culture that continues unabated today. Even in these early works it was possible to discern a relationship between organisational culture and innovation (for example, the roles of hierarchy and control in fostering or limiting innovation). Today, it is accepted that organisational culture is a determining factor in driving organisational innovation. Although some firms are renowned for being particularly innovative (e.g., Google, 3M, Apple), and pride themselves on their organisational culture that fosters innovation, theoretically the explanation of the organisational culture–innovation relationship is fraught with complexity and even contradictions.

The obvious place to start when considering how organisational culture affects innovation is to consider what organisational culture is. Here numerous definitions exist but we refer to Barney's (1986:657) given its widespread use: 'a complex set of values, beliefs, assumptions and symbols that define the way in which a firm conducts its business'.

Even simpler than this, and a definition similarly frequently quoted, is Hofstede's (1998) who suggests culture is 'the collective programming of the mind'.

Particularly this latter definition points to culture as a means of indirect control and the first definition underlines culture's importance in shaping firm behaviour and also its complexity. Culture defines what valid goals (ends) are, and equally, what acceptable means of attaining these goals are. Therefore, an organisational culture that fosters innovation is one that, in the first instance, values innovation. This may sound self-evident but creating an awareness of entrepreneurship is one of the first goals of entrepreneurship education (Quality Assurance Agency, 2018) and in fact many organisations, certainly in tourism, are not interested in innovation (or change for that matter) if we think about the many small lifestyle firms. Furthermore, as we have seen in Chapter 3, different types of innovation exist, from the incremental to the radical. An organisation's management or ownership may endorse incremental innovation while shying away from radical innovation.

Büschgens et al. (2013) offer a number of examples of potential relationships between organisational values, culture and innovation that support Gibb's (1996:314) statement that 'certain basic stimuli for entrepreneurial behaviour lie naturally within the culture, task structure and learning environment of the owner-managed company':

- An organisation that values growth and resource acquisition is in line with invention and innovation as these can be considered a means to achieve those goals (Quinn and McGrath, 1982).
- Organisations that value flexibility could be said to be accepting of deviation from existing procedures and thereby more open to the implementation of innovations.
- Tolerance for risk goes hand-in-hand with a flexibility orientation as it signifies a willingness to deal with uncertainties. It is also related to growth as only risk-taking allows seizing opportunities that appear in the market.
- An organisational culture that values organisational learning is more likely to be innovative as it allows adaptation to an external environment. An organisation that fosters training and the development of its members is equally more likely to be innovative as maintaining expertise of employees is a predictor for the generation and adoption of innovations.

We can see here how culture may support HR functions' quest to foster an entrepreneurial orientation.

Organisational learning and absorptive capacity

It can be difficult to draw clear lines between the terms organisational culture, organisational learning and absorptive capacity. They all dovetail, but for the sake of clarity, here we have separated organisational culture from organisational learning and absorptive capacity. Thus, while organisational culture is a very broad term, and touches on numerous themes, organisational learning and absorptive capacity are narrower in scope and arguably more closely connected theoretically, not always in a positive way, as we shall discuss further below.

In 1990 Peter Senge published his much acclaimed book *The Fifth Discipline: The Art and Practice of the Learning Organization* where organisational learning (as distinct from the learning organisation) is defined as 'the process of creating, retaining, and transferring knowledge within an organization.' His book established the importance of learning within organisations, a theme that is equally, if not more important, today. The importance of learning to competitive advantage and organisational success has been summarised by Hess (2014:3) in the introductory chapter to his book *Learn or Die* as follows:

> many organizations rely on operational excellence – getting better, faster, and cheaper – as the key part of their business models; many also rely on innovation to drive growth. The former requires relentless, constant improvement; the latter requires discovery and experimentation. What is the fundamental process underlying both efforts? It is learning.

Hess (2014:7) also spells out his formula for HPLOs (high performance learning organizations) as follows:

HPLO = Right People + Right Environment + Right Processes

This confirms what was already described above, i.e., it is not enough to have 'the right people on the bus' (Collins, 2001), the right conditions need to be created for learning to take place, as confirmed by Hjalager (2010) in her review of innovation in tourism. Having the 'right conditions' is the responsibility of senior managers and the human resources function in the organisation (which, depending on the size of the organisation, could be one and the same). According to Hess (2014), ensuring the environment is 'right' as well as having the right processes involves:

- High employee engagement.
- Creating an internal learning system that should consistently align the organisation's culture, structure, HR policies, leadership behaviours, measurements, and reward.
- Promoting behaviours fundamental to learning. These include foundational behaviours (e.g., open-mindedness, resilience), exploratory behaviours (e.g., being curious and inquisitive), managing self behaviours (e.g., being mindful, actively listening) and learning process behaviours (e.g., using critical thinking processes).
- A specific kind of leadership that facilitates learning and high emotional engagement.

We can see that creating a true learning organisation is no easy undertaking, and effectively many of the recommendations suggested by Hess (2014) simply appear to be good management and HR practice. However, this does not mean they are common in tourism, which does not have a particularly good reputation when it comes to employment practices despite widespread recognition that employees are key to organisational success (see start of this chapter).

The value of organisational learning becomes even more apparent when we consider the role of innovation to business performance. The need for companies to be innovative is not new, and the call to become a learning organisation in this regard is likewise not novel as the following quote by Cahill (1997:105) with reference to the millennium makes clear:

> This focus on innovativeness is one of the two strongest practical reasons to go through the pain of creating a learning organization from an existing organization. Organizations clearly need to become more innovative as we approach the millennium; they should have been more innovative all along: innovative in terms of new products and services that they offered, innovative in terms of new methods of organizing, innovative in terms of how they dealt with their employees, more innovative in general.

Creating the right conditions for innovation to occur can be difficult and not every innovation is successful. There is something to be said, therefore, for adopting innovations that have proven themselves in the so-called real world (whereby one clearly needs to be mindful of infringement of patent and copyright laws of course). Incremental innovations, particularly service innovations, are not necessarily difficult to imitate. Kotler et al. (2014) provide examples of service innovations in the airline industry where they stress this point:

- The introduction of internet access on flights
- Seats that turn into flat beds
- Offering hot showers
- Availability of cooked-to-order breakfasts.

Many people would balk at the suggestion there was anything innovative in these examples. Readers may, at least if they are in the habit of flying business or even first class, consider all of these a standard offering. However, these are all relatively recent innovations. The point is that it is not enough to innovate once. The successful company in a competitive environment must innovate continuously. The learning organisation with its external focus, its flexibility and the autonomy given to its staff is more likely to be able to fulfil these demands for continuous innovation or indeed adopt others' innovations.

Damanpour and Wischnevsky (2006) have examined the differences between innovation-generating and innovation-adopting firms. They distinguish four types of innovative organisation (Table 7.1) suggesting that the truly innovative organisation both generates and adopts innovation.

They also argue:

> The innovation-generating organization depends more heavily on its technological knowledge and market capabilities to develop and commercialize innovations; the innovation-adopting organization (IAO) relies more on its managerial and organizational capabilities to select and assimilate innovations.
>
> (Damanpour and Wischnevsky, 2006:272)

Table 7.1 Organisational type and innovation

		Generation of innovation	
		High	Low
Adoption of innovation	High	Innovative organisation	Innovation-adopting organisation
	Low	Innovation-generating organisation	Non-innovative organisation

Source: Damanpour and Wischnevsky (2006:271)

What this quote confirms is the importance of HRM in ensuring the parameters are in place for creating an organisation that can benefit from adopting, indeed absorbing, innovations. The consequence of this statement is that the ability to absorb innovations is not distributed equally across firms. Those firms that are able to learn quickly and absorb innovations are likely to achieve a competitive edge over firms that display a lower level of absorptive capacity. Organisational learning and absorptive capacity go hand-in-hand (Lane et al., 2006).

Absorptive capacity has been defined by Zahra and George (2002:186) as 'a set of organisational routines and processes by which firms acquire, assimilate, transform, and exploit knowledge'. It remains an area largely ignored by tourism scholars (Shaw, 2015) despite a more general recognition of its importance in providing competitive advantage. A notable exception is Thomas and Wood's (2015) research, which, among other things, confirms the importance of management practices and leadership in fostering absorptive capacity. Their study also provided reasons why a conceptualisation of absorptive capacity in tourism might differ from that of other sectors (they refer specifically to manufacturing).

One of the reasons why absorptive capacity as it applies to tourism may be different from that of manufacturing firms is the nature of employment in tourism, which is characterised by high levels of seasonality and staff turnover. Considering that absorptive capacity is enhanced by a culture of sharing knowledge (as is corporate entrepreneurship; Castrogiovanni et al. 2011), if those bearing that knowledge then leave, or do not stay long enough to assimilate knowledge, this should negatively impact absorptive capacity. Moreover, if those that leave then share this knowledge with the new organisation, the scope to sustain competitive advantage in the industry is diminished. A final point to note from Thomas and Wood's (2015) study is the distinction between formal systems that can facilitate knowledge acquisition and the more informal social integration that contributes to the transformation and exploitation of knowledge. This again points to the importance of HRM in providing formal systems but also, crucially, in contributing to the softer 'organisational culture' that fosters social integration.

Leadership, entrepreneurship and management

To set up a successful business from scratch and to see it grow to a large, perhaps even multinational organisation will arguably require strong leadership skills and qualities. Leadership has also been related to levels of creativity and innovation in firms (Anderson et al., 2014; Dunne et al., 2016). There are numerous examples of entrepreneurial leaders and leaders who are entrepreneurs. In fact, entrepreneurs and leaders share many characteristics. From Walt Disney, to Thomas Cook or Freddie Laker, all displayed leadership qualities such as vision, resilience and decisiveness.

The theoretical link between leadership and business start-up was made as long ago as 1943 by Sweezy, who drew attention to the entrepreneur's ability to overcome not just economic barriers, but psychological and social resistances too to a new way of doing things ('he must, in short, have the qualities of leadership'; Sweezy, 1943:94). Markides (1998) makes a very strong case for leadership with clear entrepreneurial overtones:

> it is one thing to get an early warning that trouble is brewing and another thing to decide what to do about it and then do it. This is where strong leadership comes in: being able to see a different future and having the courage to abandon the status quo for something uncertain.
>
> (Markides, 1998:36)

Although Markides (1998) may be describing leadership behaviour here, he could just as easily be describing entrepreneurial behaviour.

Managing any firm requires a range of skills. We argue that starting and running a small, and then growing business requires a particularly broad range of skills. While with firm growth tasks are usually delegated (in fact they ultimately have to be to avoid what Churchill and Lewis (1983) call the omniscience problem – the owner is unable to delegate effectively), in the small firm they assume all managerial functions. Additionally, small firms frequently face something called resource poverty (Welsh and White, 1981). This relates to conditions unique to the small firm, which are often located in highly fragmented industries, such as tourism, where cash flows are precarious, and where functions such as recruitment and marketing are often haphazard. Furthermore, small firms are more susceptible to external events, or at least impacted to a greater degree by external events. It is little surprise therefore that statements such as 'start-ups are started by leaders' (Szycher, 2015:59) or 'entrepreneurs are leaders of innovation and change' (Daft, 2008:51) abound.

Achua and Lussier (2013) expand a little on Daft's (2008) conceptualisation of the relationship between entrepreneurship and leadership. They refer to Mintzberg's (1973) leadership roles that managers perform to accomplish organisational objectives, which include the decisional role of 'entrepreneur'. According to Achua and Lussier (2013:15): 'Leaders perform the entrepreneur role when they innovate and initiate improvements.' There is clear congruence between Daft (2008) and Achua and Lussier's (2013) view that entrepreneurial leadership involves innovation and change.

Burns' (2016) discussion of entrepreneurial leadership stresses the difference between an entrepreneur who displays certain leadership qualities, and the entrepreneurial leader who creates an entrepreneurial organisation: 'to become a leader of an entrepreneurial organization you need to build an organization that is fundamentally entrepreneurial' (Burns, 2016:483). For Burns (2016) entrepreneurial leadership is very much about creating something that will endure once the owner/manager leaves the organisation, it is about creating long-term sustainable competitive advantage by creating an organisation that is systematically entrepreneurial.

It is safe to say that all textbooks on leadership will contain some discussion of the differences between managers and leaders. A common but rather crude view, expressed, for example, by Achua and Lussier (2013:21) in the summary of their discussion of the differences between the leader and the entrepreneur, is:

> managers focus on doing things right, and leaders focus on doing the right thing. Managers are concerned with stability and the best way to get the job done, and leaders place greater concern on innovation and change.

It is almost as though managers have no decision-making powers beyond the short term (they make operational and tactical but not strategic decisions).

Daft (2008) and DuBrin (2013) provide further distinctions between the manager and the leader, such as the leader focusing on the horizon, the manager keeping an eye on the bottom line, the leader acting as a coach, facilitator or even a servant, the manager acting as a boss (DuBrin, 2013, does suggest that these are stereotypical views). Kotter (1990) saw the difference between managers and leaders as so important that he even refers to this in the title of his book on leadership (*A Force for Change: How Leadership Differs from Management*). According to Kotter (1990) management is a modern invention that arose to address the emergence of large complex organisations, whereas leadership is timeless. He even recognises the role of entrepreneurs on the first page of Chapter 1: 'Modern management was invented, in a sense, to help the new railroads, steel mills, and auto companies achieve what legendary entrepreneurs had created for them' (Kotter, 1990:3). Management is seen as leadership's poorer second cousin, again something that is conveyed by Szycher (2015:5) in the first of his ten commandments of entrepreneurship: 'Thou shall be a leader first, then a manager.'

The simplistic view of the role of a manager as someone who simply makes day-to-day operational decisions, focusing only on maintenance of the status quo, goes against Mintzberg's (1973) understanding of the leadership roles of managers, which includes an entrepreneurial role, specifically the need to innovate. In fact, Andrews (1999, originally 1979) in his classic 'The concept of corporate strategy' lays out the leadership qualities of the 'entrepreneur as general manager'. The roles fall into the three domains of personal leader, organisational leader and architect of organisational purpose. As a personal leader, the entrepreneur needs to motivate and provide guidance, set standards of conduct and effectively function as a role model. As organisational leader, it is the entrepreneur's job to select the top management team as the firm expands, blending its skills and expertise. Finally, as the architect of organisational purpose, the entrepreneur needs to shape the organisation's goals and objectives, s/he needs to direct business strategy and demonstrate strategic awareness. This is where management and leadership intertwine most.

Kotter (1990) is very clear, however, that management and managers play a crucial role, especially in maintaining consistency and order, which is increasingly important as the firm grows (see also previous chapter). The owner/manager may feel torn between both roles if we consider Mintzberg's (1989) claim that it is easier for the owner/manager of a small business to display leadership because of fewer formal organisational constraints and simple structures. This is something Markides (1998), with reference to large firms, terms cultural and structural inertia. The need for bureaucracy grows with the growth of the firm, but this does not mean the firm should relinquish the entrepreneurial flair that led to its growth. Traditionally, this may not be easy to achieve as Messeghem (2003:199) suggests: 'As a smaller business is in the process of setting up a much more bureaucratic structure, one may doubt its capacity to maintain an entrepreneurial behaviour.' Although Messeghem's (2003) findings indicate that SMEs with a bureaucratic structure did in fact have a stronger entrepreneurial orientation, which goes against the grain of common wisdom.

Achua and Lussier (2013:21) suggest 'the old command-and-control model of management just doesn't work in today's global economy' and 'the management to the leadership theory paradigm is a shift from the older autocratic management style to the newer participative leadership style of management'. Whether leadership is more important in today's competitive business environment than, say, was the case ten, 20 or even 30 years ago is open to debate (although the claims that it is abound). However, it seems fair to argue that as the business environment becomes less predictable, in part because more competitive, then entrepreneurial leadership as a means of dealing with, and even seeing change as an opportunity, does become more important. Ultimately, entrepreneurs as architects of innovation and change share many characteristics with leaders.

Case study 7.1: Entrepreneurial leadership at Disney

From humble beginnings as a cartoon studio in the 1920s to one of the leading global entertainment companies, the Walt Disney Company's history offers plenty of examples of innovation and entrepreneurial leadership. Walt Disney's unwavering perseverance, optimism, innovation and risk-taking all contributed to the firm's success as documented in the *Forbes* article 'The keys of Walt Disney's Mickey Mouse leadership' (Loftus, 2014). Today, the company operates in four business segments, Media Networks, Parks and Resorts, Studio Entertainment, and Consumer Products and Interactive Media, and boasted sales of over US$55 billion in 2017. Entrepreneurial leadership has been demonstrated in particular during CEO Robert Iger's tenure, a period of rapid and trenchant changes in the marketplace. Iger, on only his second day in office, suggested a risky purchase of Pixar Animation Studios. This was to address the rut the animation unit was in, but also came upon the backdrop of a hostile takeover attempt and a shareholder revolt. Iger did worry about the directors' reaction to pursuing a high-stakes acquisition so soon after assuming office but Iger is not one for shying away from challenges. In his own words:

> I just was built with an innate ability to not let fear guide me in how I run my life. You can look at all the numbers in the world, but as some point somebody. . . needs to dig down deep, search his soul, analyse or get in touch with his own or her own instinct, and decide.
>
> (Miller, 2015)

Other acquisitions followed – Marvel Entertainment in 2009 and Lucasfilm in 2012 – and the share price has more than quadrupled since he took the reins. Iger also has an expansive vision for Disney, colleagues suggest, and is clearly not afraid to act on it. Iger has faced many obstacles, including convincing Steve Jobs to sell Pixar or similarly Isaac Perlmutter that it was time to sell Marvel.

Disney demonstrates innovation and entrepreneurial leadership across all of its business segments, including parks and resorts. This is in fact crucial for its survival as it sees competitive pressures mount from rivals such as Universal Studios. Braun and Soskin (1999) who analysed theme park competitive strategies in Florida in the 1980s and 1990s note how changes in industry structure (e.g., entry of well-heeled rivals, notably Universal Studios) and the overall market environment forced Disney to play a catch-up game. Rather than resting on its laurels, Disney recognised that it needed to continue to invest in product innovation. One of its latest investments is MagicBands. This innovation aims to provide each resort guest with an all-in-one resource, enabling him/her to make a dinner reservation, book rides and times, and access their hotel rooms all from the MyMagic+ device. The development of this device may have cost over US$1.5 billion but Disney maintains it has been worthwhile (Thorp, 2015).

For Peters (2005), leadership skills of entrepreneurs in tourism are crucial in light of the difficultly tourism firms often face in attracting and retaining staff. Peter's (2005) study, which was conducted in the Tyrol region of the Italian Alps, divided entrepreneurs into two groups: the first 'employee friendly leaders' and the second 'employee distant leaders'. Overall, apprentices managed (led) by the first group demonstrated greater levels of job satisfaction, which was particularly pronounced for the leaders who scored highly on 'fairness' and 'honesty'. While it is debatable whether these traits are exclusive to leadership it does show that for this particular group of 16–22-year-old apprentices in tourism SMEs leadership matters.

Thus, we arrive at a final consideration on the role of the entrepreneurial leader in tourism: emotional intelligence (EI). Emotional intelligence as a concept was popularised by Goleman (1996) who drew on the work of two US academics, Mayer and Salovey. Mayer and Salovey (1997:22) defined EI as 'the ability to perceive emotions, to access and generate emotions so as to assist thought, to understand emotions and emotional meanings, and to reflectively regulate emotions so as to promote both better emotion and thought'. In Peters' (2005) study we have already seen how emotional intelligence and entrepreneurship are related. In fact, Ahmetoglu et al. (2011:1029) argue that given the social nature of entrepreneurial activities, 'EI has been hypothesised to be an extremely important factor for predicting entrepreneurial success.' We have recognised the importance of social capital in entrepreneurship (see Chapter 4), whereby the social networks (i.e., capital) the entrepreneur creates may be regarded as a direct function of the entrepreneur's emotional intelligence. Nonetheless, Ahmetoglu et al. (2011) also propose that 'research examining the relationship between EI (emotional intelligence) and entrepreneurship is near to non-existent'.

As per Mayer and Salovey's (1997) definition, emotional intelligence is not just about understanding others' emotional states, but also one's own. When the entrepreneur starts his or her own venture, assuming this is done on their own, there is, however, no one else to 'lead' but oneself. We recognise that the notion of 'leading oneself' can strike people as bizarre, possibly even absurd. (A common understanding of leadership, I would argue, entails leadership and followership. MacGregor Burns (2012:25) similarly argues 'that leadership is nothing if not linked to collective purpose'.) However, the term self-leadership, although potentially confusing, does comprise important ideas for the entrepreneur as they relate to EI.

For example, McKitterick (2015): discusses self-leadership, which he links directly to EI, as being both tactical and strategic, (the ability to focus on both immediate needs, and also having a long-term perspective), and finally being resilient. These are arguably qualities an entrepreneur should have and so self-leadership conceptualised as comprising these elements is very relevant to entrepreneurship.

Zampetakis et al. (2008) were able to establish a relationship between EI and entrepreneurship behaviour within organisations. They used Pearce et al.'s (1997) Entrepreneurial Behaviour Scale, which consists of 11 items as per Table 7.2. Pearce et al. (1997) who developed this measure of entrepreneurial behaviour recognised that it needed to differentiate entrepreneurial behaviour from generally espoused management conduct.

Ahmetoglu et al. (2011) also found a link between EI and entrepreneurial outcomes, although only one of the hypothesised relationships between EI and entrepreneurship was statistically significant. They explain this by drawing on the influence of other personality factors that, in combination with EI, may lead to increased entrepreneurial outcomes. There is a more fundamental message here relating to personality traits and entrepreneurship: predicting entrepreneurial outcomes based on an analysis of a limited number of factors misunderstands the nature of entrepreneurship, which is driven by numerous internal (to the individual) and external factors (Gartner, 1985). This will make it difficult disaggregating the study of EI (or other personality traits) – it is only a combination of factors that lead to entrepreneurship or that create and entrepreneurial mindset (Davis et al., 2016).

Table 7.2 Entrepreneurial behaviour scale items (Pearce et al., 1997)

Item
Efficiently gets proposed actions through 'bureaucratic red tape' and into practice.
Displays an enthusiasm for acquiring skills.
Quickly changes course of action when results aren't being achieved.
Encourages others to take the initiative for their own ideas.
Inspires others to think about their work in new and stimulating ways.
Devotes time to helping others find ways to improve our products and services.
'Goes to bat' for the good ideas of others.
Boldly moves ahead with a promising new approach when others might be more cautious.
Vividly describes how things could be in the future and what is needed to get us there.
Gets people to rally together to meet a challenge.
Creates an environment where people get excited about making improvements.

Innovations in tourism employment

As a sector, tourism is frequently criticised for poor working conditions: long, often unsociable working hours, lack of training and development opportunities and precarious work are regularly highlighted. It is also true that many jobs in tourism pay low wages albeit with some international variation (Walmsley, 2012). Nonetheless, working in tourism does appeal to many (Nickson, 2013), and of course, a huge variety of jobs in the sector exist. Tarring all jobs with one brush, while convenient, is not appropriate. There are certainly many tourism employers, whether large or small, that are innovative in their approach to typical human resource management functions of recruitment, selection, training, performance management and ultimately separation. Here we review a handful of examples that demonstrate that innovative ways of managing (leading) employees are possible, and more importantly, are beneficial to the organisation.

The first example relates to pay and lack of affordable housing, specifically in some parts of London. It is widely acknowledge that tourism and hospitality are low wage sectors. Data from the Office for National Statistics (2016) in the UK, for example, indicate that after hairdressing and childcare, hospitality has the highest proportion of jobs that are paid below the minimum wage rate. D'Arcy (2017) also recognises the hospitality sector's reliance on employing people at the bottom of the legal wage floor.

Although pay is a fundamental aspect of employment, and counts as an extrinsic motivator (as opposed to intrinsic motivators, which are psychological, for example, feeling of accomplishment, relationships with colleagues), other extrinsic motivators can be considered, such as that by an unnamed coffee chain in a report by KPMG (2017) that offered interest-free loans on rental deposits to encourage young workers to move into those areas where they needed workers. At a time of very low interest rates, this will have cost the company very little, indeed will have saved the company money in the long run if this led to fewer staffing (recruitment and severance) costs.

Another example of employment innovation that has led to more responsible forms of employment relates to two hotels in Toronto as discussed in an OECD report by Verma (2012). What is interesting in this example is that some tangible beneficial outcomes for the firms involved are provided (rather than just suggested). The report focuses on two hotels that occupy different niches. Both hotels pride themselves on their service ethos and their recruitment, selection and training is evidence of this. In a sector renowned for its informal recruitment practices (particularly for lower-ranked jobs) both hotels place great emphasis on getting employees with the right attitudes on board (ensuring applicants undertake on average 4–5 interviews with different managers to gauge their suitability). Because of the hotels' reputation, they have a large pool of candidates to draw on. Career progression is also important, workers at all levels are encouraged to learn new skills and to bid for new positions. In-house training is promoted, and employees are encouraged to seek learning opportunities outside the organisation also. Both hotels have a Learning Manager and one of the performance measures is how much training is provided (all employees should receive a minimum of ten hours training per year, excluding job-specific training). As a consequence of their employment practices, labour turnover rates, usually staggeringly high in the sector, average out at between 8–12% for both hotels.

A further example of innovative employment practices, in relation to what we could regard as more responsible employment practices, is the approach adopted by Red Carnation Hotels. This small chain of upmarket hotels has scooped numerous awards for its employment practices including Princess Royal Training Awards 2017, ranked third in the *Sunday Times* Best Companies to Work For 2016, Human Resources Team of the Year, 2015, Hotel Cateys Awards. Similar to the two hotels in Toronto, Red Carnation Hotels emphasises exceptional service quality. Its motto is 'No request is too large, no detail too small' (Red Carnation Hotels, 2017).

Red Carnation Hotels offers an extensive internal training programme as well as encouraging its staff to pursue external personal development opportunities too. A full list of staff benefits is included on its website, which includes:

- Free meals while on duty
- Uniform provided and laundered free of charge
- 28 days holiday per year, which increases with service
- Loan offered to help buy a season ticket for travel to and from work in London
- Pension scheme
- Package of healthcare benefits
- Volunteer for a charity that Red Carnation supports for up to two days per year and get paid as a normal working day
- Stay at one of our 4-star hotels with or without your family at a heavily discounted rate
- Opportunities to travel worldwide with one of our sister companies at heavily discounted rates

Additional benefits are also offered at some properties such as free English lessons, discounted spa treatments and use of a staff car.

While the above examples are probably universally regarded as positive (for employer and employee) another aspect of work that is more controversial is the rise of the so-called gig economy. The gig economy has blurred the boundaries between employee and independent contractor. It is characterised by short-term contracts, with workers often working without formal employee status as quasi-freelancers. This has been enabled by developments in ICT, specifically here the widespread use of apps (examples hereof include well-known companies such as Uber, Deliveroo and Airbnb). Kuhn's (2016) review of the meaning of the gig economy and employment describes how politicians and activists view freelancers as vulnerable and in need of protection, but also highlights how others conceptualise these freelancers as entrepreneurs (Born and Witteloostuijn, 2013) or the 'smallest of small businesses' (Kitching and Smallbone, 2012).

A further consideration in relation to innovations in tourism employment relates to the rapid developments in technology, especially the rise of AI (artificial intelligence). This would not be the first time technological developments cause major shifts in the supply of tourism products and services (for example, the role the internet has played in disintermediation in the late 1990s, or the introduction of the jet engine on commercial flights in the 1950s). The rate of technological change continues to gather pace. What was once barely conceivable – for example, driverless cars – is now a reality. In particular, advances in machine learning (the ability of computers to learn without explicit programming) is providing for rapid advances in AI. Chapter 3 already provided a small taste of what may be heading our way as a result of the developments in AI (see Case study 3.2 Artificial intelligence: pizza robot).

Motivated by John Maynard Keynes' (2010, originally 1931) widely quoted view that as a result of advances in labour-saving technology technological, unemployment would occur, Frey and Osborne (2017) have categorised occupations according to their susceptibility to computerisation (computerisation refers to job automation by means of computer-controlled equipment). Least susceptible to computerisation are recreational therapists (P=0.0028), first-line supervisors of mechanics, installers, and repairers (P=0.003) and emergency management directors (P=0.003). Most susceptible to computerisation are 12 occupations all with probabilities of P=0.99 (i.e., almost a certain event) including telemarketers, library technicians, insurance underwriters and watch repairers. For our purposes it is interesting to note the following occupations as they relate to tourism (Table 7.3).

The possibility for technological substitution of manual labour increases with routinised work. At first glance, this may not seem to apply to the service encounter, which is currently made unpredictable by the combined elements of the service provider and the person(s) receiving the service. As Nickson et al. (2005:196) among many others have argued: 'No two service interactions are identical and this situation gives rise to uncertainty in the service delivery process.' Of course, by introducing automation to the service delivery an element of variation is reduced but the customer's variability is still present.

The non-routinised nature of much service work is offered by Autor and Dorn (2013) as an explanation for the structural shift in the labour market we are currently witnessing, from middle-income manufacturing to low-income service occupations, which is said to contribute to the hourglass economy phenomenon, i.e.,

Table 7.3 Probability of computerisation in tourism

Occupations	Probability of computerisation
Hosts and hostesses, restaurant, lounge, and coffee shop	0.97
Hotel, motel and resort desk clerks	0.94
Waiter and waitresses	0.94
Tour guides and escorts	0.91
Bartenders	0.77
Bus drivers transit and intercity	0.67
Lifeguards, ski patrol, and other recreational protective service workers	0.67
Flight attendants	0.35
Air traffic controllers	0.11
Chefs and head cooks	0.1
Travel agents	0.099
Travel guides	0.057
Lodging managers	0.0039

Source: From Frey and Osborne (2017).

a polarisation of jobs at the top and at the bottom of the occupational hierarchy (Anderson, 2009). Furthermore, there is less of an incentive to automate jobs that pay less as cost savings are lower than for high paid work. Additionally, we may query to what degree, for example, tourists want to be welcomed by a robot when checking into a hotel, regardless of how anthropomorphic that robot is. Nonetheless, as we can see in Frey and Osborne's (2017) analysis, the threat of computerisation to many forms of tourism employment is real. Numerous examples now exist of automation in tourism such as the previously mentioned (Chapter 3) Henn-na hotel in Japan, which is mainly staffed by robots. The hotel seems, according to TripAdvisor, to receive good reviews, although whether guests at the hotel visit largely because of the novelty around its adoption of robots is, of course, something to be considered when interpreting the review.

Papathanassis (2017) has reviewed developments in automation as they apply to tourism, something he calls R-Tourism, and suggests three drivers of automation/robots: productivity, accessibility and service augmentations.

- Productivity: certain routinised tasks can be performed more quickly and accurately by robots than by humans. This idea, although being used most widely in manufacturing, has found its way into tourism. Papathanassis (2017:213) highlights Royal Caribbean Cruises who have introduced robotic bartenders on their newest vessels (Quantum Class) that can mix two drinks per minute and offer a menu of 21 cocktails.
- Service augmentation: for example, via chatbots that enable users to interact with digital assistants online. They also include robotic assistance devices that can entertain or physically assist passengers. Examples include KLM's 'Spencer' (who has his[1] own blog) or Marriott's 'Mario'.
- Accessibility: here Papathanassis (2017) refers to telepresence technology that allows travellers to be virtually present in any location at any time. Although the idea that a virtual version of oneself travels in your place seems to defeat the purpose of tourism that, arguably, is about personal experiences, there are situations where having a telepresence makes sense. It would allow visits most obviously to those with access issues (e.g., wheelchair-bound) but also to all in terms of being able to visit dangerous places, to places out of hours/off peak or to environmentally or socially sensitive areas. It is all about accessibility in other words.

Voluntary work

A further important, fairly recent, innovation in employment in tourism, certainly in terms of scale and scope, is the reliance on volunteers. The innovation here is replacing 'work for wages' with 'work for experience' or 'contribution to a worthy cause'. The exchange of wages for labour has in some circumstances even been reversed where volunteers pay to be able to contribute to community projects.

Definitions of work often claim that work distinguishes itself from non-work activities because it is paid (Grint, 1991). Because volunteers by definition do not get paid, at least not directly (they may receive benefits in kind such as free food or lodging), volunteering distinguishes itself from paid work. This should not be taken to mean volunteers do not have to work hard; some volunteer work is both arduous (e.g., maintaining footpaths in mountain destinations) and potentially dangerous (e.g., working in remote, politically unstable regions of the world).

Many tourism organisations are dependent on volunteers; they have become part of the business model. In fact, businesses have been created based on matching those seeking volunteer opportunities with organisations that seek volunteers. An example of this reliance on volunteer staff is Ducks Unlimited, the world's largest private waterfowl and wetlands conservation organisation, which has a membership of over 700,000 persons and over 50,000 volunteers. In the fiscal year 2002, volunteers held over 6,000 fundraising events, which generated 32% of a total of $185.7 million in revenues and 67% of the organisation's membership (www.ducks.org). Clearly, this innovative use of and heavy reliance on volunteers at the grassroots level for such core organisational functions present a very different set of management challenges for the organisation's leadership.

Case study 7.2: National Trust volunteers

The National Trust (short for the National Trust for Places of Historic Interest or Natural Beauty) is a UK charity founded in 1895. It is a conservation organisation in England, Wales and Northern Ireland, and the largest membership organisation in the United Kingdom, with an income in excess of £500 million in 2016. The National Trust looks after:

- 775 miles of coastline
- Over 248,000 hectares of land
- Over 500 historic houses, castles, ancient monuments gardens and parks and nature reserves.

It relies heavily on volunteers in roles ranging from house guides and countryside rangers to project management and IT support. Morris (2013) suggests 70,000 individuals were volunteering for the Trust in 2013. According to its own website the figure is closer to 60,000 who contribute 3.1 million hours of their time (according to the 2015/2016 annual report it was 62,000 volunteers who contributed 4.5 million hours) – the equivalent of 1,590 full-time staff (National Trust, 2017). A calculation based on the minimum wage of £6.70 per hour for adults that came into place on 1 October puts this at a saving to the NT of over £30 million (excluding other non-wage costs). Morris (2013) quotes Helen Ghosh, the charity's director-general: 'When you visit one of our properties, for the most part the people that welcome you, explain the history of the place and look after it, are all volunteers.' The number of volunteers working for the Trust has increased by more than 30,000 in a decade. Justin Davis Smith, of the National Council of Voluntary Organisations, makes the case for volunteering thus: 'Where volunteering works well, as it clearly does within the National Trust, it benefits all concerned, including the volunteers – who learn new skills, meet new people and reap the rewards of improved physical and mental well-being.' There is an acknowledgement here, however, that it does not always work well and in fact volunteering and voluntourism have come under some criticism, again leading to another opportunity: offering responsible volunteering 'holidays' (see below).

Potential pitfalls of volunteering and voluntourism

It is possible to argue that replacing the exchange of labour for wages with an exchange of labour for an experience, gaining skills, offering a sense of contributing to society and so forth represents a sustainable tourism innovation and yet it would be remiss not to point out some of the potential dangers regarding voluntourism. There has been a growing commercialisation of volunteer tourism, which started with people's desire to do good (for whatever ulterior motive), but is now being recognised as a means to make money. In a report quoted by Coghlan and Noakes (2012) on voluntourism it was noted that the market for volunteer tourists was 1.6 million with a value of between US$1.7 billion and US$2.6 billion. The growth witnessed in volunteer tourism has also resulted in the growth of 'sending' organisations; these are organisations that, for a fee, arrange volunteer opportunities for would-be volunteers. Coghlan and Noakes (2012) explain some of the pressures non-profit organisations are under and thereby justify the more commercial stance many volunteer organisations now adopt. Here it seems they argue that as long as the profits made are invested in the organisation's social cause, increased commercialisation is not necessarily a bad thing (this echoes arguments around the nature of social enterprise). Tomazos (2012:271) in an opinion piece on Coghlan and Noakes' (2012) work is less sanguine:

> This, of course, by deduction would mean that commercialization is ok, provided the increased revenues are shared among all stakeholders, but the history of tourism development teaches us that even when the intentions are beyond reproach, things do not turn out well for all stakeholders.

Case study 7.3: Tourism Concern's volunteer tourism guidelines

Tourism Concern is a charity that campaigns for the rights of local communities. It has a vision for:

> Tourism which is ethical, fair and a positive experience for both travellers and the people and places they visit.

And likewise its mission is:

> To ensure tourism always benefits local people by challenging bad practice and promoting better tourism.

It advises potential volunteer tourists of some of the dangers of volunteering with the wrong organisation. It draws attention to:

- volunteers who have had unfulfilling and disappointing experiences
- volunteer placements that can prevent local workers from getting much-needed jobs
- hard-pressed institutions that waste time looking after them and money upgrading facilities
- abused or abandoned children forming emotional attachments to the visitors, who increase their trauma by disappearing back home after a few weeks.

It also set up an Ethical Volunteering Group whose vision is:

... to promote best practice in international volunteering, to maximise the beneficial developmental impacts in the communities where volunteering takes place, minimise the negative impacts, and to ensure volunteers have a worthwhile experience.

(Tourism Concern, 2017)

Things have now come full circle in that in response to the emergence of irresponsible volunteer tourism organisations, some volunteer organisations are now trying to distinguish themselves by drawing attention to their responsible credentials. One such organisation is People and Places: Responsible Volunteering (www.travel-peopleandplace.co.uk) who, in 2013, won a World Responsible Tourism Award. People and Places are keen to advertise their responsibility credentials, which include an independently audited responsible travel policy.

Summary

This chapter began by confirming the importance of people to organisational success in tourism, whatever the organisation's size or age. It was suggested that, because of the ongoing and rapid pace of change witnessed across all spheres of human activity (political, economic, social, technological), tourism firms will continue to face pressures for self-renewal, driven by an entrepreneurial owner/manager as well as entrepreneurial employees. Just how an entrepreneurial orientation can be fostered and maintained was a primary focus of the chapter therefore. This issue was also identified as being particularly relevant to the growing tourism firm. Within this context of change, the concepts of an entrepreneurial mindset and entrepreneurial effectiveness were discussed.

One of the key propositions of the chapter was that to foster an entrepreneurial orientation requires enterprising individuals, as well as an environment that fosters entrepreneurship. HRM has an important role to play in ensuring, via standard HR functions, the creation and maintenance of the tourism firm's entrepreneurial orientation. Within this context organisational culture was also discussed. It was recognised that organisational culture is strongly connected to organisational learning and absorptive capacity, both concepts that are fundamental to an understanding of fostering an entrepreneurial orientation within the tourism firm.

With reference to organisational learning and absorptive capacity we examined the differences between innovation-generating and innovation-adopting firms, noting again the importance of HR functions and systems in creating organisations that are able to innovate and adapt innovations to meet market needs. We noted some aspects of employment in tourism that may lead to a diminished absorptive capacity, but also that very little tourism-specific research exists in this area.

Leadership was highlighted as another critical factor in fostering an entrepreneurial orientation in firms, not least in its role in setting the foundations of organisational culture but also in HRM policy and practices. The relationship between leadership and entrepreneurship was reviewed, noting many similarities. We also noted that being an entrepreneurial leader involves creating a 'systematically entrepreneurial' organisation and provided the example of Robert Iger's tenure at Walt Disney as characterised by entrepreneurial leadership. Examples were also provided of innovations in tourism employment, ranging from the very obvious and widely reported changes in the nature of employment in the so-called gig economy, to innovations in the area of responsible tourism. The threat to tourism jobs as a result of advances in artificial intelligence was also considered whereby it was argued that while there is a threat, there are limits (at least at present) to the extent to which tourists are willing to deal with robots. Some very personalised jobs such as travel guides and lodging managers are among the least likely to be replaced by artificial intelligence/robots.

The chapter concluded with a review of another innovation in tourism employment; that of using volunteers. The innovation here lies in the removal of the traditional exchange of labour for a wage. Using volunteers is now part of the business model for many tourism organisations. Some tourism organisations would not be able to cope financially if they did not have access to volunteers. A variation on the use of volunteers is where the volunteers are tourists themselves – this may itself be regarded as an innovation in tourism. A number of ethical concerns were, however, also raised in relation to some forms of voluntourism.

Review questions/discussion points

1   Davis et al. (2016) defined an entrepreneurial mindset as including the following skills (see also Chapter 2): creativity, optimism, persistence, self-confidence, execution, future focus and interpersonal skills. So how entrepreneurial is your mindset? Score yourself on a scale of 1–10 where 1 is minimal and 10 is extremely high on these seven skills. The minimum possible score is 7, the maximum score 70 and the mid-point is 37.5. Compare your scores with others in your class. Do the results confirm your expectations of how entrepreneurial you are?

2   Review the differences and similarities between the concepts of entrepreneur and leader.

3   In your own view, what are the key barriers to creating an entrepreneurial organisation?

4 Imagine you have set up a business that uses volunteers. What managerial challenges might you face? Apart from the obvious cost-savings, why else might it make sense to hire volunteers?

Note

1 I presume as the name is Spencer, Spencer is male!

References

Accor Hotels Group. 2018. *Innovation* [Online]. Available: www.accorhotels.group/en/innovation [Accessed 22 January 2018].

Achua, C. and Lussier, R. 2013. *Effective Leadership*. New York: Cengage Learning.

Ahmetoglu, G., Leutner, F. and Chamorro-Premuzic, T. 2011. Eq-nomics: understanding the relationship between individual differences in trait emotional intelligence and entrepreneurship. *Personality and Individual Differences*, 51, 1028–1033.

Anderson, N., Potočnik, K. and Zhou, J. 2014. Innovation and creativity in organizations: a state-of-the-science review, prospective commentary, and guiding framework. *Journal of Management*, 40, 1297–1333.

Anderson, P. 2009. Intermediate occupations and the conceptual and empirical limitations of the hourglass economy thesis. *Work, Employment and Society*, 23, 169–180.

Andrews, K. 1999. The concept of corporate strategy. *In:* Mintzberg, H., Quinn, J. and Ghoshal, S. (eds.), *The Strategy Process*. Harlow: Pearson Education Limited.

Autor, D. and Dorn, D. 2013. The growth of low skill service jobs and the polarization of the US labor market. *American Economic Review*, 103, 1553–1597.

Bacon, N., Ackers, P., Storey, D. J. and Coates, D. 1996. It's a small world: managing human resources in small businesses. *The International Journal of Human Resource Management*, 7, 82–100.

Band, D. C., Scanlan, G. and Tustin, G. M. 1994. Beyond the bottom line: gainsharing and organizational development. *Personnel Review*, 23, 17–32.

Barney, J. 1986. Organizational culture: can it be a source of sustained competitive advantage? *Academy of Management Review*, 11, 656–665.

Barney, J. 1991. Firm resources and sustained competitive advantage. *Journal of Management*, 17, 99–120.

Baum, T. 2006. *Human Resource Management for Tourism Hospitality and Leisure: An International Perspective*. London: Thomson.

Baum, T. 2007. Human resources in tourism: still waiting for change. *Tourism Management*, 28, 1383–1399.

Baum, T. 2018. Sustainable human resource management as a driver in tourism policy and planning: a serious sin of omission? *Journal of Sustainable Tourism*.

Born, A. and Witteloostuijn, A. 2013. Drivers of freelance career success. *Journal of Organizational Behavior*, 34, 24–46.

Braun, B. and Soskin, M. 1999. Theme park competitive strategies. *Annals of Tourism Research*, 26, 438–422.

Burns, P. 1997. Hard-skills, soft-skills: undervaluing hospitality's 'service with a smile'. *Progress in Tourism and Hospitality Research*, 3, 239–248.

Burns, P. 2016. *Entrepreneurship and Small Business: Start-Up, Growth and Maturity.* New York: Palgrave Macmillan.

Büschgens, T., Bausch, A. and Balkin, D. 2013. Organizational culture and innovation: a meta-analytic review. *The Journal of Product Innovation Management*, 30, 763–781.

Cahill, D. 1997. The 'real world' as classroom: the learning organization and innovation. *The Learning Organization*, 4, 106–108.

Cardon, M., Wincent, J., Singh, J. and Drnovsek, M. 2009. The nature and experience of entrepreneurial passion. *Academy of Management Review*, 34, 511–532.

Castrogiovanni, G., Urbano, D. and Loras, J. 2011. Linking corporate entrepreneurship and human resource management in SMEs. *International Journal of Manpower*, 32, 34–47.

Chang, S., Gorg, Y. and Shum, C. 2011. Promoting innovation in hospitality companies through human resource management practices. *International Journal of Hospitality Management*, 30, 812–818.

Churchill, N. and Lewis, V. 1983. The five stages of small business growth. *Harvard Business Review*, 83, 30–50.

Cobble, D. S. and Merrill, M. 2009. The promise of service worker unionism. *In:* Korczynski, M. and Macdonald, C. (eds.), *Service Work: Critical Perspectives*. London: Routledge.

Coghlan, A. and Noakes, S. 2012. Towards an understanding of the drivers of commercialization in the volunteer tourism sector. *Tourism Recreation Research*, 37, 123–131.

Collins, J. 2001. *From Good To Great: Why Some Companies Make the Leap. . . and Others Don't.* London: Random House.

D'Arcy, C. 2017. *Low Pay Britain*. Resolution Foundation.

Daft, R. L. 2008. *Leadership*. New York: Cengage.

Damanpour, F. and Wischnevsky, D. 2006. Research on innovation in organizations: distinguishing innovation-generating from innovation-adopting organizations. *Journal of Engineering and Technology Management*, 23, 269–291.

Davis, M. H., Hall, J. and Mayer, P. 2016. Developing a new measure of entrepreneurial mindset: reliability, validity and implications for practitioners. *Counseling Psychology Journal: Practice and Research*, 68, 21–48.

De Bono, E. 2016. *Parallel Thinking: From Socratic Thinking to De Bono Thinking*. London: Vermilion.

Deal, T. E. and Kennedy, A. A. 1982. *Corporate Cultures: The Rites and Rituals of Corporate Life*. Reading, MA: Addison-Wesley.

Deloitte. 2016. *Global Human Capital Trends 2016*. Deloitte.

DuBrin, A. 2013. *Principles of Leadership*. Canada: Cengage Learning.

Dunne, T., Aaron, J., Mcdowell, W., Urban, D. and Geho, P. 2016. The impact of leadership on small business innovativeness. *Journal of Business Research*, 69, 4876–4881.

Frey, C. B. and Osborne, M. A. 2017. The future of employment: how susceptible are jobs to computerisation? *Techological Forecasting and Social Change*, 114, 254–280.

Gartner, W. B. 1985. A conceptual framework for describing the phenomenon of new venture creation. *Academy of Management Review*, 10, 696–706.

Gibb, A. A. 1996. Entrepreneurship and small business management: can we afford to neglect them in the twenty-first century business school? *British Journal of Management*, 7, 309–321.

Goleman, D. 1996. *Emotional Intelligence: Why It Can Matter More Than IQ*. London: Bloomsbury Publishing.

Grint, K. 1991. *The Sociology of Work: An Introduction*. Cambridge: Polity Press.

Hagel, I. J. 2016. We need to expand our definition of entrepreneurship. *Harvard Business Review* [Online]. Available: https://hbr.org/2016/09/we-need-to-expand-our-definition-of-entrepreneurship [Accessed 28 September 2016].

Handy, C. 1978. *Gods of Management*. London: Souvenir Press.

Hess, P. 2014. *Learn or Die: Using Science to Build a Leading-Edge Learning Organization*. New York: Columbia University Press.

Hjalager, A. M. 2010. A review of innovation research in tourism. *Tourism Management*, 31, 1–12.

Hofstede, G. 1998. Attitudes, values and organizational culture: disentangling the concepts. *Organization Studies*, 19, 477–493.

Intercontinental Hotels Group. 2018. *Join IHG®, One of the World's Leading Hotel Companies* [Online]. Available: http://careers.ihg.com/ [Accessed 21 January 2018].

Kallmuenzer, A. and Peters, M. 2018. Entrepreneurial behaviour, firm size and financial performance: the case of rural tourism firms. *Tourism Recreation Research*, 43, 2–14.

Kaspar, C. 1989. The significance of enterprise culture for tourism enterprises. *The Tourist Review*, 44, 204.

Keynes, J. M. 2010 (originally 1931). Economic possibilities for our grandchildren. *Essays In Persuasion*. Basingstoke: Palgrave Macmillan.

Kitching, J. and Smallbone, D. 2012. Are freelancers a neglected form of small business? *Journal of Small Business and Enterprise Development*, 19, 74–91.

Kotler, P., Bowen, J. and Makens, J. 2014. *Marketing for Hospitality and Tourism*. Harlow: Pearson.

Kotter, J. 1990. *A Force for Change: How Leadership Differs From Management*. New York: The Free Press.

KPMG. 2017. *The Brexit Effect on EU Nationals:A Survey on What European Workers Will Do Now* [Online]. Available: https://assets.kpmg.com/content/dam/kpmg/uk/pdf/2017/08/the-brexit-effect-on-eu-nationals.pdf [Accessed 23 August 2018].

Kuhn, K. 2016. The rise of the 'gig economy' and implications for understanding work and workers. *Industrial and Organizational Psychology*, 9, 157–162.

Kuoni. 2018. *Join The Kuoni Family: We Live and Love Travel* [Online]. Kuoni. Available: www.kuoni.co.uk/careers [Accessed 21 January 2018].

Lane, P., Koka, B. and Pathak, S. 2006. The reification of absorptive capacity: a critical review and rejuvenation of the construct. *Academcy of Management Review*, 31, 833–863.

Loftus, G. 2014. The keys of Walt Disney's Mickey Mouse leadership. *Forbes*.

Lucas, R. 2004. *Employment Relations in the Hospitality and Tourism Industries*. London: Routledge.

MacGregor Burns, J. 2012. *Leadership*. New York: Open Road Media.

Margolis, J. D. and Walsh, J. P. 2001. *People and Profits: The Search for a Link Between a Company's Social And Financial Performance*. Mahway, NJ: Lawrence Erlbaum.

Markides, C. 1998. Strategic innovation in established companies. *Sloan Management Review*, 39, 31–42.

Marriott. 2018. *Marriott Careers* [Online]. Available: www.careers.marriott.co.uk/ [Accessed 21 January 2018].

Mayer, J. and Salovey, P. 1997. What is emotional intelligence? In: Salovey, P. and Sluyter, D. (eds.), *Emotional Development and Emotional Intelligence: Educational Implications*. New York: Basic Books.

McKitterick, B. 2015. *Self-Leadership in Social Work: Reflections From Practice*. Bristol: Policy Press.

Messeghem, K. 2003. Strategic entrepreneurship and managerial activities in SMEs. *International Small Business Journal*, 21, 197–212.

Miller, D. 1983. The correlates of entrepreneurship in three types of firms. *Management Science*, 29, 770–791.

Miller, D. 2015. How Robert Iger's 'fearless' deal-making transformed Disney. *Los Angeles Times* [Online]. Available: www.latimes.com/entertainment/envelope/cotown/la-et-ct-disney-iger-20150607-story.html [Accessed 18 February 2018].

Mintzberg, H. 1973. *The Nature of Managerial Work*. New York: Harper and Row.

Mintzberg, H. 1989. *Mintzberg on Management*. New York: The Free Press.

Morris, S. 2013. National Trust volunteer numbers hit record high. *The Guardian*, 12 September 2013.

Mumford, M. 2000. Managing creative people: strategies and tactics for innovation. *Human Resource Management Review*, 10, 313–351.

Nabi, G., Liñan, F., Fayolle, A., Krueger, N. and Walmsley, A. 2017. The impact of entrepreneurship education in higher education: a systematic review and research agenda. *Academy of Management Learning and Education*, 16, 277–299.

National Trust. 2017. *Fascinating Facts and Figures* [Online]. Available: www.nationaltrust.org.uk/lists/fascinating-facts-and-figures [Accessed 1 September 2017].

Nickson, D. 2013. *Human Resource Management for the Hospitality and Tourism Industries*. London: Routledge.

Nickson, D., Warhurst, C. and Dutton, E. 2005. The importance of attitude and appearance in the service encounter in retail and hospitality. *Managing Service Quality*, 15, 195–208.

Office for National Statistics. 2016. *Statistical Bulletin: Low Pay in the UK: Apr 2016*. London: HMSO.

Ottenbacher, M. 2007. Innovation management in the hospitality industry: different strategies for achieving success. *Journal of Hospitality and Tourism Research*, 31, 431–454.

Ottenbacher, M., Gnoth, J. and Jones, P. 2006. Identifying determinants of success in development of new high-contact services: insight from the hospitality industry. *International Journal of Service Industry Management*, 17, 344–363.

Page, S., Forer, P. and Lawton, G. R. 1999. Small business development and tourism: terra incognita? *Tourism Management*, 20, 435–459.

Papathanassis, A. 2017. R-tourism: introducing the potential impact of robotics and service automation in tourism. *Ovidius University Annals*, 12, 211–216.

Pearce, D., Kramer, T. and Robbins, K. 1997. Effects of managers' entrepreneurial behavior on subordinates. *Journal of Business Venturing*, 12, 147–160.

Peters, M. 2005. Entrepreneurial skills in leadership and human resource management evaluated by apprentices in small tourism businesses. *Education & Training*, 47, 575–591.

Peters, T. and Waterman, R. 1982. *In Search of Excellence: Lessons From America's Best-Run Companies*. New York: Harper & Rowe.

Quality Assurance Agency. 2018. *Enterprise and Entrepreneurship Education: Guidance for UK Higher Education Providers*. Gloucester: Quality Assurance Agency for Higher Education.

Quinn, R. E. and Mcgrath, M. R. 1982. Moving beyond the single solution perspective: the competing values approach as a diagnostic tool. *Journal of Applied Behavioral Science*, 18, 463–472.

Rainnie, A. 1989. *Industrial Relations in Small Firms: Small Isn't Beautiful*. London: Routledge.

Red Carnation Hotels. 2017. *What We Offer Our Employees* [Online]. Available: www.redcarnationhotels.com/careers/whats-in-it-for-you/employee-benefits [Accessed 27 November 2017].

Senge, P. 1990. *The Fifth Discipline: The Art and Practice of the Learning Organization*. New York: Doubleday.

Shaw, G. 2015. Tourism networks, knowledge dynamics and co-creation. *In:* Mcleod, M. and Vaughan, R. (Eds.) *Knowledge Networks and Tourism*. London: Routledge.

Smith, N. 1967. *The Entrepreneur and His Firm: The Relationship Between Type of Man and Type of Company*. East Lansing: Michigan State University.

Stevenson, H. and Jarillo, C. 1991. A new entrepreneurial paradigm. *In:* Etzioni, A. and Lawrence, P. (Eds.), *Socio-Economics: Toward a New Synthesis*. New York: M. E. Sharpe.

Storey, D. J. 1994. *Understanding the Small Business Sector*. London: Routledge.

Sweezy, P. M. 1943. Professor Schumpeter's theory of innovation. *The Review of Economics and Statistics*, 25, 93–96.

Szycher, M. 2015. *The Guide to Entrepreneurship: How to Create Wealth for Your Company and Stakeholders*. Boca Raton: CRC Press.

Thomas, R. and Wood, E. 2015. The absorptive capacity of tourism organisations. *Annals of Tourism Research*, 54, 84–99.

Thomas, R., Shaw, G. and Page, S. 2011. Understanding small firms in tourism: a perspective on research trends and challenges. *Tourism Management*, 32, 963–976.

Thorp, J. 2015. What would Walt do? Universal and Disney battle to be US's best theme park. *The Guardian*, 21 July 2015.

Tomazos, K. 2012. The commercialization of voluntourism money vs mission. *Tourism Recreation Research*, 37, 271–272.

Tourism Concern. 2017. *Ethical Volunteering* [Online]. Available: www.tourismconcern.org.uk/ethical-volunteering/ [Accessed 3 September 2017].

TUI Group. 2018. *Careers At TUI* [Online]. TUI Group. Available: www.tuigroup.com/en-en/careers [Accessed 21 January 2018].

Urbano, D. and Yordanova, D. 2008. Determinants of the adoption of HRM practices in tourism SMEs in Spain: an exploratory study. *Service Business*, 2, 167–185.

Verma, A. 2012. Skills for competitiveness: country report for Canada. *OECD Local Economic and Employment Development (Leed) Working Papers*. OECD.

Walmsley, A. 2012. Decent work and tourism wages: an international comparison. *Progress in Responsible Tourism*, 1, 90–99.

Walmsley, A. 2015. *Youth Employment in Tourism: A Critical Review*. Oxford: Goodfellow Publishers.

Walmsley, A. and Partington, S. N. 2014. *A Stakeholder Approach to Working Conditions in the Tourism and Hospitality Sector*. 2nd International Hospitality & Tourism Conference 2014, Penang, Malaysia.

Walmsley, A., Thomas, R. and Jameson, S. 2012. Internships in SMEs and career intentions. *Journal of Education and Work*, 25, 185–204.

Walmsley, A., Partington, S., Armstrong, R. and Goodwin, H. 2018. Reactions to the national living wage in hospitality. *Employee Relations*.

Welsh, J. and White, J. 1981. A small business is not a little big business. *Harvard Business Review*, 59, 18–27.

Wernerfelt, B. 1984. A resource-based view of the firm. *Strategic Management Journal*, 5, 171–180.

Wiklund, J. and Shepherd, D. 2005. Entrepreneurial orientation and small business performance: a configurational approach. *Journal of Business Venturing*, 20, 71–91.

Wood, R. C. 1997. *Working in Hotels and Catering*. London: Routledge.

Zahra, S. and George, G. 2002. Absorptive capacity: a review, reconceptualization, and extension. *Academy of Management Review*, 27, 185–203.

Zampetakis, L. A., Beldekos, P. and Moustakis, V. S. 2008. 'Day-to-day' entrepreneurship within organisations: the role of trait emotional intelligence and perceived organisational support. *European Management Journal*, 27, 165–175.

Chapter 8

Strategy and entrepreneurship

Effective Entrepreneurs know where they are going, and why. They are focussed on the achievement of specific goals.

(Wickham, 2006:321)

Perception is strong and sight weak. In strategy it is important to see distant things as if they were close and to take a distanced view of close things.

Miyamoto Musashi (philosopher and writer)

Introduction

Today, the importance of strategy and strategic management continues to engender much debate. This is particularly true in relation to large firms that have traditionally provided the context within which strategy has been explored, including in tourism (Evans, 2015). However, many of the principles of strategic management apply as much to small as to large organisations even though a deliberate, strategic approach to managing organisations is not the norm in small firms. For Gibb and Davies (1990) it is in fact strategic management, as employed by innovative owners of small businesses, that distinguishes them from 'regular' small businesses. Others (e.g., Ireland et al., 2003) directly acknowledge the complementarity of strategic management and entrepreneurship. This view is justified if we consider that the exploitation of entrepreneurial opportunities will contribute to the efforts to create sustainable competitive advantage.

There are grounds to believe that the implementation of strategy may be simplified in small firms given the absence of complex organisational hierarchies. The path from strategic decision-makers to the final point of delivery, the contact with customers, is more direct and passes through fewer intermediaries. In addition to 'simpler structures', McAdam (2000), with reference to organisational reengineering suggests a 'dynamic SME culture' can also assist with this process, i.e., ensuring the business is prepared to take on new challenges in a changing business environment. Although not all tourism SMEs will have a 'dynamic SME culture', for those that do, the willingness and ability to change strategic direction should be more prevalent.

Chapter 8 seeks to outline the relationship between strategy/strategic management and entrepreneurship. The chapter will review different approaches to business strategy and how they might be applied to the entrepreneurial tourism firm. It considers the role strategic thinking can play in ensuring sustainability of the business as it moves from birth to growth, or as it simply seeks to survive in rough and uncharted waters that are characteristic of our times. Strategic awareness capability as a concept is discussed and different entry strategies for the fledgling tourism firm are also reviewed. Finally, the chapter reviews a frequently overlooked resource, particularly in small firms: time. Owners/managers of small firms are regularly tied up to such an extent in operational duties that they can easily miss the need to take a step back and consider the strategic direction of their enterprise.

Learning outcomes

At the end of this chapter, the reader should be able to:

- Explain various interpretations of strategy and how strategy relates to entrepreneurship.
- Understand the role of vision and strategic awareness capability for the small or fledgling tourism firm.
- Outline the components of strategic entrepreneurship.
- Appreciate the importance of time as a resource to the small business owner.

Strategic planning

Theorising about strategy extends into ancient history with early writings and their martial focus (e.g., Sun Tzu's *The Art of War* written in the sixth century BC and Von Clausewitz's *On War* compiled posthumously in the nineteenth century) finding renewed relevance and appeal in the world of business.[1] These foundations of modern writings on strategy share the premise that action should follow a plan. This is the common view of strategy, that of a plan, which sets out, over a certain period of time (medium to long term), what the business wants to achieve, and how it is going to achieve this. This planning perspective appeals to what some may regard as a unique human trait, that is the ability to envision alternative future scenarios and then plan to bring a desired future scenario about (Taylor et al., 1998).

The typical strategic planning process involves the three questions depicted in Figure 8.1. With further reference to Figure 8.1, strategic planning and with it strategic management have often been likened to a roadmap: a path is charted from where the business currently finds itself, to where it wants to be and how it will navigate the terrain to get there. The starting point is environmental analysis, both to answer the question about current position, and then also in considering where one wants to be and how one is going to get there. The key idea behind this planned view of strategy is the prediction of a future scenario and so many tools have been offered to assist the firm in environmental scanning such as SWOT, PESTEL, SCEPTICAL[2] to help ascertain what that future scenario might look like.

Figure 8.1 Strategic planning

While this planning interpretation of strategy is intuitive, and has appeal because of its rational, ordered approach, this is not its only meaning. Mintzberg (1999) famously proposed the five Ps of strategy, illustrating the varied uses of the term. Strategy according to Mintzberg can be thought of in a number of ways, namely as:

- A plan (as used above)
- A ploy (a manoeuvre that is more short term and tactical, designed to outwit a competitor)
- A pattern of behaviour (this contrasts directly with the rational planned approach to strategy – it represents a consistent set of behaviours that lead to success whereby the behaviour is intuitive/habitual)
- A position in respect to others (this view takes a product-market approach; the strategic decisions revolve around which products to place in which markets and how these positions may then be defended against the competition)
- A perspective (this is about organisational culture, 'the way things are perceived' collectively; for example, this could be whether the organisation supports a risk-taking culture, how much emphasis is placed on quality, etc.).

Another seminal paper by Mintzberg (Mintzberg and Waters, 1985), suggests strategies range on a continuum from the entirely deliberate to the entirely emergent. What their paper emphasises is the unpredictability of the external environment (external to the organisation) and the difficulty this creates for any kind of planning, which assumes fairly predictable environmental parameters. A rigid plan only really works in a rigid environment. Any strategy, or plan, must grapple with this issue of flexibility versus rigidity. This issue is critical to tourism firms, many of which operate in very unpredictable environments, where demand for the tourism product/service may fluctuate widely with changes in external conditions, whether these be man-made (e.g., political unrest, changes in fashion) or natural (e.g., natural disasters, epidemics), not to forget changes in consumer tastes and trends. Developments in technology likewise have had dramatic impacts on tourism demand, as well as supply. Moreover, as advances in technology continue apace, the tourism market continues to change. It is because of the changing environmental parameters that Evans (2015:2) in his book on strategic management in tourism writes of 'The Strategy Process'; 'it is never a once-and-for-all event – it goes on and on'. Similarly, Moutinho et al. (2011a:18) point out: 'Essentially, the whole process of tourism strategic planning boils down to planning on uncertainty.' For Moutinho et al. (2011b) it is, however, precisely the fickleness of the environment that calls for a long-term, strategic approach to decision-making in tourism.

Johnson et al. (2014) in an attempt to overcome some of the limitations of others' definitions of strategy define it as the long-term direction of an organisation. They argue this definition has two advantages:

- It may include both deliberate as well as emergent strategies.
- It may include strategies that focus on differentiation and competition as well as cooperation and even imitation.

Debates around the nature of strategy, strategic management and their impact on firm performance are unlikely to abate in the near future. This does not mean that the issue of strategy and how it relates to entrepreneurship in tourism should be ignored. A consideration of the role of strategy helps us make sense of the world of the entrepreneur and his/her enterprise (descriptive theory) and it can also serve as a tool for the entrepreneur (normative theory). It offers a standpoint from which we can critique, but also offer solutions, to the tourism entrepreneur who faces short-term and long-term business challenges.

Case study 8.1: Boeing and obliquity

In 2011 John Kay published a book called *Obliquity: Why Our Goals Are Best Achieved Indirectly*. In this book Kay provides numerous examples of how companies have made substantial profits by not primarily focusing on profits. A telling example is Boeing, which grew to be the market leader in the second half of the twentieth century. Bill Allen who was chief executive of Boeing from 1945 to 1968 established the corporate purpose as to 'eat, sleep and breathe aeronautics' – there was no mention of profits. Under Allen's stewardship, Boeing developed the 737 and 747 jumbo jet, arguably the most successful commercial aeroplane at the time. In the early 1990s Boeing's lead in the civil aviation market seemed virtually unassailable. However, it took just ten years for this to change.

The company's new CEO, Phil Condit, brought about a culture change in the airline, arguing that the company's preoccupation with meeting 'technological challenges of supreme magnitude would have to change'. He argued: 'We are going into a value-based environment where unit cost, return on investment, shareholder return are the measures by which you will be judged. That's a big shift.' The company moved its headquarters from Seattle, where its production facilities were, to Chicago, which is closer to Washington, underpinning a new focus on military projects, which were supposedly lower financial risk. This move was, however, counterproductive in that stories of corruption soon emerged. How did the market assess Condit's focus on profit? When he took over Boeing stock traded at $32, it then rose sharply to $59 as he affirmed commitment to shareholder value; when he was ousted in 2003 it had fallen to $34. Kay argues that the Boeing story is just another example where shareholder value was most effectively created when sought obliquely. Although on a much smaller scale, what Kay argues is reflected in Ateljevic and Doorne's (2000) description of small tourism firms in New Zealand who despite not having a growth or profit, but rather a lifestyle orientation, were commercially very successful precisely because of this. These firms' closeness to the consumer, sharing their ideology, helped them create products and services that more directly met these consumers' needs.

With reference to Figure 8.1, we can see that a starting point for strategy is an understanding of firm context and then market positioning. Here Johnson et al. (2014) recognise that strategy may apply differently to small firms, in part because small firms are susceptible to environmental change. They also make reference to strategic purpose as many small firms will not necessarily focus so heavily on profit but on such things as independence, family control, handing over to the next generation 'and maybe even lifestyle'(Johnson et al., 2014:20).

Strategic vision

The human ability to imagine future scenarios has been discussed in virtually every area of psychology (Taylor et al., 1998). Visualisation, as a form of imagining future scenarios, has been linked to goal achievement in a number of fields, especially in sports and in career development (Fanning, 1994), studies of leadership (see previous chapter), but also in entrepreneurship (e.g., Wickham's, 2006, quote at the beginning of this chapter). All entrepreneurs will have a vision that they are striving towards, whether this involves making as much money as possible, being able to pursue a passion or hobby, or being able to 'make a difference' via a social/environmental cause. Irrespective of whether the vision is detailed or vague, it may not necessarily offer an understanding of the steps required to reach the 'promised land' (which is where the business plan can come in use).

The benefits to the entrepreneur of having a vision are nonetheless manifold. The vision can serve to encourage, to help clarify goals and strategy, to set a direction for the business. Crucially, it may also provide a moral context (Wickham, 2006) as well as a tool to help communicate what the business is about to key stakeholders (e.g., investors, employees, customers). Entrepreneurial vision is not necessarily something that comes about quickly, it can take time to develop and refine as one explores and evaluates opportunities. It is unlikely Thomas Cook anticipated the success he was going to have, nor did Ray Kroc when he went into business with Dick and Mac McDonald foresee that this would result in the world's largest restaurant franchise.

What a vision should do is identify how value is going to be created for the customer, in our case the tourist. The entrepreneur has, after all, been defined (e.g., Hagel, 2016) as someone who sees an opportunity to create value and is willing to take a risk to capitalise on that opportunity. Entrepreneurship is, as discussed previously, not simply coming up with something new, but something new that has value to the consumer.

Notwithstanding the benefits of a strategic vision, vision without some consideration of how the vision is to be realised is merely a conjuring up of pipe dreams. A vision should therefore be followed by a mission that begins to operationalise, i.e., make practical, the vision. Examples of mission statements across a range of tourism organisations are as follows:

- Japanese Airlines Group: Pursue the material and intellectual growth of all our employees; deliver unparalleled service to our customers; and increase corporate value and contribute to the betterment of society.
- QHotels (a chain of four-star hotels in the UK): Our mission is to make your stay as stress-free and enjoyable as possible, whatever your reason for visiting us.
- Kuoni Group (upmarket tour operator): Aspires to become a leading service provider to the global travel industry and to grow significantly faster than the travel market as a whole.
- Tourism Australia: To make Australia the most desirable destination on earth.
- Ministry of Tourism, Malta: To establish and execute a tourism policy which is based on the principles of sustainable tourism development to contribute to economic growth whilst respecting the heritage and environment of the Maltese islands.
- Discover Mongolia (inbound tour operator): To offer our customers the best, most unforgettable travel experience of their lives.

This selection of mission statements was chosen to demonstrate the diversity inherent in mission statements in tourism. Some are very short, some a little more expansive, some are very precise in terms of what success means and how it is to be measured, others offer a sense of values. Of particular interest is Japanese Airlines' mission statement, which puts the employees first, in a sector that is not renowned for its positive employment practices (Nickson, 2013).

Vision and mission statements, although more common in large corporations, can still be of use to the tourism entrepreneur. In large corporations, vision and mission statements provide a guide for senior managers in determining strategy as well as, in theory at least, for employees (the extent to which they actually influence employee behaviour is a moot point). However, a vision, and concomitant mission, can also assist the entrepreneur in not losing sight of the goal. This is particularly important as the firm expands. As we saw in the previous chapters, a key challenge for the growing firm is how to maintain its entrepreneurial orientation.

Strategic awareness capability

As we have seen above, different views of strategy exist. Part of the difference in the interpretations lies in the varying purposes of the definitions: some try to describe strategy as it happens in organisations, others take a more prescriptive approach, suggesting how it should happen. Hannon and Atherton (1998) do not jettison the idea of the planned approach to strategy, but offer in addition to this the notion of strategic awareness capability (SAC). They do so within the context of business plans by comparing the role of the business person or entrepreneur to that of an orienteer, traversing undiscovered, or unknown, territory with just the aid of a compass. The compass is strategic awareness capability (while the map would be a business plan). 'The compass would appear to be an ideal tool for the myriad of small firms trying to navigate their way through complex environments towards destinations that may not be visible and with limited resources' (Hannon and Atherton, 1998:103).

Strategic awareness capability is different to business planning, which is an embedded process. Strategic awareness capability can be likened to 'having your finger on the pulse'. It connects the owner-manager's opportunity recognition with action planning. It is formally defined as:

> The process of continually improving how one identifies and conceptualises one's own world, recognises events in this world, interprets these events and makes decisions on taking appropriate action to achieve positive business outcomes.
>
> (Hannon and Atherton, 1998:112)

The growing need for managers to sensitise themselves to what is a turbulent and increasingly competitive environment has long been recognised (and as a theme has run throughout this book). There is a direct link here to Miyamoto Musashi's quote at the start of the chapter. Strategic awareness capability involves looking beyond the immediate, perceiving the distant and trying to make sense of it. In a similar way it aligns with notions of an entrepreneurial organisation that focuses on opportunities not just resources (Austin et al., 2006).

Figure 8.2 identifies four types of firm based on their planning effectiveness (PE) and strategic awareness capability (SAC). As we can see, both planning and SAC are important. The firm characterised by high levels of SAC but low PE, the 'visionary

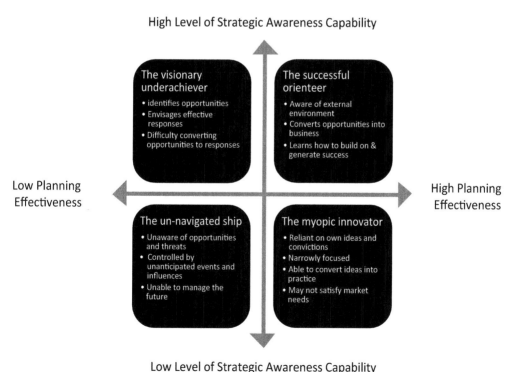

Figure 8.2 Linking strategic awareness capability to business planning
Source: Hannon and Atherton (1998).

underachiever', is one where opportunities are readily identified but where the firm lacks the ability to see any of these opportunities realised. The 'myopic innovator' on the other hand is thinking about its future and has a plan which it follows, albeit not one that is particularly innovative or meets market needs. The danger is that the market's needs, i.e., consumers' needs, gradually drift away from the kinds of products or services the firm offers.

Strategic entrepreneurship

Ireland et al. (2003) discuss the notion of strategic entrepreneurship, stressing that both entrepreneurship and strategic management are necessary for firm growth and wealth creation, whether this be a small, newly established firm, or a large corporation. They argue: 'both opportunity-seeking (i.e., entrepreneurship) and advantage-seeking (i.e., strategic management) behaviours are necessary for wealth creation, yet neither alone is sufficient' (Ireland et al., 2003:965). Strategic entrepreneurship then draws on the integration of knowledge of strategic management and entrepreneurship.

Ireland et al. (2003) offer a framework of strategic entrepreneurship as depicted in Figure 8.3. Accordingly, the development of an entrepreneurial mindset in employees goes hand-in-hand with a culture of entrepreneurship and entrepreneurial leadership. Both then combine with the strategic management approach of managing

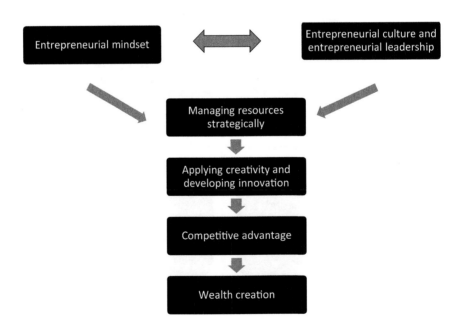

Figure 8.3 A theoretical framework of strategic entrepreneurship

Source: Ireland et al. (2003)

resources, resulting in the application of creativity and the development of innovation, which in turn leads to competitive advantage and subsequently wealth creation.

The importance of Ireland et al.'s (2003) work resides not so much perhaps in the recognition of the importance of innovation and creating a culture in the organisation to foster innovation (this has been recognised by others as outlined in Chapter 7). Rather, the bringing together of entrepreneurship and strategic management in a formal framework offers a recognition of their joint importance in helping firms address the challenges of operating in a competitive environment. To the author's knowledge, strategic entrepreneurship has yet to be explicitly addressed in tourism.

Entry strategies

A further feature of strategy as it relates to the small and/or start-up firm relates to entry strategies, or 'entry wedges' (Dollinger, 2003). Market entry strategies apply also to the established firm that is seeking to enter new markets, but they are part and parcel of the start-up. According to Dollinger (2003:92) all new ventures employ one or more of the following three major entry wedges.

New product or service

Offering a new product or service to the market is perhaps the most commonly imagined entry strategy, if not the most common in practice; in fact, few examples of an entirely new product or service exist. The entry wedge strategy here is to be first with a new product or service (or product–service combination) thereby offering a potentially insurmountable leadership position. This is akin to the first-mover advantage, where the first-mover firm is able to establish a client base, supplier relationships, expertise and so forth that make it very difficult, ideally impossible, for others to gain a competitive edge subsequently.

Parallel competition

Parallel competition is a far more common entry wedge strategy for the start-up firm. It involves competitive duplication, with the enterprise offering a very similar, albeit not identical, product or service. This is the most common entry wedge strategy in tourism and occurs where, for example, the tourism entrepreneur sees the success of a new hotel and decides to establish his/her own hotel. A further example is where the tourism entrepreneur sees how an existing enterprise has developed a new product, which seems to be attracting plenty of tourists and decides to offer a very similar product.

A real example of parallel competition in tourism are tours to glacier caves in Iceland, which were originally only offered by local providers, but which have grown in popularity and are now being offered by providers based in Iceland's capital Reykjavik (Welling and Arnason, 2017). As Butler (1980) recognised and has been confirmed elsewhere (Barr, 1990), small-scale local tourism development is frequently superseded by large-scale externally funded development. There will usually be some difference between suppliers of the tourism product, but these can be very small (the danger here is increased competition based on price). Rather than pure

Figure 8.4 Tourists visiting glacier caves, Iceland

Credit: Thorvardur Árnason

imitation, the tourism entrepreneur can be a 'creative imitator'. Creative imitation involves spotting some weakness in the tourism product that can be exploited. The basic business idea is copied, with the addition of creativity to exploit a gap but could also relate to a blind spot, things the incumbent firm does not see about the market, the competition, or themselves (Dollinger, 2003). Applied to the glacier cave tour example, a weakness could be offering tours only once a day (something it could do but for whatever reason chooses not to), a blind spot could be existing providers' lack of marketing prowess, (e.g., not attracting customers earlier than the competition).

Franchising

The final entry wedge strategy is franchising. This offers opportunities for both the franchisor and the franchisee. For the franchisor it offers scope for expansion using another's resources. The franchisees on the other hand also gain by reducing risk (there is usually a tried and tested product/service) along with a reduction in costs by drawing on the franchisor's resources and systems (training, advertising, HR, etc.). Franchising is less common in tourism, although with the emergence of the sharing economy one could argue that offering a spare room on Airbnb shares many characteristics of franchising.

An alternative approach to understanding entry strategies is proposed by Wickham (2006) who focuses on product–market combinations. Whichever entry strategy is pursued, it is important to consider how competitive advantage is going to be achieved, i.e., how value is going to be created for the consumer. Wickham (2006:362) proposed the following five entry strategies:

1   Focused entry – addressing a single, well-defined product-market domain.
2   Product spread – offering a wide range of products to a single, well-defined market.
3   Customer spread – delivering a single or narrow range of products to a wide base of customers.
4   Adjacency – offering a wide range of products to a broad customer base. All product–market combinations are adjacent in that the characterising features of each segment are continuous or can be related to each other.
5   Scatter – a variety of different products are offered to a variety of different customers. The segments are not adjacent.

A focused entry strategy in tourism could comprise the offer of skiing holidays to the French Alps to the British family market. A product spread entry strategy might involve offering a range of winter/snow sport holidays to the British family market. Customer spread would then comprise the offer of skiing holidays to the entire British winter/snow sports market, or indeed to the entire northern European market. An adjacency entry strategy would be to offer a range of snow/winter sport holidays (e.g., tobogganing, cross-country skiing, walking, husky experience, etc.) to the British/northern European market. Finally, a scatter entry strategy could include the offer of winter sports holidays as well as cultural tours and culinary holidays.

With regard to strategic entrepreneurship, Wickham (2006) also very usefully draws attention to the role of heuristics. Heuristics can be described as a means of simplifying decision-making (a mental short-cut). They are akin to rules-of-thumb, enabling decisions to be made without having to understand the finer details of a situation. They have played an important role in the emergence of behavioural economics that question the rationality of individual decision-making as taken for granted in much traditional economic theory (Wilkinson, 2008).[3] With regard to heuristics simplifying decision-making, Busentiz and Barney (1997) identified that entrepreneurs did make recourse to heuristics more than managers, which can come in handy in situations where quick decision-making is required. An entirely rational decision-making approach would require the collection and careful weighing up of information, which may be a luxury in a rapidly changing environment. Busenitz and Barney (1997) therefore argue that the recourse to heuristics entrepreneurs make could be a reason why they do not make for good managers.

Heuristics may, however, be confused with biases that cloud decision-making (in fact, sometimes the two are used interchangeably in the literature). Table 8.1 provides examples of heuristics and counter-heuristics in entrepreneurship.

The inclusion of Table 8.1 addresses one of the key themes of the book as mentioned in the Preface. Tourism entrepreneurship is contingent on the environment and the entrepreneur (aspiring entrepreneur). Catch-all solutions do not exist; situations need to be assessed on their own merits. Tourism entrepreneurs differ by their preferences or attitudes towards profit, growth, lifestyle aspirations, risk, sustainability, family-orientation and so forth. Given the complexity of entrepreneurial

Table 8.1 Heuristics in strategic entrepreneurship

Theme	Heuristic	Counter-heuristic
Innovation	Avoid standard products	Stick with the tried and tested
Flexibility	Success comes from continual improvement	'Don't fix what ain't broke'
Vision	Never compromise your vision	Be willing to adapt your vision
Start-up strategy	Start small and build	Go for it big time before someone else does
Expansion	Grow in sure-footed steps	Don't let anything hold growth back
Competition	Avoid competing head-on	Business is about competition, embrace it
Investment	Only borrow when you have to	You have to borrow to expand, use others' money to grow your business

Source: Adapted from Wickham (2006:365–366)

motivations, the offering of generic advice needs to be undertaken with a degree of caution.

Time as a resource

> Yet, the importance of the effective use of managerial time cannot be over-emphasised. Time is important and the only economic resource which is common to all managers.
>
> (Oshagbemi, 1995:31)

> If you're not being seen as enough of a strategic thinker, my guess is that it's because you're so busy. What percentage of your workweek is spent in meetings? How much of the time left over is a mad dash to respond to emails, make phone calls, and do some actual work? Is there anything left? Under the guise of productivity, you have probably squeezed out thinking time.
>
> (Davey, 2014)

The relationship between valuing time and strategic thinking is critical as the quotations by Oshagbemi (1995) and Davey (2014) suggest, which is why this section on time as a resource has been included here. 'Time is money', so the well-worn adage goes, and yet still there is no resource as under-valued as time. While some individuals start businesses to give themselves more time, and many more think about how setting up a business could lead to a life of leisure, in reality entrepreneurs often find they have less spare time than when they were in employment. The world of work may be changing, with more of us taking work home with us (thanks to developments in technology, work can accompany us wherever we go), but for the entrepreneur, drawing a clear demarcation line between work and home has never, or rarely at least, been a viable option. Often in tourism, it is precisely when others have their 'down time' that many tourism firms are at their busiest.

The focus on time might strike the reader as peculiar in a chapter on the 'bigger picture', i.e., strategy. However, the consequences for entrepreneurs as well as for managers of not allocating time to tasks according to their importance, rather allocating based on short-term needs, can have dire consequences for the new or the established enterprise. Specifically, managers are regularly reproached for lacking strategic thinking. After all, it is managers, especially senior managers who are tasked with setting the course upon which the organisation should sail (we can see this as a rebuff to those who interpret managerial roles as solely operational, see previous chapter). However, the entrepreneur must also be a strategic thinker in the sense that they are able to spot, or create, opportunities, have a long-term vision and are willing to see this implemented. It is this latter point, however, that often detracts from thinking strategically; that is, being so tied up with day-to-day operations that one fails to consider the long-term needs of the new venture, or indeed the existing firm.

Keegan (2017) has termed this 'working in' and 'working on' the business. Working in the business entails the day-to-day stuff (replying to emails, paying bills, creating staff rotas, etc.), but working on the business is to set time aside to think about questions like 'do I have a strategic plan for my department?' or 'this account has been growing tremendously, do I have an account plan?' In a way then, there are overlaps with the process of systematic innovation (e.g., Chapter 3), one could say it is about 'connecting the dots'. Birkenshaw and Caulkin (2012) write of 'pull' activities, which are things others have requested the manager does such as meetings, filling in reports and answering emails. 'Push' activities on the other hand are driven by the manager (e.g., coaching members of the team or meeting with customers), but in their study of a Swedish insurance company managers only spent 29 per cent of their time on these push activities.

It is precisely the difference between a short-term focus (tactical planning) and the long-term focus (strategic planning) that is at stake here. It is too easy for the entrepreneur running a small business to get involved in all aspects of the business. While in a large firm strategic planning is left to senior management, and tactical planning to middle management (Moutinho et al., 2011b), this 'luxury' is not afforded the small business manager/owner.

It is precisely one of the reasons (frequently the key reason) the entrepreneur decides to hire additional staff, i.e., because of the lack of his/her ability to cope on their own (Churchill and Lewis, 1983, refer to the aforementioned omniscience problem). The relinquishing of control can be difficult but needs to be achieved to free up some of their time to consider firm strategy (Smallbone and Wyer, 2012). The following statistics provide some further evidence as to the challenging relationship between time and strategic management:

- The typical company's senior executives spend less than three days each month working together as a team – and in that time they devote less than three *hours* to strategic issues (Mankins, 2004).
- With almost 50% of executives saying that they're not spending enough time on strategic priorities, time challenges are a concern for companies, not just individuals (Bevins and De Smet, 2013).
- Based on two independent surveys of senior executives, Clark (2018) claims 97% believed being strategic was the most important leadership behaviour for their

firm's success, and yet in the second survey 96% claimed to lack the time for strategic thinking.

Summary

This chapter began by setting out key perspectives of strategy and strategic management. It was recognised that even though strategy is often viewed through the lens of a plan, there is an inherent tension in strategy between rigidity and flexibility. Although a changing business environment might suggest plans should be flexible, Moutinho et al. (2011b) have argued it is precisely because of this fickleness of the environment that a course needs to be charted and stuck to.

The chapter then moved on to discuss strategic vision whereby this was linked to the vision of the entrepreneur (entrepreneurial vision). Here it was noted that the vision should include how value is created for the tourist and how an accompanying mission may help in its implementation. Examples of mission statements in tourism provided testimony to their diversity.

Strategic awareness capability was loosely defined as 'having one's finger on the pulse'. Together with the planned approach to strategy (a roadmap), strategic awareness capability (a compass) can assist the entrepreneur in identifying changes that are likely to affect his/her enterprise. It also offers early detection of opportunities. We referred to Hannon and Atherton's (1998) framework of small firms based on their planning effectiveness and strategic awareness capability. Ireland et al.'s (2003) view of strategic entrepreneurship was reviewed whereby the concept drew on the need for both enterprising (opportunity-seeking) and managerial (advantage-seeking) behaviour.

Entry strategies were reviewed that are of particular relevance to start-up firms who must find a market to enter. We identified three market entry strategies: new product/service, parallel competition and franchising (Dollinger, 2003). We also reviewed different entry modes (focused, product spread, customer spread, adjacency and scatter) as discussed by Wickham (2006).

Finally, the chapter focused on the role of heuristics in entrepreneurship, whereby we highlighted the varying nature and often contradictory advice offered to entrepreneurs. One thing that is not contentious is that time as a resource is undervalued. Entrepreneurs and managers are in the habit of complaining that a lack of time prevents them from thinking strategically, which carries risks to the tourism venture.

Review questions/discussion points

1   Moutinho et al. (2011b) suggest that because of turbulent markets, companies need to have a long-term plan. Others might argue that the fickleness of the environment means firms should not stick to any long-term plan but be flexible to respond to changing circumstances. Who is right?

2   Find examples of Wickham's (2006) five entry strategies in tourism. What might the advantages/disadvantages be for the tourism entrepreneur of adopting focused entry as opposed to customer spread and vice versa?

3   Find a vision and mission statement of two tourism firms of your choice. Compare them as to their focus, and the extent to which the mission statement offers guidelines of how the vision is to be implemented. Issues you could compare, for example, are whose needs the firm is serving, their clarity and ambition, and whether they say anything about the competition.

Notes

1   Sun Tzu's work was ranked 330 in Amazon's list of bestselling books, and number one in the Defence Strategy and Research rubric.
2   See Chapter 10.
3   In fact, a number of Nobel Prizes in Economics have been awarded for the work undertaken in behavioural economics, e.g., Thaler in 2017, Kahneman in 2002, and Simon in 1978.

References

Ateljevic, I. and Doorne, S. 2000. Staying within the fence: lifestyle entrepreneurship in tourism. *Journal of Sustainable Tourism*, 8, 378–392.

Austin, J., Stevenson, H. and Wei-Silkern, J. 2006. Social and commercial entrepreneurship: same, different or both? *Entrepreneurship Theory and Practice*, 30, 1–22.

Barr, T. 1990. From quirky islanders to entrepreneurial magnates: the transition of the Whitsundays. *Journal of Tourism Studies*, 1, 26–32.

Bevins, F. and De Smet, A. 2013. Making time management the organization's priority. *The McKinsey Quarterly*, 1, 26–41.

Birkenshaw, J. and Caulkin, S. 2012. How should managers spend their time? Finding more time for real management. *Business Strategy Review*, 23, 62–65.

Busentiz, L. and Barney, J. 1997. Differences between entrepreneurs and managers in large organizations: biases and heuristics in strategic decision-making. *Journal of Business Venturing*, 12, 9–30.

Butler, D. 1980. The concept of a tourist area cycle of evolution: implications for management of resources. *Canadian Geographer*, 24, 5–12.

Churchill, N. and Lewis, V. 1983. The five stages of small business growth. *Harvard Business Review*, 83, 30–50.

Clark, D. 2018. If strategy is so important, why don't we make more time for it? [Online]. *Harvard Business Review*. Available: https://hbr.org/2018/06/if-strategy-is-so-important-why-dont-we-make-time-for-it [Accessed 24 June 2018].

Davey, L. 2014. Strengthen your strategic thinking muscles. *Harvard Business Review*, 2–4.

Dollinger, M. J. 2003. *Entrepreneurship: Strategies and Resources*. New Jersey: Prentice Hall.

Evans, N. 2015. *Strategic Management for Tourism, Hospitality and Events*. London: Routledge.

Fanning, P. 1994. *Visualization for Change*. Oakland, CA: New Harbinger.

Gibb, A. and Davies, L. 1990. In pursuit of frameworks for the development of growth models of the small business. *International Small Business Journal*, 9, 15–31.

Hagel, I. J. 2016. We need to expand our definition of entrepreneurship. *Harvard Business Review* [Online]. Available: https://hbr.org/2016/09/we-need-to-expand-our-definition-of-entrepreneurship [Accessed 28 September 2016].

Hannon, P. and Atherton, A. 1998. Small firm success and the art of orienteering: the value of plans, planning, and strategic awareness in the competitive small firm. *Journal of Small Business and Enterprise Development*, 5, 102–119.

Ireland, R. D., Hitt, M. and Simon, D. G. 2003. A model of strategic entrepreneurship: the construct and its dimensions. *Journal of Management*, 29, 963–989.

Johnson, G., Whittington, R., Scholes, K., Angwin, D. and Regner, P. 2014. *Exploring Strategy: Texts and Cases*. Harlow: Pearson.

Kay, J. 2011. *Obliquity: Why Our Goals Are Best Achieved Indirectly*. London: Penguin.

Keegan, B. 2017. The value of strategic thinking [Online]. *Forbes*. Available: www.forbes.com/sites/forbescoachescouncil/2017/04/26/the-value-of-strategic-thinking/#5831e854430b [Accessed 4 September 2017].

Mankins, M. C. 2004. Stop wasting valuable time. *Harvard Business Review*, 89, 58–65.

McAdam, R. 2000. The implementation of reengineering in SMEs: a grounded study. *International Small Business Journal*, 18, 29–45.

Mintzberg, H. 1999. Five Ps for strategy. *In:* Mintzberg, H., Quinn, J. and Ghoshal, S. (eds.), *The Strategy Process*. Harlow: Pearson.

Mintzberg, H. and Waters, J. 1985. Of strategies, deliberate and emergent. *Strategic Management Journal*, 6, 257–272.

Moutinho, L., Ballantyne, R. and Rate, S. 2011a. The new business environment and trends in tourism. *In:* Moutinho, L. (ed.), *Strategic Management in Tourism*. Wallingford: CABI.

Moutinho, L., Rate, S. and Ballantyne, R. 2011b. Strategic planning and performance management. *In:* Moutinho, L. (ed.), *Strategic Management in Tourism*. Wallingford: CABI.

Nickson, D. 2013. *Human Resource Management for the Hospitality and Tourism Industries*. London: Routledge.

Oshagbemi, T. 1995. Management development and managers' use of their time. *Journal of Management Development*, 14, 19–34.

Smallbone, D. and Wyer, P. 2012. Growth and development in the small firm. *In:* Carter, S. and Jones-Evans, D. (eds.), *Entrepreneurship and Small Business: Principles, Practice and Policy*, 3rd edn. Harlow: Pearson.

Taylor, S., Pham, L., Rivkin, I. and Armor, D. 1998. Harnessing the imagination. Mental stimulation, self-regulation, and coping. *American Psychologist*, 53, 429–439.

Welling, J. T. and Arnason, T. 2017. Dealing with chaos in Icelandic glacier caves: exploring a resilience approach to manage rapidly emerging tourist destinations. *13th International Conference on Responsible Tourism in Destinations: Tackling Overtourism – Local Responses*. Reykjavik, Iceland.

Wickham, P. 2006. *Strategic Entrepreneurship*. Harlow: Pearson Education/Prentice Hall.

Wilkinson, N. 2008. *An Introduction to Behavioral Economics*. Basingstoke: Palgrave Macmillan.

Chapter 9

Social entrepreneurship in tourism

Introduction

Recently there has been a growth in interest in social enterprises generally, and in tourism specifically. This interest is fuelled by concerns that the current economic system is not meeting the needs of wider society, that in many countries inequalities are growing, and that environmental degradation continues largely unabated. Social entrepreneurship with its focus on leveraging entrepreneurial drive and innovation for a wider social good, directly rather than implicitly, is finding greater recognition in policy-making circles, offering an alternative form of economic organisation. Tourism, because of its global nature, its ability to reach into the farthest-flung corners of the planet, as well as its (relatively) low barriers to entry, lends itself to social entrepreneurship. Tourism can and does make a real difference to the people 'on the ground', to local communities and also marginalised groups.

This chapter therefore seeks to provide an overview of social entrepreneurship in tourism, to link social entrepreneurship in tourism to wider movements surrounding the notion of responsibility and sustainability in society, and to demonstrate how social innovations can begin to address some of the challenges faced by society today. The chapter also discusses cooperatives in tourism as a distinct form of economic organisation, similar to the social enterprise, and as an example of how enterprise and entrepreneurship can be encountered in all types of organisation, even those not traditionally associated with a capitalist system.

Learning outcomes

At the end of the chapter the reader should be able to:

- Critically evaluate different conceptions of social entrepreneurship.
- Explain why tourism in particular lends itself to social entrepreneurship.
- Distinguish different types of social enterprises in tourism.

Social entrepreneurship

Similar to the concepts of entrepreneurship and tourism, social entrepreneurship has been variously described, defined and measured. To offer a flavour of its broad scope, Mair et al. (2006:1) propose that social entrepreneurship may encompass:

> a wide range of activities: enterprising individuals devoted to making a difference; social purpose business ventures dedicated to adding for-profit motivations to the nonprofit sector; new types of philanthropists supporting venture capital-like 'investment' portfolios; and nonprofit organizations that are reinventing themselves by drawing on lessons learned from the business world. In the past decade 'social entrepreneurship' has made a popular name for itself on the global scene as a 'new phenomenon' that is reshaping the way we think about social value creation.

Notwithstanding a range of definitions, a dominant theme underpinning the concept of social entrepreneurship is its emphasis on increasing social value rather than profits to owners or shareholders (Zahra et al., 2009). While traditional conceptions of the entrepreneur are premised on a profit motive (see von Mises, 1949, or Harper, 1996:3, who defines entrepreneurship as 'a profit-seeking activity'), this view may strike us today as somewhat removed from the vast array of entrepreneurial motivations. Nonetheless, the profit-seeking view of the entrepreneur still features prominently in policy-making circles. The United Nations Conference on Trade and Development (UNCTAD, 2012:1), for example, draws on this profit motive in defining the entrepreneur and entrepreneurship: 'Entrepreneurship – the act of being an entrepreneur – implies the capacity and willingness to undertake conception, organization, and management of a productive new venture, accepting all attendant risks *and seeking profit as a reward*' (emphasis added).

By way of contrast, social entrepreneurship is regarded by many as a means to promote more equitable forms of economic development, as an alternative to a culture of greed and selfishness (Mintzberg et al., 2002; Hemingway, 2005) often associated with the profit motive. It has been argued (Weisbrod, 1977) that social entrepreneurship arises where the market mechanism fails to meet social needs. As such, the growth in interest in social entrepreneurship following the global financial crisis of 2007/2008, which has brought forth wider discussions around economic justice, indeed alternative models to a winner-takes-all form of capitalism, should not come as a surprise. Before we review how social entrepreneurship has been discussed and applied within a tourism context, a discussion of definitions is provided that offer a flavour of what lies at the heart of the concept.

Austin et al. (2006) suggest that definitions of social entrepreneurship range from the very narrow to the very broad; the broad covering both for-profit and non-profit sectors, corporate social entrepreneurship and ventures with a predominantly social purpose. The narrow perspective focuses only on the phenomenon of applying business expertise and market-based skills in the non-profit sector.

Austin et al.'s own work provides an example of an extremely succinct definition of social entrepreneurship: 'entrepreneurial activity with an embedded social purpose' (Austin et al., 2006:1). This aligns with a more extensive example of a definition offered by the United Kingdom government's Department for Business,

Innovation and Skills (2011:2): 'a business with primarily social objectives whose surpluses are principally reinvested for that purpose in the business or in the community, rather than being driven by the need to maximise profit for shareholder and owners'.

These types of definition, i.e., that place at their core social objectives, are common. What this definition also proposes, perhaps more tacitly, is that social ends and profit motives do not necessarily contradict each other, but rather have complementary outcomes, and constitute a 'double bottom line'. More fundamentally, 'Social enterprises, and the social economy, to which they contribute, are concepts that challenge the traditional division of organisational activity into the separate categories of economic or social purpose' (Bridge et al., 2003:157). The fact that this point is highlighted draws attention to an alternative view encompassed by the ubiquitous concept of the triple bottom line (also people, profit, planet), in that firms have responsibilities that extend beyond the economic domain. While this view may, today, appear self-evident, this was not always the case. Milton Friedman's (1970) widely cited quotation that 'the business of business is business' argues that anything but a focus on shareholder value (within the confines of legal boundaries) would be irresponsible. This view is open to various interpretations, one of which is that business left to its own devices is able to generate greater wealth for all (e.g., via trickle-down).

The foregoing definition also implies that effective financial management for social purposes is a key feature of sustainability (i.e., the financial stability of an organisation to trade over the long term); economic sustainability underpins social sustainability. The term 'non-profit' is something of a misnomer, as all businesses, including social enterprises, do seek to make a profit (at least cover costs), and indeed require surpluses for long-term survival. It may be more helpful therefore to consider a continuum rather than a dichotomy when dealing with the distinction between social and for-profit enterprises; placing enterprises at different points depending where their focus lies. Indeed, Dees (1998) and Chell (2007) have written about a continuum between social enterprises and economic enterprises in recognition of the questionable either-or approach at defining enterprises.

Because of this, the question as to whether enterprises that are not 'profitable' can in fact be social enterprises is worth considering. Some social enterprises are not financially viable, i.e., without state support (be that in subsidies, reduced business rates, cheap loans and so forth) or other forms of financial support (e.g., individual contributions, foundation grants, member dues, user fees, and government payments; Austin et al. 2006). Viability here comes not so much from generating profits, which are then either ploughed back into the enterprise or distributed to social causes, but from state and others' largesse.

This draws the discussion to the ethics of social entrepreneurship, which will be discussed in greater detail in the next section. However, to demonstrate the intricate nature of the issue at hand we need only consider the net benefits to society. If the aim of the social enterprise is to provide a greater social contribution than it receives, in other words if its net social contribution is positive (after government support has been factored into this calculation, whereby we need to consider opportunity costs associated with this support) then a case can be made for government support. Zahra et al. (2009:522) argue any definition, measurement or evaluation of social entrepreneurship should reflect both social and economic considerations.

They propose Total Wealth (TW) as a standard to evaluate those opportunities and organisational processes related to social entrepreneurship:

Total Wealth (TW) = Economic Wealth (EW) + Social Wealth (SW)

In turn,

Economic Wealth (EW) = Economic Value (EV) – Economic Costs (EC) – Opportunity Costs (OC)

Social Wealth (SW) = Social Value (SV) – Social Costs (SC)

As a result:

TW = EV + SV – (EC + OC + SC)

This definition of total wealth can help us understand the nature of social enterprise:

- Both economic and social wealth can be created by entrepreneurial entities in the pursuit of total wealth maximisation.
- Indicates how entrepreneurs can shift resources in a manner that enhances wealth in one category at the expense of another.
- Indicates how social value may offset economic costs, as well as social costs (e.g., social discord) incurred in generating social value.

Trying to calculate the net benefits can then be quite a complicated affair. Indeed, *performance measurement* is one of four differentiators between for-profit and non-profit firms explored by Austin et al. (2006), the others being *market failure, mission* (as discussed above) and *resource mobilisation* (see also Table 9.1). Similar to Gartner's (1985) framework for new venture creation (Chapter 2), Austin et al. (2006:4) do not claim their framework is exhaustive or definitive, 'but rather provide us with a theoretical frame with which to engage in the subsequent comparative analysis'.

A critique of social enterprise

Despite social entrepreneurship's widespread appeal and recognition as offering an alternative to commercial entrepreneurship, it is an area that has not gone without criticism. Chell et al. (2016) have noted that the ethical underpinnings of social enterprises remain under-explored; there is an assumption that because something is socially orientated it is ethically sound. Chell et al. (2016) query whether the notion of the ethical social entrepreneur is a further myth to add to the list of myths in entrepreneurship, and it is clear from what they write that they believe the relationship between social entrepreneurship and ethics is anything but straightforward.

At a fundamental level, and following on from Friedman's querying of developments around corporate social responsibility in the 1970s, it may be argued that business left to its own devices, not tying it down with regulations and red tape, will result in a thriving economy which then benefits society (by, for example, offering

Table 9.1 Austin et al.'s (2006) framework for comparing commercial with non-profit organisations

Market failure	Social enterprises emerge where there is a social need that is not being met by the market. A problem for the commercial entrepreneur is an opportunity for the social entrepreneur.
Mission	Social enterprises create social value for a public good, whereas commercial enterprises seek profitable opportunities for private gain.
Resource mobilisation	Social enterprises have different access to capital/capital markets and are also usually unable to pay market rates to employees (who tend to place greater emphasis on non-pecuniary benefits when working for social enterprises).
Performance measurement	Performance measurement of social impacts is more complicated than traditional measures of commercial enterprises (profits, market share, customer satisfaction). Accountability and stakeholder relations are also more complicated.

products and services to the consumer and jobs to its employees, as well as taxes to the state coffers). Anything that detracts businesses from focusing on profit maximisation is detrimental to society, including trying to realign business with so-called societal goals. This is the traditional, neoliberal economic approach that has dominated much thinking in the developed and developing world in the past four decades (see, for example, Chang, 2011).

A further consideration that offers a counter-discourse to social entrepreneurship is an acknowledgement that in practice there are no definitive boundaries between many social enterprises and other small businesses (Bridge et al., 2003:158). What Bridge et al. (2003) are referring to here specifically is the distinction between profit-driven and non-profit-driven (i.e., social) enterprises. Especially in tourism, many, if not the majority, of businesses are started for reasons other than profit maximisation as lifestyle businesses (Morrison et al., 1999). Lifestyle entrepreneurship is of particular relevance to tourism (e.g., Shaw and Williams, 2004; and will be discussed further in Chapter 11). Profit orientation as the distinguishing factor between 'traditional' enterprises and social enterprises loses some of its significance once it is recognised that enterprises are rarely created with a sole purpose of profit maximisation.

The application of social entrepreneurship in tourism

According to Von der Weppen and Cochrane (2012:498), tourism lends itself to the study of social entrepreneurship because of its potential for stimulating 'both social and financial added value along the supply chain'. Effectively, what Von der Weppen and Cochrane are arguing here is that tourism firms may ensure social value (as well as financial value) is added at various stages in the provision of the tourism product. Thus the hotel can source the food on its menus locally, thereby saving on food miles and the pollution associated with transport, as well as supporting local producers. A tour operator may stipulate its hotels have a policy in place that requires a percentage of its workforce to come from the local population, particularly in supervisory or senior roles.

It is recognised that tourism is a key economic activity and foreign revenue earner for many low- and middle-income countries and so ways of promoting more equitable means of tourism development can make a real difference (Mitchell and Ashley, 2010). It is perhaps not surprising then that social enterprise and entrepreneurship feature regularly in the tourism literature. In fact, if we extend the definition of social enterprise as per Austin et al.'s (2006) framework to include the adoption of socially responsible activities in existing organisations (not just the new firm), the number of articles in tourism on social entrepreneurship may be regarded as substantial. This 'intrapreneurship' interpretation of social entrepreneurship is the case, for example, in Ikwaye, Ogembo and Kiarie's (2016) study of 'socially entrepreneurial activities' of hospitality organisations within the coastal tourism circuit in Kenya (here, 56% of businesses had a social enterprise strategy). What we can see is a merging of social entrepreneurship and a sustainability orientation. Theoretically, both social enterprise and corporate social responsibility/business ethics share much common ground in that they see non-profit goals of organisations as legitimate ends, and so this overlap is not surprising. In terms of conceptual clarity, however, this is not an ideal situation. Despite sharing a common concern for non-economic goals, social entrepreneurship does not equate to sustainable tourism.

Von der Weppen and Cochrane's (2012) study is instructive in trying to address the question of how social enterprises in tourism might differ from social enterprises per se. Although their study only drew on a sample of 11 tourism firms (who had won or were shortlisted awards for their efforts in social enterprise) it does tackle the issue of tourism-specificity directly. Their case study firms included a range of business types (e.g., accommodation providers, tour operators, a destination management organisation and a visitor attraction) with a wide geographic spread. Their study applied Alter's (2006) framework of operational models of social enterprise to this sample of tourism firms. Findings illustrated the adoption of a variety of models, frequently simultaneously. This demonstrates how these businesses, as a whole, tackled issues surrounding employment (assisting marginalised groups – such as youth, women or those from ethnic minorities – to find work), diminishing the exploitation of a natural resource (e.g., providing alternative income for villagers), or simply using the proceeds from the sale of products and services of the business to support local initiatives. The extent to which 'the business' can be separated from the social mission is open to debate (see introductory section to this chapter). Overall, their study offered a useful insight into the tourism-specificity of social enterprise, arguing that three of Alter's (2006) seven models of social enterprise operations are potentially more relevant to tourism:

- The Employment Model: Provides employment opportunities/job training for people with high barriers to employment through enterprises that sell products or services on the open market.
- The Service Subsidisation Model: Selling products/services externally. Business mandate is separate from social mission, but business activities are often mission-related.
- Organisational Support Model: Selling products/services externally. Business activities are separate from social programmes and unrelated to the mission. Income is used to cover programme costs and operating expenses of parent organisation.

Alter's (2006) operational modes of social entrepreneurship again highlight the fuzzy boundary between a social enterprise with a mission that reflects this, and a for-profit enterprise with social elements attached. In light of the introduction to this chapter, where a common definition of a social enterprise was found to be one about organisational focus (profit or social purpose), it is difficult to reconcile Alter's (2006) operational modes of social enterprises with what others might regard to be a social enterprise; the distinction between for-profit or not-for-profit is not made directly.

Similar to success factors of for-profit businesses, the authors (Von der Weppen and Cochrane, 2012) argue that awareness of market conditions, including the need for a good product, and strong leadership are key. The successful social enterprise in tourism will also create a balance between financial and social/environmental aims. This latter point is particularly interesting as it highlights the at times competing social and economic facets of enterprise (see Zahra et al.'s, 2009, discussion of firm's Total Wealth creation above).

Social enterprises have been explored in other tourism contexts. Examples include Kimbu and Ngoasong's (2016) research on female social entrepreneurs in Cameroon. Here it appeared that participants felt that general barriers to entrepreneurship (e.g., access to finance, excessive regulations and taxes) played a far more important role than gender discrimination. There appeared to be little that was tourism-specific in this study's findings, i.e., that pointed to how social enterprises in tourism might be different from non-tourism firms. What is, however, very clear to see are the opportunities tourism provides to social entrepreneurs within a developing country context.

A final point to note, two key challenges to the social entrepreneur in tourism involve overcoming a reliance on donations or state funding, and the other, as highlighted by Von der Weppen and Cochrane (2012), trying to meet competing economic and social needs. As Zahra et al. (2009:520) have claimed: 'Because the goals of social ventures are deeply rooted in the values of their founders, balancing the motives to create social wealth with the need for profits and economic efficiency can be tricky.'

Both of these issues are highlighted, for example, in Laeis and Lemke's (2016) study of a tourism social enterprise in South Africa. Their study, which focused on a tourism lodge, demonstrates how the project did not reach its full potential because of a lack of clarity in its mission. The for-profit side of the business was competing with the non-profit side of the business. The dependence on external funding also presented challenges and was the cause of the initiative not developing fully. The study demonstrates that where key stakeholder views conflict as to the organisation's mission/purpose the ultimate outcome is unlikely to be positive.

Cooperatives in tourism

Tourism is often promoted as a means of alleviating poverty, particularly in less developed countries. At first glance, considering tourism's importance in generating foreign earnings, its positive effect on countries' balance of payments, the relationship between tourism development and poverty reduction would appear straightforward. However, the link between capital flows and benefits 'on the ground', i.e., in the communities where the income generated by tourism could be needed most, is anything but straightforward (e.g., Goodwin, 2011: Mitchell and Ashley, 2010). Issues such as lack of skills and expertise, and (capital) leakages due to foreign ownership of tourism assets can severely curtail benefits accruing to host communities. One way of tackling the leakage issue, but also to an extent the lack of skills and expertise, is cooperatives.

An interest in cooperatives has grown as concerns about the 'liberal capitalist model' have grown, and may in fact be seen as its oldest and largest alternative (Kaswan, 2012). The term 'cooperative' has clear political connotations. Marx himself regarded the 'cooperative mode of production' as a valid form of economic organisation, with Jossa (2005) arguing Marx even saw cooperatives eventually supplanting capitalist firms. He quotes Marx (1894:571, in Jossa, 2005:3) referring to cooperatives as firms in which workers are 'their own capitalists'.

The cooperative movement is vast. The International Co-operative Alliance, the apex organisation for cooperatives worldwide, suggests that through its membership it represents 1.2 billion people from any of the 2.6 million cooperatives worldwide (ICA, 2018). According to the ICA, cooperatives are 'people-centred enterprises owned and run by and for their members to realise their common dreams. Profits generated are either reinvested in the enterprise or returned to the members.' There are many similarities to social enterprises although a difference is the cooperatives' focus on the needs of their members, whereas the beneficiaries of the social enterprise are usually found outside the organisation (see Table 9.2).

Table 9.2 For-profit, not-for-profit and cooperatives

	For-profit/ investor-owned	Not-for-profit/social enterprise	Cooperative
Ownership	Investor-owned	Generally not 'owned' by a person or members	Member-owned
Control	Controlled by shareholders according to their investment share. Business decisions and policy are made by a board of directors and corporate officers.	May be controlled by members who elect a board of directors or, in non-membership organisations, the board of directors may elect its own successors. Control is maintained by those not receiving the services.	Democratically controlled; one member, one vote basis; equal voice regardless of their equity share. Members are involved in the day-to-day business operations and receive services for their input.
Purpose/ motivation	Maximise shareholder returns	Primary motivation is to serve in the public interest. Redistribute resources to provide educational, charitable and other services.	Maximise customer service and satisfaction

Source: Adapted from ICA (2007).

There are clear overtones to community-based tourism here (and community-based enterprises; Harrison, 2008); that is, tourism that empowers the host community at four levels – economic, psychological, social and political (Scheyvens, 2002). It is about greater participation of the community in tourism development (Brohman, 1996).

Although not numerous, studies of cooperatives in tourism exist. Yang and Hung (2014) mention Iakovidou's (1997) study of women's cooperatives in Greece that have developed agro-tourism businesses, thereby also promoting their social and economic roles in rural areas. Verma's (2006) study of tourism cooperatives in India demonstrated how they were able to protect ethnic cultures, and Gorman et al.'s (1997) study showed how cooperatives can help farmers, again in remote rural areas, market accommodation to tourists.

Looking at these studies in a little more detail, Iakovidou (1997) suggests that women's agro-tourism cooperatives are the most traditional form of agro-tourism in Greece. This cooperative was not formed spontaneously, but was instigated by the Greek government, specifically the General Secretariat for Equality, in an attempt to improve the lives of women in rural areas. Rather than an organically formed, local-led initiative, as cooperatives frequently are, the opposite is the case here. Verma's (2006) paper offers a perspective on tourism cooperatives in India. He suggests that the Indian cooperative movement is the largest movement in the world, and emphasises the role cooperatives can have in promoting peace, which we understand to mean social harmony within the context of his paper. Yang and Hung's (2014) study of accommodation cooperatives in rural China argues that using a range of poverty measures (e.g., resource poverty, poverty of skills and economic poverty) the adoption of a cooperative model has led to an overall reduction of poverty.

Until now, the reader would be excused for understanding cooperatives as a quasi-panacea to the negative impacts of tourism. Just as the benefits of community-based tourism have rarely been rigorously assessed (Goodwin, 2011), the benefits of tourism cooperatives have yet to be fully explored. Yang and Hung (2014) also point out that different forms of tourism cooperatives exist, some which they regard as 'fake'. These are cooperatives that have been established solely to benefit from government funding. They also identify why the cooperative they focused on in China worked, highlighting a number of conditions including the desire for equality, participation in tourism and democratic management. Successfully creating and then sustaining a tourism cooperative also requires strong leadership/management as well as depending on levels of market competition.

Social entrepreneurship and responsible tourism

Advances in social entrepreneurship in tourism tap into a broader movement towards more sustainable/responsible forms of tourism. The distinction between sustainable/responsible tourism generally and social entrepreneurship in tourism specifically is not always discernible, and frequently they are mentioned in the same breath. The World Travel and Tourism Council (2018) with reference to the Tourism for Tomorrow Awards suggests: 'all over the world travellers can use their trips to directly support social enterprises and responsible tourism businesses'.

Responsible and sustainable tourism may be seen to reflect wider societal discussions around the role of businesses in society and the meaning of development. Just as the focus on corporate social responsibility (CSR) today tries to draw attention to the social and environmental responsibilities of the corporation (the economic are largely taken for granted), so does social entrepreneurship focus on non-economic goals and wider societal impacts. We could say that both responsible tourism and social entrepreneurship in tourism are united by a common focus on the social (to include the environment).

Tourism development, from a Western perspective at least, is said to have gone through a number of phases that reflect wider societal perceptions and attitudes towards the environment and development. For example, Jafari (2001) suggests that in the 1950s and 1960s tourism was undertaken on what he terms an advocacy platform. In the advocacy platform, tourism was by-and-large only associated with positive impacts, economic foremost (income and employment) and then via the economic also the social (e.g., improved healthcare and education). The advocacy platform then ceded to the cautionary platform (late 1960s–1970s), which stresses the often-negative impacts tourism can have on destinations, particularly as a result of unplanned and rapid development (Jafari, 2001). The adaptancy platform focuses on 'alternative' forms of tourism to mass tourism and the final platform, 'knowledge-based', suggests a more realistic understanding of tourism as a holistic and systematic phenomenon requiring detailed knowledge of what works in a specific context. The move in particular from an advocacy platform to a cautionary and then adaptancy platform develops in tandem with a growing awareness and concern of business' impact on the environment. This is reflected in the notion of sustainable development (see, for example, the UNWCED, 1987, report *Our Common Future: Report of the World Commission on Environment and Development*, and the 1992 report from United Nations Conference on Environment and Development commonly referred to as the Rio Summit) from which the notion of sustainable tourism then also emerges (e.g., founding of the *Journal of Sustainable Tourism* in 1993).

In a similar manner Ateljevic and Li (2009) offer four phases of tourism development that they link to entrepreneurship in tourism:

1   **Boosterism** – the emergence of mass tourism, with a focus only on tourism's benefits not negative impacts (this is very similar to Jafari's, 2001, advocacy platform).
2   **Expansion of mass tourism** – advances in technology lead to the replication of mass tourism on a global scale. Tourism offers many characteristics of mass manufacturing: standardisation and rigid packaging (Poon, 1993).
3   **Tourism as a resource user** – tourism's negative impacts on the environment are increasingly visible and recognised. A questioning of traditional top-down development models took place. Public–private partnerships are increasingly common. Crucially for entrepreneurship, cut-backs to the welfare state resulted in an increasing number of individuals seeking self-employment in tourism.
4   **Alternative approaches to tourism development** – sustainable tourism development is now firmly on the agenda as manifested in a proliferation of sister concepts such as alternative tourism, eco-tourism, green tourism and community-based tourism. The emergence of new markets, destinations and consumer preferences has led to a greater diversification of the tourism product. Tourism planning becomes more complex with a range of public–private partnerships in evidence. The opportunities for entrepreneurship in tourism abound.

Innovations in sustainable tourism

From a developmental policy perspective, the potential of entrepreneurship as a means of linking private sector development with the goals of inclusive and sustainable development is widely recognised (UNCTAD, 2012). The coming together of sustainability considerations with entrepreneurship offers much potential to improve business' social and environmental performance. In fact, entrepreneurship and innovation are in a position to drive the sustainability agenda forward (Auerswald, 2012). Some social/environmental innovations may be driven by the desire to make money, an admittedly very myopic view of the 'green economy', but equally some innovations are driven by the desire to 'do good'. Using innovations to improve tourism's sustainability specifically has gained much traction recently. For example, in June 2017 a conference held at the University of Mauritius, 'Innovation and Progress in Sustainable Tourism', is indicative of developments in this area.

For Moscardo (2008) innovation in sustainable tourism must start with a new way of thinking, a willingness to challenge the view that sees tourism solely as a development option separate from other activities in a destination region. We need to 'reconceptualise tourism as a tool to support the development of activities such as traditional or specialist agriculture, craft, education, health or other socio-economic activities' (Moscardo, 2008:9). An entire reconceptualisation of the relationship between tourism and sustainability is likely to lead to innovations in sustainable tourism, but this is not to say traditional forms of tourism cannot be adjusted to make them more responsible. Plenty of examples exist of innovations, particularly in the environmental sphere, that have led to more responsible forms of tourism because they have reduced negative impacts and/or enhanced benefits to the local community.

We find this perspective of innovation in sustainable tourism represented, for example, in Booyens and Rogerson's (2017) paper at the aforementioned conference in Mauritius. The paper focused on 'responsible tourism and innovation practices by tourism enterprises in the Western Cape (South Africa)' but has wider implications in terms of our understanding of responsible tourism innovation. Booyens and Rogerson (2017:226) described innovation in responsible tourism as follows:

> Tourism entities are considered to be innovative in terms of responsible tourism if they exhibit economically sustainable behaviour by introducing innovations or significant improvements to their products, processes or business practices in order to maintain their competitiveness and/or enhance their socially or environmentally sustainable practices.

What is slightly confusing here is the use of the 'and/or' because if a tourism firm innovates to achieve competitive advantage, but is no more socially or environmentally responsible, then it is unclear why this is specifically a responsible tourism innovation. Moreover, from Booyens and Rogerson's (2017) paper, what is novel is gauged at the level of the individual firm, as opposed to the market or geographical location. In other words, if it is new to the firm it is an innovation, irrespective of whether other firms in the sector are doing the same thing. This would seem to be quite a weak definition of what counts as an innovation.

Examples of environmental innovations offered by Booyens and Rogerson (2017) fall into the categories of water and energy savings, waste management, reducing a firm's carbon footprint and enhancing biodiversity. Social innovations on the other hand appear to be akin to the undertakings of social enterprises as described above, i.e., they are led by organisations that have a primarily social purpose. Specifically, Booyens and Rogerson (2017:232) write: 'It is observed that social innovation is in most cases implemented by entities whose main motivation is not a profit orientation.' The boundaries between social enterprises in tourism, and tourism enterprises that offer social innovations are blurred. This should not necessarily be the case though. Based on Booyens and Rogerson's (2017) definition of innovations in responsible tourism, any tourism firm that introduces an innovation that improves that firm's social impact is engaging in sustainable tourism innovation irrespective of whether the firm is a social enterprise or not. We encounter again the difficulty

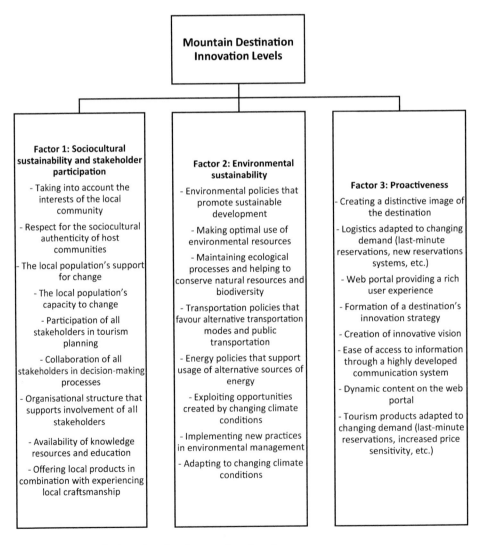

Figure 9.1 Mountain Destination Innovation Levels

distinguishing between a social enterprise per se, and an enterprise that displays some social innovations.

Innovations in sustainable tourism may also be analysed at the level of the destination. Such a focus is taken by Kuščer et al. (2017) in a comparison of Alpine resorts in Slovenia, Austria and Switzerland. These resorts must innovate given the already clearly observed climatic changes, where prognostications indicate that only 63% of Swiss ski resorts will receive enough snowfall if the average temperature rises by 2°C (Koenig and Abegg, 1997, in Kuščer et al. 2017). Technological advances are permitting more environmentally friendly forms of transport and ski-infrastructure (e.g., electric cars and bikes, solar-powered lifts and more efficient snow-making equipment) alongside more sustainable transport management.

Kuščer et al. (2017) offer the construct of 'Mountain Destination Innovation Levels' (which is itself part of a larger Mountain Destination Innovation Model, MDIM). This may help us understand how sustainable tourism innovations may be measured at a destination level as depicted in Figure 9.1. The items themselves do not necessarily reflect innovation, but managers were asked about the extent to which they felt their destination compared with others on these items in terms of innovation. This formed the basis of Kuščer et al.'s (2017) comparison of destinations' innovativeness.

Summary

This chapter has moved away from an exclusive small firm focus in its efforts to explore the relationship between responsible tourism and entrepreneurship. The main focus has been on social entrepreneurship in tourism and the concept of social entrepreneurship was discussed in some detail prior to exploring how social enterprises in tourism may differ from social enterprises generally. Here we acknowledge that while differences arguably exist, tourism is certainly a sector that lends itself to social entrepreneurship. The chapter took a critical stance towards social enterprises that are unsustainable financially; in other words, those social enterprises that consistently rely on donations, whether from the public directly, or from the public purse. The chapter also looked at cooperatives as an alternative, if not entirely new, form of tourism organisation. It was argued that social enterprises and cooperatives share many characteristics, foremost a desire to share more equitably the rewards of economic activity. The chapter concluded with a review of the relationship between social entrepreneurship and responsible and sustainable tourism, culminating in an overview of how innovation can serve the desire for a more responsible and sustainable tourism sector. Just as the gales of creative destruction (Schumpeter, 1934) can serve as a means of economic renewal, gales of innovation may provide for a more responsible tourism sector, and for more sustainable tourism development.

Review questions/discussion points

1 How might you respond to the suggestion that because for-profit firms pay taxes, give people jobs and provide consumers with goods and services, they are in fact no different to 'so-called' social enterprises?

2 List characteristics of social enterprises that distinguish them from traditional for-profit firms.
3 Do you think passion for a social/environmental cause is required to start a social enterprise in tourism?
4 Why might tourism present an ideal sector for the promotion of social entrepreneurship?
5 Imagine you set up a social enterprise in tourism with a friend. How would you calculate your salary?

References

Alter, S. K. 2006. Social enterprise models and their mission and money relationships. *In:* Nicholls, A. (ed.), *Social Entrepreneurship: New Models of Sustainable Change.* Oxford: Oxford University Press.

Ateljevic, J. and Li, L. 2009. Tourism entrepreneurship – concepts and issues. *In:* Page, S. and Ateljevic, J. (eds.), *Tourism and Entrepreneurship: International Perspectives.* London: Routledge.

Auerswald, P. 2012. *The Coming Prosperity: How Entrepreneurs Are Transforming the Global Economy.* Oxford: Oxford University Press.

Austin, J., Stevenson, H. and Wei-Silkern, J. 2006. Social and commercial entrepreneurship: same, different or both? *Entrepreneurship Theory and Practice*, 30, 1–22.

Belhassen, Y. and Caton, K. 2011. On the need for critical pedagogy in tourism education. *Tourism Management*, 32, 1389–1396.

Booyens, I. and Rogerson, C. 2017. Responsible tourism and innovation practices by tourism enterprises in the Western Cape. *BEST EN Think Tank XVII. Innovation and Progress in Sustainable.* Mauritius: University of Mauritius.

Bridge, S., O'Neill, K. and Cromie, S. 2003. *Understanding Enterprise, Entrepreneurship and Small Business.* Basingstoke: Palgrave Macmillan.

Brohman, J. 1996. New directions in tourism for the Third World. *Annals of Tourism Research*, 23, 48–70.

Chang, H.-J. 2011. *23 Things They Don't Tell You About Capitalism.* London: Penguin Books.

Chell, E. 2007. Social enterprise and entrepreneurship: towards a convergent theory of the entrepreneurial process. *International Small Business Journal*, 25, 3–19.

Chell, E., Spence, L., Perrini, F. and Harris, J. 2016. Social entrepreneurship and business ethics: does social equal ethical? *Journal of Business Ethics*, 133, 619–625.

Dees, J. G. 1998. Enteprising nonprofits. *Harvard Business Review*, 76, 55–67.

Department for Business Innovation and Skills. 2011. *A Guide to Legal Forms for Social Enterprise.* London: DBIS.

Friedman, M. 1970. The social responsibility of business is to increase its profits. *The New York Times Magazine.*

Gartner, W. B. 1985. A conceptual framework for describing the phenomenon of new venture creation. *Academy of Management Review*, 10, 696–706.

Goodwin, H. 2011. *Taking Responsibility for Tourism.* Oxford: Goodfellow Publishing Ltd.

Gorman, G., Hanlon, D. and King, W. 1997. Some research perspectives on entrepreneurship education, enterprise education and education for small business management: a ten-year literature review. *International Small Business Journal*, 15, 56–77.

Harper, D. A. 1996. *Entrepreneurship and the Market Process*. London: Routledge.

Harrison, D. 2008. Pro-poor tourism: a critique. *Third World Quarterly*, 5.

Hemingway, C. 2005. Personal values as a catalyst for corporate social entrepreneurship. *Journal of Business Ethics*, 60, 233–249.

Iakovidou, O. 1997. Agro-tourism in Greece: the case of women agro-tourism co-operatives of Ambelakia. *Medit*, 8, 44–47.

ICA. 2007. *Factsheet: Differences between Co-operatives, Corporations and Non-Profit Organisations*. US Overseas Cooperative Development Council, ICA.

ICA. 2018. *International Co-operative Alliance About Us* [Online]. Available: https://ica.coop/en/the-alliance/about-us [Accessed 15 March 2018].

Ikwaye, S., Ogembo, J. and Kiarie, B. 2016. Social entrepreneurship in hospitality industry: the case of operators at the coastal tourism circuit in Kenya. *International Journal of Humanities Social Sciences and Education*, 3, 115–121.

Jafari, J. 2001. The scientification of tourism. *In:* Smith, V. L. and Brent, M. (eds.), *Hosts and Guests Revisited: Tourism Issues of the 21st Century*. New York: Cognizant.

Jossa, B. 2005. Marx, Marxism and the cooperative movement. *Cambridge Journal of Economics*, 29, 3–18.

Kaswan, M. 2012. Awakening the sleeping giant: interstitial transformation and the cooperative movement. *New Political Science*, 34, 366–372.

Kimbu, A. N. and Ngoasong, M. Z. 2016. Women as vectors of social entrepreneurship. *Annals of Tourism Research*, 22, 63–79.

Kuščer, K., Mihalič, T. and Pechlaner, H. 2017. Innovation, sustainable tourism and environments in mountain destination development: a comparative analysis of Austria, Slovenia and Switzerland. *Journal of Sustainable Tourism*, 25, 489–504.

Laeis, G. C. M. and Lemke, S. 2016. Social entrepreneurship in tourism: applying sustainable livelihoods approaches. *International Journal of Contemporary Hospitality Management*, 28, 1076–1093.

Mair, J., Robinson, J. and Hockerts, K. 2006. *Social Entrepreneurship*. London: Palgrave Macmillan.

Mintzberg, H., Simons, R. and Basu, K. 2002. Beyond selfishness. *Sloan Management Review*, 44, 67–74.

Mitchell, J. and Ashley, C. 2010. *Tourism and Poverty Reduction: Pathways to Prosperity*. London: Earthscan.

Morrison, A., Rimmington, M. and Williams, C. 1999. *Entrepreneurship in the Hospitality, Tourism and Leisure Industries*. Oxford: Butterworth-Heinemann.

Moscardo, G. 2008. Sustainable tourism innovation: challenging basic assumptions. *Tourism and Hospitality Resarch*, 8, 4–13.

Poon, A. 1993. *Tourism, Technology and Competitive Strategies*. Wallingford: CAB.

Scheyvens, R. 2002. Backpacker tourism and Third World development. *Annals of Tourism Research*, 29, 144–164.

Schumpeter, J. 1934. *The Theory of Economic Development*. New York: Oxford University Press/Galaxy 1961.

Shaw, G. and Williams, A. 2004. From lifestyle consumption to lifestyle production: changing patterns of tourism entrepreneurship. *In:* Thomas, R. (ed.), *Small Firms in Tourism. International Perspectives*. London: Elsevier.

UNCTAD. 2012. *Entrerpreneurship Policy Framework and Implementation Guidance*. New York and Geneva: United Nations Conference on Trade and Development.

Verma, S. K. 2006. Promoting peace through tourism: a role for co-operatives. *The International Journal of Co-operative Management*, 3, 54–59.

Von der Weppen, J. and Cochrane, J. 2012. Social enterprises in tourism: an exploratory study of operational models and success factors. *Journal of Sustainable Tourism*, 20, 497–511.

von Mises, L. 1949. *Human Action*. New Haven: Yale University Press.

Weisbrod, B. 1977. *The Voluntary Nonprofit Sector.* Lexington, MA: DC Heath & Co.

World Travel and Tourism Council. 2018. *When Tourism Meets Microfinance* [Online]. Available: https://medium.com/@WTTC/when-tourism-meets-microfinance-a78a8d38fc81 [Accessed 10 April 2018].

Yang, X. and Hung, K. 2014. Poverty alleviation via tourism cooperatives in China: the story of Yuhu. *International Journal of Contemporary Hospitality Management*, 26, 879–906.

Zahra, S., Gedajlovic, E., Neubaum, D. and Schulman, J. 2009. A typology of social entrepreneurs: motives, search processes and ethical challenges. *Journal of Business Venturing*, 24, 519–532.

Chapter 10

Public policy and entrepreneurship in tourism

Virtually every country in the developed and developing world is now intervening in some way to promote enterprise skills, to encourage more entrepreneurs and the development of more self-employment, and to grow more indigenous businesses.

(Bridge et al., 2003:402)

During the last 30 years, entrepreneurship has become what most nations would call a socially desirable action and thus target for planned social change.

(Dreisler et al., 2003:383)

Introduction

This chapter will expand upon the idea offered in Chapter 1 that tourism entrepreneurship can play an important role in promoting economic growth and regeneration. It will look at policy-makers' stance on enterprise including attempts at inculcating an enterprise culture. The premise underpinning the chapter is that entrepreneurship is affected by the contexts within which it occurs (Gartner, 1985; Autio et al., 2014; Smallbone et al., 2014). If this were not the case, there would be no cause for government intervention (as level of enterprise would be independent of environmental circumstances). As self-evident as this sounds, the majority of the entrepreneurship literature takes the individual rather than his/her context as its focus (Autio et al., 2014). The same cannot be said of the tourism policy literature, where it could be argued the opposite is the case: the emphasis has been on context, less on the individual owner/manager of the tourism firm, with exceptions of course (e.g., Russell and Faulkner, 2004, who look at the interplay between the entrepreneur and his/her context). The chapter will review policy tools governments have introduced in an attempt to foster enterprise and entrepreneurship, such as financial, information and counselling, education and training and deregulation. The chapter will also review development theory and its relationship to the small tourism firm, providing a link to tourism in emerging and developing countries.

The role of the entrepreneur and entrepreneurship in economic development

Both tourism and entrepreneurship tend to be valued by policy-makers as a means to promote economic growth and development (Russell and Faulkner, 2004); tourism more frequently in a regional or destination-specific context, enterprise and entrepreneurship more at a national level. The combination therefore of tourism and entrepreneurship might appear to be quite a potent mix in terms of policy tools for economic regeneration and development. A hypothetical example was provided in Chapter 2 of how, using Butler's (1980) Tourism Area Lifecycle, entrepreneurs drive tourism development. The role of tourism entrepreneurs has been recognised by some, such as Koh and Hatten (2002:21) who call the tourism entrepreneur 'persona causa' or Ryan et al. (2012:120) who use the term 'tourism influentials' when referring to tourism entrepreneurs' role in destination development. Despite this crucial role, Ryan et al. (2012) also point to the lack of research into how precisely tourism entrepreneurs drive destination development.

We should acknowledge that support for tourism does tend to vary; it can be seen as a solution, but also as part of 'the' problem in terms of overreliance on a single sector and its negative impacts (for example, in recent discussions of the issue of overtourism). Where tourism is frowned upon as a means of development this is often because its impacts are not well documented or understood (Moutinho et al., 2011). Enterprise and entrepreneurship are viewed almost entirely positively on the other hand.

Taking a lead from Schumpeter's (1934) 'gales of creative destruction', others such as William Baumol (2002) have argued entrepreneurial innovation is the true source of national competitive advantage. Disruptive innovations introduced by entrepreneurs continue to reshape the competitive landscape, some in very profound ways (examples of such innovations that have brought about dramatic changes in tourism include the development of the jet engine for use in commercial flights, and, more recently, the internet). Today, policy-makers continue in their attempts to foster innovation in entrepreneurial firms. This is evident in the promotion of university-based start-ups (Grimaldi et al., 2011), for example.

Although one might imagine that since Schumpeter's (1934) work entrepreneurship, and with it innovation (Autio et al., 2014),[1] has been recognised as the driving force of economic development, traditional microeconomics with its emphasis on the general equilibrium model provides little scope for the role of the entrepreneur (Kirzner, 1997). This contrasts with other schools of economic thought (notably the so-called Austrian School) where the entrepreneur has always played a dominant role as the following quote by Von Mises (1949:325–326) indicates:

> The driving force of the market process is provided neither by the consumers nor by the owners of the means of production – land, capital goods, and labour – but by the promoting and speculating entrepreneurs. . . Profit-seeking speculation is the driving force of the market as it is the driving force of production.

Put simply, the entrepreneur and the entrepreneurial process have not always been afforded the place they, arguably, deserve in economic development, which has led to calls from some (e.g., Peters, 2005) that the entrepreneurial process should constitute a major focus of research in tourism. Today most governments recognise the importance of entrepreneurship, which is even equated by some with other traditional factors of production, i.e., land, labour and capital (UNCTAD, 2012). Entrepreneurship plays a key role in policy discourses in emerging, developing and developed economies alike. This is not to say that the causal relationship between entrepreneurship and economic growth is entirely understood, at least not according to Smallbone and Wyer (2012:404) who maintain that despite 'a growing body of research evidence that demonstrates a positive relationship between entrepreneurship and economic growth. . . there is limited causal understanding of precisely how this occurs'.

The veracity of Smallbone and Wyer's (2012) claim is open to debate and certainly may be questioned if we consider in more detail why entrepreneurship is promoted. Here we can identify a number of causal connections between entrepreneurship and other factors associated with economic development more generally. The first is the seemingly obvious relationship between entrepreneurship and job creation. Viewed from the perspective of the individual firm, if a firm is created, grows and hires staff then the mechanism by which entrepreneurship leads to job creation is clear. However, it is not a given that firms grow, many try and fail, many do not even try. One could even argue that a particularly entrepreneurial tourism firm may use developments in technology to replace staff (there are downsides to productivity growth).

Indeed, small firms have not always been of immediate interest to policy-makers because for a period in history they were regarded as in decline, and their employment creation potential was equally unrecognised. Storey (1994) describes how the post-war period saw the rise of the corporation and with it the view that these were the drivers of economic growth; small firms were largely ignored. This changed with the publication in the USA of the Birch Report (1979), which indicated that the majority of jobs created between 1969 and 1976 occurred in small firms, and also because of the 'oil crisis-ridden' 1970s (Curran and Blackburn, 1991). Suddenly small firms were in vogue, as the title of Bannock's (1981) book of the time suggests: *The Economics of Small Firms: Return From the Wilderness*.

Audretsch (2009), describing the role of small firms in the United States, suggests the policy emphasis on small and new firms as engines of dynamic efficiency may seem startling after decades of looking to the corporate giants to bestow efficiency. He refers, however, to Alexis de Tocqueville's claim – 'What astonishes me in the

United States is not so much the marvellous grandeur of some undertakings as the innumerable multitude of small ones' – made in 1935 to demonstrate that the view of small firms as engines of growth is anything but new. In fact, given continued low growth rates in developed countries in particular, governments are reconsidering their economic development strategies and increasingly placing their hopes in entrepreneurship and small firms.

Of all of these reasons, employment generation, arguably, stands to the fore in policy-makers' minds. Because of tourism's low human capital requirements to gain entry (Szivas and Riley, 1999), as well as its labour intensity, the theoretical case for supporting tourism entrepreneurship is strong. Opportunities for the substitution of labour by technology exist, but only to a degree (see Chapter 7). Koh (1996) in a rare mention of tourism entrepreneurship specifically within a policy context argues that policy-makers need to improve their understanding of the 'tourism entrepreneurial process' to raise the number of tourism firms created by the indigenous population. As tourism grows it is often money from outside the destination that flows into the destination to exploit opportunities. The fostering of indigenous entrepreneurship may alleviate this situation.

Job creation is then a key policy objective behind stimulating entrepreneurship and supporting small businesses in tourism but job creation aside, entrepreneurship is promoted for a range of social and economic reasons. In addition to job creation, Wanhill (2004) regards the promotion of tourism SMEs by policy-makers as a result of their ability to meet market (i.e., customer) needs in a post-Fordist economy. Other reasons for the promotion of SMEs are provided by West et al. (2008:15) who suggest:

> Entrepreneurial development is seen by many government and community leaders as a gateway to economic vitality, leading to a growing tax revenue base, enhancing prospects for self-generating innovation and future growth, and yielding qualitative improvements to an area's social and economic fabric.

Entrepreneurship can then serve as a means of solving social and environmental problems as discussed in Chapter 9 as well as stimulating wealth creation. Entrepreneurship is promoted because it supports innovation and creativity (especially on the understanding that small firms are more agile/flexible/innovative than large firms). Related to this, new firms function as agents of economic change and restructuring, particularly in emerging and developing economies (De Clercq et al., 2010). Wanhill (2004) also mentions European policy-makers' support for tourism SMEs because they can lead to economic diversification. Allied to this is the promotion of entrepreneurship as a means to combat regional economic decline (it is often believed small businesses will enter markets that are not seen as profitable by large firms, usually because these markets are too small), and also increasing competition (sometimes the argument is made that start-ups need support to be able to compete with larger, more established firms).

The rationale for government intervention

Up until this point, we have assumed government intervention is of itself a good thing, something that is universally desired; but this view is anything but universal.

With regard to support for entrepreneurship specifically, Hall (2009b) in a contemplation on the nature of public policy in tourism entrepreneurship suggests that, at first glance, one might see a discrepancy between government's involvement in entrepreneurship, given its perceived bureaucratic stance, and the entrepreneur who is nimble and dynamic. To illustrate he quotes former US President Ronald Reagan: 'Government is not the solution to our problem, government is the problem.' To illustrate further, we may consider legislation that governs employment. Thus, hiring staff, if done formally,[2] i.e., within the regulative ambit of the state (Harris-White, 2010) can involve the entrepreneur having to first understand and then adhere to a slew of legislation. Sometimes owners of small firms can feel overwhelmed with the wealth of employment legislation that typically covers things like: recruitment; the terms and conditions of employment; holidays, working hours and pay; health and safety regulations; maternity and parental rights; discrimination; discipline, grievance and dismissal procedures; redundancy; and latterly GDPR (General Data Protection Regulation).

The perception of a bureaucratic, heavy-handed and anti-entrepreneurial state is not necessarily borne out in reality, however, where 'nothing could be further from the truth than a supposed dichotomy of individuals as entrepreneurial and government as anti-entrepreneurial' (Hall, 2009b:243). This is recognised in particular in tourism where we can find many examples of firms that are neither particularly entrepreneurial, nor innovative in their approach to meeting market needs.

Ronald Reagan's quote has far wider implications than entrepreneurship as it embodies a more general laissez-faire, non-interventionist approach to economic policy (also referred to as 'Small Government'). From this perspective, the best way to stimulate economic growth is to leave the economy, or rather markets, to their own devices (the so-called 'invisible hand' regulates markets, i.e., supply and demand). This may result in the demise of weaker firms, but drawing on neo-Darwinist principles business is about survival of the fittest – in theory at least. However, even the most ardent free-market adherents recognise some intervention is necessary to avoid, for example, excessive negative externalities (untrammelled pollution is a case in point). Despite the liberalisation of global trade, no markets are truly free from government intervention, nor would free-market adherents wish for an entirely government-free zone (Chang, 2011).

Markets left to their own devices may not result in a 'societally optimal' outcome.[3] A key justification for state intervention then is to address market failure or market imperfections (in a capitalist system at least). As we acknowledge in relation to social enterprise (see previous chapter) the market left entirely to its own devices is unable to meet all human needs. We have also come across the 'liability of newness' (Stinchcombe, 1965) idea, which argues small firms are, because of their newness and size, often at a competitive disadvantage. Thus, one of the most consistent and compelling findings to emerge over a rich body of literature is that potential entrepreneurs with innovative ideas are frequently unable to attract adequate resources – financial, management, technical and human capital – impeding their ability to launch, sustain or grow a new venture (Gompers and Lerner, 2001). A level playing field does not exist; small firms are unable to compete on equal terms. This situation may then lead to reduced competition with the emergence of monopolies and oligopolies, a scenario familiar to tourism where the so-called 'big four' tour operators (First Choice, TUI, Thomas Cook and MyTravel) merged to become just two in 2007. Despite their large share of the package holiday market, regulators recognised the continued high levels of competition and pressure on profit margins, driven by low-cost airlines and the increased disintermediation offered by the internet. Profit margins will vary depending on market segment (e.g., offering food tours compared to an operator offering skiing breaks) but for the mass-market package travel segment margins rarely rise above 5%.

Interestingly, support for entrepreneurs can stumble across a (mythical) view of the entrepreneur, one that portrays the entrepreneur as hero in their own epic (Gibb, 2002). Why would the go-getter, the tenacious maverick require support? As we have argued throughout the book, see in particular Chapter 4 and the discussion of social capital, entrepreneurship does not occur in a vacuum. While a perspective exists that portrays the entrepreneur as a hero, the go-it-alone entrepreneur seldom, if ever, exists.

Figure 10.1 provides a graphical illustration of the policy environment for entrepreneurship in tourism. We identify three distinct yet overlapping policy areas, which on their own, and in conjunction, will shape the policy environment for tourism entrepreneurs and their businesses. Crucial to an understanding of the impact of policy and the policy environment on tourism entrepreneurship is the role generic – i.e., non-sector-specific – policy plays in determining levels and nature of entrepreneurship in tourism. Arguably, non-tourism policies and regulations might have more impact on the tourism firm than tourism-specific policies. This issue is highlighted directly by Hall (2009a) and Shaw and Williams (2010) who suggest the impact of mainstream SME policy on tourism businesses remains a valuable area for

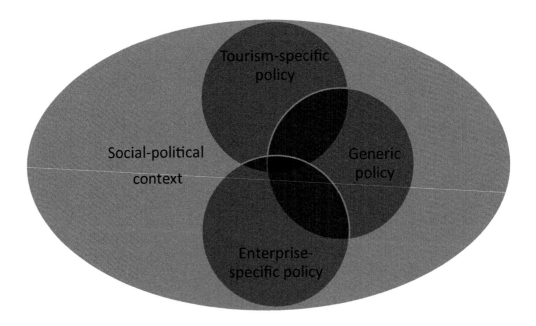

Figure 10.1 The policy context of entrepreneurship in tourism

further enquiry. Hall (2009a) in his review of innovation policy in tourism in Australia and New Zealand confirms that tourism is not regarded as being a particularly innovative field.

To illustrate the role non-tourism-specific policy can play in tourism we have seen (Chapter 4) how regulations governing banks' minimum reserve requirements will affect banks' willingness and ability to lend. This affects firms across all sectors, not just tourism. Similarly, regulations governing the employment of staff can affect whether a tourism lifestyle enterprise decides to expand or not, seeing excessive regulation and the need to comply with it (time, effort and money) as inimical to the desire to pursue an envisaged lifestyle.

Policies, whether tourism-specific, entrepreneurship/SME-specific, or generic, are couched within a broader socio-political context, which is important to consider if policy is to be understood (Mason, 2008). Thus, governments in different countries will have divergent views on the role of the state itself, which will shape economic, social and environmental policy. The state could, for example, take a more hands-on, interventionist stance to tourism such as the Republic of Ireland or India have done (Kerr, 2003), or decide to intervene less such as the Reagan government in the United States in the 1980s, which abolished the United States Travel Service. At a time of austerity, such as that faced by many developed economies after the global financial crisis of 2007/2008, governments that believe they should be actively supporting tourism may find they are unable to do so (this could be seen as an excuse of course, it depends on what a government's priorities are) such as the Conservative government under Cameron in the UK (Kennell and Chaperon, 2011).

Hall and Williams (2008) note that in tourism the entrepreneur and the firm are often treated in relative isolation from their contexts. This is a serious omission as it is recognised that firm context is a determinant of firm behaviour. Firm context can itself be categorised based on how global/local the context is. Commonly, firms may be understood as being part of an industry (or sector), and the industry is placed within a wider macro context (national and international levels). Sometimes the analysis refers to micro (i.e., firm), meso (i.e., industry) and macro (economy) levels. Unsurprisingly, numerous models and frameworks exist that help make sense of the context of the firm (these can be used both descriptively and prescriptively). Most, probably all, strategy and marketing textbooks will make reference, for example, to PESTEL analysis, which covers political, economic, social, technological, environmental and legal forces affecting the firm. PESTEL is not the only framework of course and others, such as Scott's (2001) three-pillar institutional framework, which distinguishes between regulatory, normative and cultural cognitive institutional factors. Moutinho et al. (2011) suggest a revised form of PESTEL analysis should apply to tourism given its uniqueness, which they term SCEPTICAL, and which appears to link PESTEL with Scott's (2001) institutional framework:

- Social factors
- Cultural factors
- Economic factors
- Physical factors
- Technological factors
- International factors
- Communications and infrastructure factors

- Administrative and institutional factors (culture is part of Scott's, 2001, institutional framework as are the legal)
- Legal and political factors

It is clear that government with its legislative powers directly shapes the regulatory environment and yet the influence of government and policy-makers extends far beyond just the legal aspects that promote or inhibit entrepreneurship in tourism as we shall see below. A meso-level analysis is offered, for example, by the long-standing SCP (structure-conduct-performance) paradigm of industrial economics, which suggests market structures affect market conduct, which in turn affects market performance. Much of Michael Porter's work on competitive advantage (e.g., Porter's Five Forces[4]) draws on SCP.

Just as the environmental context surrounding the new venture may be assessed at different levels, so public policy occurs at different levels (e.g., international, national, regional and local). Just how multi-layered policy-making is will differ from one nation to another, but to understand policy-making and entrepreneurship it is necessary to comprehend variation at all levels.

Another complication, and an important one, in helping us understand the policy context of entrepreneurship in tourism is the acknowledgement that the impact of policy is both intentional and unintentional (Davis et al., 1993) as evidenced in the case of the ban on term-time holidays (Walmsley, 2018). The law of unintended consequences is one that policy-makers grapple with constantly in an attempt to ensure that measures introduced to solve one issue do not result in an exacerbation of another issue. In fact, the complexity of the economy is sometimes suggested by adherents of a laissez-faire approach as a reason why state intervention should be minimised.

To illustrate, we offer some examples of policy at different levels and the policy context, which all have an impact on the tourism entrepreneur.

- **Generic policy:** The state has many responsibilities including education, health, defence, environmental protection, supply of infrastructure and essential services and law and order. It determines therefore issues such as tax rates, interest rates, planning guidelines, environmental legislation, foreign property ownership regulations, employment law.
- **Entrepreneurship policy:** start-up support (financial), value added tax/sales tax thresholds for small firms, accounting regulations relating to research and development, business rates, laws governing intellectual property and patents.
- **Tourism policy:** tax breaks for tourism firms or special dispensation from certain taxes, funding for capital investments in tourism (e.g., government match funding for tourism projects), visa restrictions, air passenger duty, marketing budgets to promote national and/or regional tourism, access to national parks or environmentally sensitive areas, the development of public–private partnerships in tourism marketing and development, rights of indigenous peoples (Jenkins, 2006).
- **Socio-political context:** policy affected by attitudes of the populace (e.g., towards immigration, climate change, inequalities in society), by levels of support for the incumbent government and proximity to a general election (it has been argued governments tend to implement less popular legislation shortly after an election and

hence further away from the next general election), or, for example, by economic trends (levels of national debt, growth forecasts, balance of payments).

We have now drawn attention to numerous factors that add to the complexity of the tourism policy environment and tourism policy itself, especially as it relates to entrepreneurship. However, further complications arise. As Thomas et al. (2011) clarify, policy-making for tourism can be jeopardised by the diversity inherent in tourism SMEs as well as in the diversity of owner/managers that run tourism SMEs. Morrison and Teixeira (2004:166) also draw attention to this:

> Therefore, if enterprise policy is to be effective, formulation needs to be fully cognizant of complex business and humanistic impediments to the accomplishment of the commercial pursuit of enterprise as viewed through the eyes of the small tourism business owner-managers who collectively contribute a significant critical mass within this industry sector.

This could explain the lack of take up of training or collective marketing activities and quality networks, for example. It is also noted that policy is as much about what government decides not to do, as what to do. So, for example, the decision of the UK government not to take advantage of an EU dispensation on VAT is a decision not to do something with implications for the competitiveness of the UK tourism sector (Seely, 2015).

The state itself has been likened to an 'undertaker of works to support private enterprise' (Jenkins, 2006:51).The result of a shift in the political landscape for tourism allied with a need to tackle regional economic decline can result in the public sector becoming an 'entrepreneur' itself, a so-called 'tourism industry entrepreneur' (Shone, 2011). Shone (2011) describes a situation in the Huruni district in New Zealand, which suffered a decline in agriculture, its primary industry, in the 1980s and early 1990s. The local district council recognised that tourism could offer a means of offsetting this decline, providing locals with income and employment. The council opened a tourism information centre in 1991, followed by a newspaper advertising campaign promoting the North Canterbury Triangle touring route, of which Huruni was the principal attraction. Further marketing campaigns followed, a visitor strategy was created. Collaboration with the neighbouring area of Kaikoura was established (Kaikoura could offer marine-based attractions, Huruni alpine spa attractions and food and wine tourism), leading in 1999 to the creation of the Huruni District tourism promotions agency and management structure (also known as APT – Alpine Pacific Tourism). The North Canterbury Triangle tourist route was rebranded as the Alpine Pacific Triangle touring route. Today the route has been lengthened and re-branded again as the Alpine Pacific Tourism Route (www.visithuruni.co.nz), which now starts in Christchurch.

However, as Shone (2011) demonstrates in the analysis but as recognised more generally (Coles and Church, 2007), tourism development invariably involves issues around power and politics. A criticism levied against the Huruni government's increased focus on and promotion of tourism was thus not wholly endorsed by others in the locale. Mihalič (2015) also draws attention to the often-false promises of high-quality, permanent jobs made by policy-makers when promoting tourism. The impartiality of the Huruni District Council was questioned as it was itself a primary beneficiary of ongoing tourism development and growth. What is illustrated by the

Huruni case is the important, even critical, role the public sector can play in shaping the context for tourism development. This context can determine the success or failure of a fledgling tourism enterprise, as well as encourage or detract from tourism businesses being established in the first place.

Frequently, despite plenty of initiatives (Bridge et al., 2003, suggest there have been hundreds of initiatives to support SME and entrepreneurship since the 1970s in the UK), what is often lacking is an overall coherent policy or strategy in terms of a set of coherent objectives with a common aim. Part of the reason for this could be the very diverse range of start-ups and SMEs to be found in an economy (e.g., different sectors, levels of capitalisation, owner/manager motivations). In fact, we do not need to look beyond tourism to see that the sector itself is incredibly diverse and that it can therefore be difficult to devise an overarching policy to support tourism start-ups and/or tourism SMEs. Figure 10.2 suggests an entrepreneurship policy framework that we can apply to tourism.

One of the key characteristics of tourism is its place specificity; tourism is tied to place. In admittedly simplistic terms, if you want to experience London, you have

Figure 10.2 UNCTAD'S Entrepreneurship Policy Framework

Table 10.1 Example policies applying UNCTAD's Entrepreneurship Policy Framework

Optimising the regulatory environment	This could involve removing legislation that is seen as inimical to the sector, or ensuring current legislation is taken advantage of, such as applying dispensations on value-added tax permitted by EU regulators. It could also involve introducing regulations that might support small tourism firms such as putting constraints on the sharing economy, notably the private lettings market (as a number of cities such as Berlin have done).
Enhancing entrepreneurship education and skills development	Offering more start-up courses in schools and universities. Offering subsidised training courses for tourism entrepreneurs and their staff. Offering mentors to assist start-ups, or incubation space alongside entrepreneurship/business workshops.
Facilitating technology exchange and innovation	Providing tax breaks for firms that invest in research and development. Providing grants for technology adoption. Offering funding to universities to research best practice and then share findings within a region.
Improving access to finance	Providing loan guarantees, including export guarantees. Regulating venture capital funding as well as providing incentives to attract venture capital.
Promoting awareness and networking	Launch entrepreneurial awareness campaigns. Celebrate entrepreneur role models through awards. Facilitate business exchange platforms.

to go to London. If you want to experience the Machu Picchu Trail, you have to go to Peru. If you want to see the Great Wall of China, you have to go to China. While it is possible to experience representations of place (e.g., in a film, in a book) and while the expansion of virtual reality offers scope to experience places virtually, to date there is no evidence that this is stopping people travelling. In fact, film- and literature-induced tourism suggests the opposite. Arguably, place specificity is not an absolute but exists along a continuum. While the features of the above destinations are highly place-specific, if it is sun, sea and sand that the tourist wants, s/he has an almost endless list of possible destinations to choose from. The crucial thing for policy-makers, however, is that at a time when much work can be outsourced, it is not possible to outsource a destination or attraction. The greater the place specificity, the more difficult/impossible it is to do.

Case Study 10.1: Term-time holiday bans

In 2013 the Education Secretary in the UK, Michael Gove, introduced regulations to address truancy in schools. Henceforth, any unauthorised absence of children during term time could result in a fine of up to £60 per day. Failure to pay could even result in prosecution and, in theory at least, a custodial sentence. What appears not to have been considered by policy-makers are impacts on tourism, particularly in very heavily tourism-dependent parts of the country, such as the south west, which in 2014 accounted for 18% of domestic tourism expenditure (Tourism Alliance, 2017). The fall-out of the change in regulations was such that it even received its own name, the so-called 'Gove Effect'. Few studies exist that attempted to assess the impact of the banning of term-time holidays, one exception being a study conducted by the author where responses were received from 260 businesses in the south west. The intention is not to dwell on the actual findings here (the reader can find further details in Walmsley, 2018), save to acknowledge that two-thirds of tourism firms believed they had been negatively affected by the change in regulations and that the change in regulations had led to a fall in income of over 30% for a fifth of respondents (a reduction of income was noted for nearly two-thirds).

The reason for covering this story here is first to illustrate how governments can introduce legislation without appreciating fully the implications for tourism, and second, to also highlight how tourism SMEs respond to such changes. Responses to the latter include the completely downbeat:

> There are no tourists about outside school holidays I do not know how attractions are surviving. The roads are going to be terrible over the school holidays as the whole country is on the move at the same time.

And

> It is a short sighted policy driven by educational targets and implemented without any recognition of the wider consequences on the tourism industry. It has reduced the earnings period, reduced the price of the shoulder weeks,

resulting in a downwards impact on revenue potential, and driven up the cost of business acquisition.

Not all tourism businesses were this negative about the changes with a hint of seeking alternative means of addressing any new challenge (one could argue in a spirit of enterprise):

> Instead of griping about school holidays we should all be encouraging people to holiday in the UK! If the 'new policy' were amended or less rigorously enforced it still wouldn't help the UK tourism industry as it is likely these families will go abroad.

> We benefit a lot from staggered holidays in countries such as Germany and Netherlands, who help fill our shoulder season. They have been staggering holidays for donkey's years, and prove it works! Also, I believe that if Britain aligned its time zone with CET (so ditch GMT), tourism would benefit hugely because of longer evenings.

What these examples highlight is the different responses elicited by the same piece of legislation; some enterprising, others less so. At an event hosted by the Tourism Society Westcountry on 11 June 2015 in response to the legislation, suggestions on how the 'Gove Effect' could be tackled were offered by some tourism entrepreneurs. Thus, one business owner had started to shift his product away from the family market and focused instead on offering dog-friendly holidays – this appears to be a growing trend, with a number of accommodation providers across the UK now offering dog-friendly accommodation, where dogs stay for free, and other enticements such as homemade dog biscuits on arrival (Overwater Hall in the Lake District), a doggy goody box and a sausage at breakfast (Trigony House Hotel, Scotland). Another was trying to make more of visitors from the EU where holidays are staggered. Another was considering offering educational packages to schools.

Entrepreneurship in emerging and developing economies

The final part of this chapter addresses how entrepreneurship in tourism may differ in an emerging and developing economy (EDE) context from that in a developed economy setting. Considering differences between the application of entrepreneurship theory in EDEs compared to developed economies is more than just an academic exercise. The key to growing economies in EDEs is entrepreneurship, in rural and urban areas (Hagel, 2016). Tourism has been regarded as a sector of choice for many non-developed economies. It is labour intensive, has low barriers to entry, draws on natural resources which are often untapped, and requires relatively small amounts of investment (depending on the nature of the tourism product). According to Bhuiyan et al. (2011), governments in developing economies are more directly involved in the planning of tourism. This may be the case given its importance to the economies of many developing countries, if not because without appropriate planning, management and governance tourism may also bear the seeds of its own destruction. Tourism continues to play a role in enhancing economic well-being in many communities around the world.

The original classification of countries into developed and less developed based on economic measures alone (notably per capita GDP) reflects beliefs about the meaning of development itself (Potter, 2014). Just as perceptions of tourism development have evolved (e.g., Jafari, 2001; Ateljevic and Li, 2009), so has the understanding of what development encompasses. Whereas per capita measures of economic output used to be the sole measure of development, today these have been included within broader indices such as the Human Development Index (HDI), which offers an alternative and more balanced approach to assessing development (the HDI focuses on three key dimensions: health, education and wealth).

Emerging economies are said to comprise both developing nations and post-communist transition countries characterised by 'low-income, rapid-growth. . . using economic liberalization as their primary engine of growth' (Hoskisson et al., 2000:249). Their growing economic importance and integration on the world stage is widely acknowledged (Aulakh and Kotabe, 2008). This shift towards economic liberalisation from post-Soviet (e.g., Iorio and Corsale, 2010) and (post)communist countries (e.g., China; Yang and Wall, 2008) has opened up opportunities for entrepreneurship generally (Peng, 2001) to include tourism entrepreneurs specifically. The largest of these economies (i.e., China, India, Russia, Brazil, Mexico, South Korea, Turkey, Indonesia, and Poland) 'now comprise over a third of the world's 25 largest economies and are growing at around three times the pace of the advanced ones' (Kiss et al., 2012:266). Indeed, some of these so-called emerging markets are very much emerged now (Dodds, 2014). Considering the development of international travel, as we have seen in Chapter 1, emerging markets are taking a growing share of this, both as source markets and as receiving markets, with growth rates outstripping those of more established tourist destinations.

Academia is currently playing a catch-up game as research on these emerging and developing countries begins to proliferate. In entrepreneurship, the vast majority of studies to date, especially academic studies, have had developed economies as their focus. In a review of leading entrepreneurship journals between 1990 and 2006, Bruton et al. (2008) found that less than one half of one percent of the articles in this time period addressed entrepreneurship in emerging economies. Loayza et al. (2000:7) second this, pointing out: 'Entrepreneurship in developing countries is the most understudied important global economic phenomenon today.' In tourism, which by definition involves mobility, the overemphasis on developed economy research is perhaps not as stark, although the phenomenon of tourism might have been interpreted largely from a developed economy perspective.

Drawing on Peng (2000), who, with regard to research in the area of strategy, suggests findings in a developed economy will not be equally applicable in an emerging economy, we argue that entrepreneurship in tourism will vary depending on stage of economic development of the country where entrepreneurship is taking place. The Global Entrepreneurship Monitor (GEM) provides evidence that aspects of entrepreneurship differ across countries. Thus, the rates of entrepreneurial intentions in factor-driven economies at 30.3% is twice as high (15.2%) as that in innovation driven economies.[5] As a so-called 'unit of analysis', emerging and developing economies are sufficiently distinct with regard to entrepreneurship as to merit their own attention.

The main theme we explore here relates to barriers and enablers of entrepreneurship in tourism in EDEs. Before we start this discussion, we draw attention to the scale of informal economic activity in EDEs in particular. Schneider and Enste (2002) argue that informal activity accounts for as much as 60% of employment in emerging economies. In tourism much employment and self-employment is informal (Walmsley, 2015). Any discussion of entrepreneurship in EDEs needs, we would argue, to take this into account although this is difficult in a sense that precisely because of its informality, this type of entrepreneurship is seldom discussed in the literature – data on this phenomenon are hard to come by.

Fogel et al. (2006:2) in a review of obstacles to entrepreneurship begin their discussion thus:

> An entrepreneur carries out a highly complicated composite act. She needs intelligence to collect and digest information about business opportunities. She needs foresight about the possibilities new technologies and other developments create. She needs judgment and leadership skills to found a company and guide its growth. She needs communication skills to enthuse financiers to back her vision.

This describes the entrepreneur in a very 'Western'-centric way, focusing on a very niche type of enterprise (one that does not just survive, but grows). If all of these requirements have to be met before entrepreneurship can take place, we would not witness much entrepreneurship in EDEs!

As has been argued throughout, entrepreneurship is something that happens in its own context, it is situational. Every start-up in tourism will be shaped by a set of unique circumstances. The circumstances in EDEs tend to be quite different from those in developed economies. As a guide to understanding the nature of these environments, many scholars have referred to the institutional environment, which at its simplest can be defined as societal constraints on behaviour, whether legal or based on norms (North, 1991). Scott (2001) extends North's (1991) work by offering three pillars of institutional theory: regulative, normative and cultural-cognitive. It is then possible to assess the institutional environment along these three dimensions and try to offer some indication of how they may differ in EDEs compared to developed economies.

Returning to North's (1991) definition of institutions as constraints, one may wonder why they are conceived of at all. Arguably, institutions may be regarded as inhibiting enterprise, as placing 'red tape' whether this be legal red tape or normative and cultural red tape, around the fledgling tourism enterprise. However, the overall purpose of institutions is 'to create order and reduce uncertainty in exchange' (North, 1991:97). Within the sphere of business, rules, regulations and norms are intended to oil the wheels of enterprise rather than clog them up. Who would spend vast amounts of money on research and innovation without a law (patent) to protect this investment? Who would enter a contract if there were no legal as well as social obligations to fulfil it – in fact, without the institutional support contracts would be meaningless.

This is not to suggest that the institutional frameworks are somehow value-neutral. Being by definition culturally embedded they reflect the values of a society at a given point in time. There is also a strong political dimension to the institutional framework and coercion and power are key underpinnings of the regulative pillar in particular (North, 1990). The normative and cultural-cognitive also, but more

Table 10.2 Institutional pillars

	Pillar one: Regulative	Pillar two: Normative	Pillar three: Cultural Cognitive
Basis of compliance	Expedience	Social obligation	Taken-for-grantedness, Shared understanding
Indicators	Rules, Laws, Sanctions	Certification, Accreditation	Common beliefs
Basis of legitimacy	Legally sanctioned	Morally governed	Culturally supported

Source: Scott (2001:52)

tacitly, uphold the status quo potentially in favour of a ruling elite. As Weber (1968, originally 1924) argues, few rulers are content to base their regime on force alone; all attempt to cultivate a belief in its legitimacy. A full discussion of power in tourism development, how it is distributed and upheld goes beyond our text here (we refer the reader here to Coles and Church's (2007) edited tome, which is very useful in this regard), but we acknowledge North's (1990:73) point that it is the creation as well as enactment of rules and regulations where power is displayed: 'enforcement is undertaken by agents whose own utility functions influence outcomes'.

If institutions should facilitate commerce, then their absence, an absence of implementation, or their ill-design may result in what we term institutional burdens that inhibit enterprise. Focusing on entrepreneurship, De Clercq et al. (2010:86) define institutional burdens as 'obstacles derived from underdeveloped or absent institutional structures, which can hinder aspiring entrepreneurs from exploiting new business opportunities fully'. We argue that institutional burdens tend to be more prevalent in developing than in developed economies and provide some examples below to illustrate.

Making use of Scott's (2001) framework both Kiss et al. (2012) and De Clercq et al. (2010) describe regulatory, normative and cognitive burdens. Regulatory burdens may present themselves in a number of ways. For example, they could reflect an absence of appropriate laws, but equally may refer to an absence of sanctions for failure to comply with existing legislation.

An example of a combination of both normative and cognitive burdens can be seen in Baker et al. (2005), who extend Shane and Venkataraman's (2000) Discovery, Evaluation, Exploitation framework with their Comparative Discovery, Exploitation and Evaluation (CDEE) framework. CDEE is more appropriate for the comparison of entrepreneurship across countries' institutional contexts because it recognises that both the character of opportunities available and the individuals who discover, evaluate and exploit them are institutionally bound. They argue that different countries will have different levels of social stratification and that this stratification affects who does, and who does not, have access to opportunities. Crucially, however, Baker et al. (2005) also posit that social structures inhibit the recognition of opportunities (it is not just about having access in other words):

> The process of evaluating an opportunity may range from a successful technology entrepreneur's musings about which project will be most satisfying (financially

or otherwise) to an impoverished farmer's anxious decision about what course of action will provide more reliable support for her family.

(Baker et al., 2005:501)

The important role social norms play in influencing entrepreneurial intentions has likewise been recognised in numerous studies based on Ajzen's Theory of Planned Behaviour (Ajzen, 1987). Social norms explain generally lower entrepreneurial intentions among females than males. This socio-cultural issue is more pronounced in countries with a clear gender role segregation. This is encountered in many patriarchal societies where women tend to see their role in society as one of wife, housekeeper, and mother (e.g., Mehtap et al., 2017, who studied female entrrpeneurship in Jordan).

Paradoxically perhaps, barriers in one area may foster entrepreneurship in another. Exclusion of groups in society from certain roles or occupations can function as a push into entrepreneurship, a form of necessity entrepreneurship (Nabi et al., 2013). Tourism offers many examples of how an entrepreneurial spirit, combined with restricted access to professional occupations or mainstream forms of employment, has resulted in successful tourism enterprise ventures or initiatives:

Woodcarving in South Africa

Christian et al. (2008) discuss the woodcarving trade's role in tourism in South Africa. These authors noted that the opportunities for self-employment in a growing tourism industry in the Western Cape were drawing entrepreneurs from a range of countries belonging to the Southern African Development Community. Using the word 'draw' is perhaps a little misplaced, as it is more of a push, necessity entrepreneurship, whereby these woodcarvers were seeking a relatively secure form of income that they were unable to find in their home countries. 'The lack of job opportunities in the formal economy rather than poor education acted as a driving force for the involvement of reasonably educated people in the Trade' (Christian et al., 2008:582).

Sapa O'Chau (www.sapaochau.org); silver award 2016 in the World Responsible Tourism Awards

As tourism grows in Vietnam many of its ethnic minorities are excluded from this new economy. Shu Tan, from the Black Hmon ethnic minority, is the founder of the tour company Sapa O'Chau. Shu Tan is a former handicraft street vendor and tour guide and her company now offers guided treks in the Sapa region of Northern Vietnam. This tourism firm is owned and managed by individuals from this ethnic minority, which is remarkable in that many locals from the Black Hmon region are not even able to go to school. Shu Tan's first step was to make that happen and hence won an award for her efforts at the 2016 World Responsible Tourism Awards.

Village Ways (www.villageways.com)

Village Ways is an example of collaboration between an outside provider and the local community in a responsible way (the initiative has won numerous awards including the 'Best for Poverty Reduction' category in the 2017 Responsible Tourism Awards). Village Ways offers tailor-made holidays in India and Nepal that focus on authenticity, which in this case means experiencing community life in the village, it offers to take the tourist 'to the heart of village life'. A local guide is provided who helps tourists interact with their hosts. Each village owns and manages the accommodation, which is run as a village homestay by the village committee, benefiting the community rather than a single family. This is an example of how tourism can be more responsible by ensuring the local community receives more of the revenue generated by the tourist, as well as an example of how institutional (here cultural) barriers can be overcome. The founders have been able to understand what the tourist wants (authentic and responsible tourism), understand what the local community wants, and have brought the two together.

Culture may serve as a barrier to entrepreneurship in two further ways in that it may:

(a) Go against the grain of commerce/entrepreneurship in a general sense
(b) Fail to align with the values of the tourists.

With regard to (a), the perceived need to inculcate an enterprise culture as has been witnessed in the UK (Gibb, 1999) and indicates that cultures may be if not antagonistic towards enterprise, at least apathetic towards it. There is widespread agreement that the development of an entrepreneurial culture matters for development (UNCTAD, 2012). Chakraborty et al. (2015) write of an anti-capitalist culture that inhibits enterprise and provide examples of Weber's writing on India (1958) and China (1961) where the caste system and Confucian values respectively are deemed hostile to capitalist values. Chakraborty et al. (2015) also go on to argue that these cultural values can change; looking at the rapid development of India and China today this interjection is timely as otherwise either the premise is wrong or these values have been diluted or superseded.

In the latter case (b) there are often opportunities that lie dormant because the local population places a different value on its natural and cultural assets than the tourist might. An example of this can be found in Ladakh, specifically the 'Himalayan-Homestays Initiative' where the innovation involves changing local mindsets towards snow leopards from that of a pest to an invaluable tourism asset. As initiator of the project, Wangchuk (2008:1) explains:

> The Himalayan-Homestays initiative emerged out of a series of brainstorming sessions with villagers in Hemis National Park on how best to resolve conflicts with snow leopards and other predators that were killing 12% of their livestock annually. The SLC and local communities developed alternatives that would transform a centuries-old problem into an opportunity.

Naturally, many people might feel slightly uneasy about questioning cultural values of a host population. There is indeed a whiff of neo-colonialism here, or what Burns (2008) refers to as tourism as a 'cultural pollutant'. In tourism's defence, we offer the argument that in some instances, certainly not all, tourism can contribute to an enhanced valuation of a destination's heritage. With reference to the Ladakh

Homestay programme Wangchuk (2008:4) quotes a local farmer, Skarma Lungstar pa from Yangthang village, who says:

> I was born in this valley and lived as a farmer all my life here. I hated it. Now that visitors come from distant places and appreciate our mountains and culture it makes me proud to be a Yangthang pa.

Barriers to entrepreneurship in tourism in subsistence economies in particular do not have to fall within the sphere of social institutions. An absence of infrastructure is a characteristic of non-developed economies, an issue that is acute in subsistence economies and prevents many forms of commerce including most forms of tourism. Put simply, there is no point having a resort ready to receive tourists if the transport infrastructure is not in place to get tourists from an airport to the resort safely and in a reasonable amount of comfort and time.

Another key feature of entrepreneurship in EDEs is resource scarcity (Kiss et al., 2012). Lack of access to finance is one of the key challenges that entrepreneurs in EDEs face. According to the International Finance Corporation of the World Bank Group, nearly three billion people in developing countries have little or no access to formal financial services (IFC, 2018). The financial infrastructure tends to be less developed in EDEs, and a requirement for a smooth functioning of the financial system is a certain amount of regulation thereof (see Scott's, 2001, first institutional pillar). The availability of non-bank finance instruments such as leasing, hire purchases, factoring and invoice discounting[6] may be more limited in EDEs. Lingelbach et al. (2005:4) have suggested that while entrepreneurial opportunities are broader in developing countries, limited personal and family savings and an absence of financial innovation severely limit the growth prospects of promising start-ups. What many small and new tourism firms may lack in EDEs are assets that can be used to secure borrowing. Furthermore, weak balance sheets translate into a reduction in the availability of credit, at higher interest rates and more stringent conditions (OECD, 2015). Because SMEs have fewer financing alternatives than large firms, they are likely to be more impacted by credit market conditions also.

A number of tools lie at the policy-maker's disposal to try to assist SMEs' need for finance such as loan guarantees, counter-guarantee schemes, direct loans, micro loans and tax exemptions and deferments (OECD, 2015). Microfinance, a source of financial services for entrepreneurs and small businesses lacking traditional access to banking and related services, is frequently promoted as an invaluable financial innovation for EDEs. In 2005 the World Tourism Organization published a report on microfinance available to tourism firms and the relationship to poverty alleviation (World Tourism Organization, 2005). It recognises that SMEs and microenterprises form the basis of tourism development in most countries. Consequently, creating the conditions in which tourism microenterprises can be created and flourish is a prerequisite to fighting poverty.

The Grameen Bank and its founder Muhammad Yunus who together won the Nobel Peace Prize in 2006 'for their efforts to create economic and social development from below' are commonly mentioned in the same breath as microfinance. Microfinance, while sometimes held up as *the* solution, does not always work, however, and has come in for some criticism (Chang, 2011). A review of microfinance in Benin, Pakistan, Peru and Georgia conducted by 'The Smart Campaign' (Meka and

Sanford, 2016), while supportive of microfinance overall, did highlight a number of difficulties, including:

- Clients frequently lack essential information (such as the precise terms of the loan, including what penalties arise for missed or delayed payments).
- Microfinance staff frequently lack human decency when dealing with clients who have problems paying their loans (those approving the loans are in a position of power and may exploit this).
- There are few channels for filing a complaint.

The WTTC describes a microfinance initiative in tourism in the Oaxaca Valley region of Mexico established by the non-profit organisation Fundación En Vía (www.envia. org). It raises funds through responsible tourism projects which are then used to provide interest-free loans and education to support women entrepreneurs. This set-up is unusual in that finance available for the loans it provides is generated through tours to visit some of the women who receive them (e.g., artisans, cooks, business owners). The WTO's (2005) report on microfinance in tourism offers some examples of how microfinance has supported tourism entrepreneurs in Morocco. Karim,[7] a tour guide, received a small loan to purchase two mountain bikes, a telescope and binoculars. In order to receive tourists, he bought a bed and a mattress and financed the construction of a shower in his brother's house. In the same locale, Soraya (who is 54) obtained funding (€2,800) to renovate a rural guesthouse she owns (creating partitioning walls, a tent for the garden and traditional cooking utensils). In a different location, the Ourika mountains close to Marrakech, Mohammed received a microcredit of €450 to consolidate his pottery souvenir production business. He used the money to purchase paint and to take on one worker. He had hoped to receive €900, which would have let him purchase a small gas stove, which would have allowed him greater precision in the manufacture of his pottery. However, microenterprises in tourism face a number of challenges such as seasonality and difficulty in estimating accurately tourism demand. Without robust financial estimates gaining access to finance, even microfinance, can be challenging.

Alongside lack of access to resources, including financial resource, the political situation in many EDEs lacks stability. It has been claimed the first condition for entrepreneurship is found in the economic situation (Spilling, 1998, cited in Dreisler et al., 2003). Levels of political instability have been related to the economic condition, not least levels and consistency of economic growth: Alesina et al. (1996) analysed data from 113 countries between 1950 and 1982 that indicated growth levels were lower for countries with higher levels of political instability.[8] Developing economies tend to be less politically stable than developed and so this can have a direct impact on the tourism entrepreneur. Thus, in relation to the regulative pillar of institutional theory (Scott, 2001), we find greater levels of political instability result in less regulative certainty. A high propensity of a change of government is associated with uncertainty about the new policies of a potential new government. Uncertainty is not conducive to business. Investment tends to decrease as uncertainty grows. With regard to tourism, Moutinho et al. (2011:17) go so far as to suggest that 'political instability and conflict between and within countries will always have a devastating effect on the tourist trade'.

What Moutinho et al. (2011) have argued can be illustrated with numerous examples. Thus, it is little consolation to the hotel owner that his/her hotel is 'kitted out' with the latest in-room technology if the levels of crime or political unrest make the destination itself unappealing to tourists. Unfortunately, many developing countries such those North African countries that were part of the Arab Spring have suffered because of an overreliance on tourism combined with a highly unstable political environment. It will be 'interesting' to note which developing countries' tourist industries suffer most as a result of climate change.

Another key area where entrepreneurs in tourism and small tourism firms are likely to face more challenges in terms of resource scarcity than those in developed economies is human capital. Human capital relates to knowledge, skills, competencies and attributes embodied in individuals that facilitate the creation of personal, social and economic well-being (OECD, 2001). Levels of education and formal training tend to be lower in developing economies, as does the provision of healthcare (a fully trained employee is of little use if they are not fit for work). Although the provision of entrepreneurship education has expanded globally, there is still a need for more to be done in this area (see for example Kaijage et al.'s, 2013, review of entrepreneurship education in East Africa). Because tourism is commonly regarded as a low-skill sector, the challenges presented by low levels of human capital are perhaps of less concern here. That said, capacity-building is an important element of tourism development. Without the development of the requisite skills in the local population, calls for increased community participation in tourism are likely to lead to disappointment. Tourism entrepreneurs, and their staff, require training on tourists' customs, especially with regard to food and their reasons for travelling, things as seemingly straightforward as 'peace and quiet' and security (World Tourism Organization, 2005:41).

Case Study 10.2: Dayak homestay entrepreneurs

The term Dayak is commonly used to categorise a group of indigenous peoples of the island of Borneo. There are by some estimates approximately 450 ethnolinguistic Dayak groups living in Borneo, though they are generally regarded as sharing a number of similarities in languages, living styles (most of these groups traditionally lived in longhouses) and customary laws (known as adat) (Minority Rights Group International, 2017). Nonetheless, according to the Encyclopaedia Britannica (2017) the term has no ethnic or tribal significance and has been widely used in studies of 'indigenous' tourism activities in Borneo (e.g. Kelling and Entebang, 2017; Kaur et al., undated) (itself split between three countries: Indonesia, the Malaysian Federated States of Sabah and Sarawak, and Brunei Darussalam).

In particular the homestay activities of the Dayak in Sarawak have received attention from tourism scholars and the Malaysian government alike as an innovative way to tap into growth of tourists wanting more authentic experiences. This reflects wider support by the Malaysian Ministry of Culture, Art and Heritage (MOCAT), which has attempted to diversify many tourism products in Malaysia, including homestay tourism (Kaur et al., undated; Ibrahim and Abdul Razzaq, 2010). The Malaysian government has, and continues to, focus on supporting ecotourism and within this supporting local, small-scale entrepreneurs (Bhuiyan et al., 2011).

According to Amran (1997, cited in Ibrahim and Abdul Razzaq, 2010) the homestay programme in Malaysia can be traced back to the early 1970s at the then drifter enclave of Kampung Cherating Lama in Pahang, when a local lady by the name of Mak Long took in long-staying drifters/hippies and provided breakfast, dinner and accommodation within her kampong house (Kampung means 'village' in Malay). Ibrahim and Abdul Razzaq (2010) further describe the development of the homestay sector in Malaysia as having emerged from an overspill of tourism in terms of overflow of tourists that could not be handled by the big entrepreneurs. Initially the product offered was merely accommodation. The operator of the homestay also sometimes extended his services as a tourist guide to the guests. In the early 1990s, in the Seventh Malaysia Plan, the government took the initiative to upgrade and improve this sector of tourism. The strategies included the introduction of new products and services and increase in the involvement of the local population, especially small entrepreneurs in the development of distinct and localised tourism products and services. In 1993, MOCAT formed a special unit to oversee the growth of the program, which was officially launched on 3 December 1995.

A Dayak Homestay Programme has been supported by the regional government, and training courses are provided by the Dayak Chamber of Commerce and Industry (DCCI) (Yi, 2016). These training programmes cover food preparation and traditional handicrafts (weaving, ceramics, bead making) thereby also contributing to the preservation of local culture and heritage. The DCCI also assists local homestay entrepreneurs in promoting and marketing their products. According to studies of the Dayak Homestay Programme (e.g., Pusiran and Xiao, 2013; Kunjuraman and Hussin, 2017) it does face certain challenges, which strengthens the case for government intervention. Pusiran and Xiao (2013:7) suggest:

> there are many challenges affecting the effectiveness of the homestay programme and each one could be different from one community to another and research needs to address the challenges found from previous studies and explore other challenges that may influence the success or failures of homestay operations.

Kunjuraman and Hussin (2017), who subsequently investigated the homestay programme in Dagat Village, Sabah, concluded that of the numerous difficulties the local community faced in implementing the homestay programme, a lack of trained human resources and a lack of financial resources were the main challenges.

Summary

This chapter has offered a review of the policy context of tourism entrepreneurship. It has laid out why governments support entrepreneurship, and why they might support tourism. Currently, support for the former is unequivocal, support for tourism is more context-specific. While tourism can be seen as a panacea in regions experiencing economic decline, frequently as a result of economic restructuring, it may also be regarded as a sector of last resort, one that 'will do for now' but not one for the long term. The chapter has clearly demonstrated the complexity inherent in policy-making for entrepreneurship in tourism. Generic policy can have greater impact on tourism than policy designed specifically for tourism. Government may be seen as bureaucratic, and by definition anti-entrepreneurial, and yet the same can be said of many tourism firms. Overall the chapter has sided with the view that tourism entrepreneurs and small tourism firms should and can usefully be supported by the state. This is primarily due to imperfect markets and liabilities of newness. Support can take a number of forms in a number of domains (e.g. financial, regulatory, training, infrastructure). The chapter also spent some time discussing the nature of entrepreneurship in emerging and developing economies as these contexts result in additional barriers but also enablers compared to developed economies. Institutional Theory (Scott, 2001; North, 1991) was offered as a framework upon which different contexts for entrepreneurship can be compared and understood. Because of tourism's potential for poverty alleviation more research should focus on barriers and enablers of entrepreneurship in tourism in emerging and developing economies specifically.

Review questions/discussion points

1 Why are policy-makers interested in supporting entrepreneurship?
2 Why might tourism be regarded as of particular interest to policy-makers when it comes to promoting entrepreneurship?
3 Is the promotion of entrepreneurship in emerging and developing economies a form of cultural colonialism?
4 In your own words, explain the distinction between the cultural-cognitive and normative constraints on entrepreneurship.
5 Identify three key barriers to entrepreneurship in tourism in emerging and developing economies.

Notes

1 Unless otherwise specified, for the sake of brevity the remainder of this chapter implies entrepreneurship and innovation when entrepreneurship/enterprise are mentioned. The two are distinct, see Chapter 3, but are amalgamated here.
2 We make this point here because much tourism employment occurs informally, partially as a result of a perceived excessive legislative burden
3 Space constraints prevent a full discussion of this point of moral philosophy, as interesting as it is.
4 Porter's Five Forces comprise competitive rivalry, supplier power, buyer power, threat of substitutes, threat of new entrants. We have desisted from a discussion here as the issue is covered elsewhere in strategy books, such as Evans' (2015) *Strategic Management in Tourism*.

5   Factor-driven countries compete based on their factor endowments – primarily unskilled labour and natural resources. Countries will then move into the *efficiency-driven* stage of development, when they must begin to develop more-efficient production processes. In the innovation-drive stage businesses are able to compete using the most sophisticated production processes and by innovating new ones (WEF, 2016)
6   Factoring means using a company's accounts receivable to secure funding. Invoice discounting is similar to factoring, it uses cash tied up in a company's assets rather than accounts receivable. See also Chapter 4.
7   None of the names here are the original names.
8   They also mention the problem of 'joint endogeneity between the economy and the polity', which effectively means that low levels of growth may in turn cause political instability.

References

Ajzen, I. 1987. Attitudes, traits, and actions: dispositional prediction of behaviour in social psychology. *Advances in Experimental Social Psychology*, 20, 1–63.

Alesina, A., Ozler, S., Roubini, N. and Swagel, P. 1996. Political instability and economic growth. *Journal of Economic Growth*, 1, 189–211.

Ateljevic, J. and Li, L. 2009. Tourism entrepreneurship – concepts and issues. In: Page, S. and Ateljevic, J. (eds.), *Tourism and Entrepreneurship: International Perspectives*. London: Routledge.

Audretsch, D. 2009. The entrepreneurial society. In: Audretsch, D., Dagnino, G. B., Faraci, R. and Hoskisson, R. (eds.), *New Frontiers in Entrepreneurship: Recognizing, Seizing, and Executing Opportunities*. New York: Springer.

Aulakh, P. and Kotabe, M. 2008. Institutional changes and organizational transformation in developing economies. *Journal of International Management*, 14, 209–216.

Autio, E., Kenney, M., Mustar, P., Siegel, D. and Wright, M. 2014. Entrepreneurial innovation: the importance of context. *Research Policy*, 43, 1097–1108.

Baker, T., Gedajlovic, E. and Lubatkin, M. 2005. A framework for comparing entrepreneurship processes across nations. *Journal of International Business Studies*, 36, 492–504.

Bannock, G. 1981. *The Economics of Small Firms: Return From the Wilderness*. Oxford: Basil Blackwell.

Baumol, W. 2002. *The Free-Market Innovation Machine: Analyzing the Growth Miracle of Capitalism*. Princeton: Princeton University Press.

Bhuiyan, A. H., Siwar, C., Ismail, S. M. and Islam, R. 2011. The role of government in ecotourism development: focusing on east coast economic regions. *Journal of Social Sciences*, 7, 557–564.

Birch, D. 1979. *The Job Generation Process*. Cambridge, MA: MIT Press.

Bridge, S., O'Neill, K. and Cromie, S. 2003. *Understanding Enterprise, Entrepreneurship and Small Business*. Basingstoke: Palgrave Macmillan.

Bruton, G., Ahlstrom, D. and Obloj, K. 2008. Entrepreneurship in emerging economies: where are we today and where should the research go in the future. *Entrepreneurship Theory and Practice*, 32, 1–14.

Burns, P. 2008. Tourism, political discourse, and post-colonialism. *Tourism and Hospitality Planning & Development*, 5, 61–71.

Butler, D. 1980. The concept of a tourist area cycle of evolution: implications for management of resources. *Canadian Geographer*, 24, 5–12.

Chakraborty, S., Thompson, J. C. and Yehou, E. B. 2015. Culture in development. *The World Bank Economic Review*.

Chang, H.-J. 2011. *23 Things They Don't Tell You About Capitalism*. London: Penguin.

Christian, M. Y., Chirwa, P. and Ham, C. 2008. The influence of tourism on the woodcarving trade around Cape Town and implications for forest resources in southern Africa. *Development Southern Africa*, 25, 577–588.

Coles, T. and Church, A. 2007. Tourism, politics and the forgotten entanglements of power. *In:* Church, A. and Coles, T. (eds.), *Tourism, Power and Space*. London: Routledge.

Curran, J. and Blackburn, R. 1991. *Paths of Enterprise: The Future of Small Businesses*. London: Routledge.

Davis, G., Wanna, J., Warhurst, J. and Weller, P. 1993. *Public Policy in Australia*. North Sydney: Allen and Unwin.

De Clercq, D., Danis, W. and Dakhli, M. 2010. The moderating effect of institutional context on the relationship between associational activity and new business activity in emerging economies. *International Business Review*, 19, 85–101.

Dodds, K. 2014. The Third World, developing countries, the South, emerging markets and rising powers. *In:* Potter, R. and Desai, V. (eds.), *The Companion to Development Studies*. London: Routledge.

Dreisler, P., Blenker, P. and Nielsen, K. 2003. Promoting entrepreneurship – changing attitudes or behaviour? *Journal of Small Business and Enterprise Development*, 10, 383–392.

Encyclopaedia Britannica. 2017. *Dayak People* [Online]. Available: www.britannica.com/topic/Dayak [Accessed 18 June 2017].

Evans, N. 2015. *Strategic Management for Tourism, Hospitality and Events*. London: Routledge.

Fogel, K., Hawk, A., Morck, R. and Yeung, B. 2006. Institutional obstacles to entrepreneurship. *In:* Mark Casson, B. Y., Basu, A. and Wadeson, N. (eds.), *Oxford Handbook of Entrepreneurship*. Oxford: Oxford University Press.

Gartner, W. B. 1985. A conceptual framework for describing the phenomenon of new venture creation. *Academy of Management Review*, 10, 696–706.

Gibb, A. 1999. Creating an entrepreneurial culture in support of SMEs. *Small Enterprise Development*, 10, 27–99.

Gibb, A. 2002. In pursuit of a new 'enterprise' and 'entrepreneurship' paradigm for learning: creative destruction, new values, new ways of doing things and new combinations of knowledge. *International Journal of Management Reviews*, 4, 233–269.

Gompers, P. and Lerner, J. 2001. The venture capital revolution. *Journal of Economic Perspectives*, 15, 145–168.

Grimaldi, R., Kenney, M., Siegal, D. and Wright, M. 2011. 30 years after Bayh–Dole: reassessing academic entrepreneurship. *Research Policy*, 40, 1045–1057.

Hagel, I. J. 2016. We need to expand our definition of entrepreneurship. *Harvard Business Review* [Online]. Available: https://hbr.org/2016/09/we-need-to-expand-our-definition-of-entrepreneurship [Accessed 28 September 2016].

Hall, C. M. 2009a. Innovation and tourism policy in Australia and New Zealand: never the twain shall meet? *Journal of Policy Research in Tourism, Hospitality and Events*, 1, 2–18.

Hall, C. M. 2009b. The public policy context of tourism entrepreneurship. *In:* Ateljevic, J. and Page, S. (eds.), *Tourism Entrepreneurship*. London: Routledge.

Hall, C. M. and Williams, A. 2008. *Tourism and Innovation*. London: Routledge.

Harris-White, B. 2010. Work and wellbeing in informal economies: the regulative roles of institutions of identity and the state. *World Development*, 38, 170–183.

Hoskisson, R. E., Eden, L., Lau, C. M. and Wright, M. 2000. Strategy in emerging economies. *Academy of Management Journal*, 43, 249–267.

Ibrahim, Y. and Abdul Razzaq, A. R. 2010. Homestay programme and rural community development in Malaysia. *Jounal of Ritsumeikan Social Sciences and Humanities*, 2, 7–24.

IFC. 2018. *Microfinance* [Online]. International Finance Corporation. Available: www.ifc.org/wps/wcm/connect/Industry_EXT_Content/IFC_External_Corporate_Site/Industries/Financial+Markets/MSME+Finance/Microfinance/ [Accessed 09 March 2018].

Iorio, M. and Corsale, A. 2010. Rural tourism and livelihood strategies in Romania. *Journal of Rural Studies*, 26, 152–162.

Jafari, J. 2001. The scientification of tourism. *In:* Smith, V. L. and Brent, M. (eds.), *Hosts and Guests Revisited: Tourism Issues of the 21st Century*. New York: Cognizant.

Jenkins, J. 2006. The role of the state in tourism. *In:* Beech, J. and Chadwick, S. (eds.), *The Business of Tourism*. Harlow: Pearson Education.

Kaijage, E., Wheeler, D. and Newbery, R. 2013. *Supporting Entrepreneurship Education in East Africa*. Institute for Sustainability Solutions Research, Plymouth University and the University of Nairobi.

Kaur, P., Jawaid, A. and Othman, N. B. A. undated. The impact of community based tourism on community development in Sarawak. *Journal of Borneo Kalimantan*.

Kelling, W. and Entebang, H. 2017. Dayak homestay entrepreneurs innovation characteristics. *Ottoman Journal of Tourism and Management Research*, 2.

Kennell, J. and Chaperon, S. 2011. Analysis of the UK government's 2011 tourism policy. *Cultural Trends*, 22, 278–284.

Kerr, W. R. 2003. *Tourism Public Policy, and the Strategic Management of Failure*. Oxford: Elsevier.

Kirzner, I. M. 1997. Entrepreneurial discovery and the competitive market process: an Austrian approach. *Journal of Economic Literature*, 35, 60–85.

Kiss, A., Danis, W. and Cavusgil, T. 2012. International entrepreneurship research in emerging economies: a critical review and research agenda. *Journal of Business Venturing*, 27, 266–290.

Koh, K. 1996. The tourism entrepreneurial process: a conceptualization and implications for research and development. *The Tourist Review*, 51, 24–41.

Koh, K. and Hatten, T. S. 2002. The tourism entrepreneur: the overlooked player in tourism development studies. *International Journal of Hospitality and Tourism Administration*, 3, 21–48.

Kunjuraman, V. and Hussin, R. 2017. Challenges of community-based homestay programme in Sabah, Malaysia: hopeful or hopeless? *Tourism Management Perspectives*, 21, 1–9.

Lingelbach, D., de la Vina, L. and Asel, P. 2005. *What's Distinctive about Growth-Oriented Entrepreneurship in Developing Countries?* UTSA College of Business Center for Global Entrepreneurship Working Paper No. 1.

Loayza, N., Schmidt-Hebbel, K. and Serven, L. 2000. What drives private savings across the world? *Reveiw of Economics & Statistics*, 82, 165–181.

Mason, P. 2008. *Tourism Impacts, Planning and Management*. Oxford: Butterworth-Heinemann.

Mehtap, S., Pellegrini, M., Caputo, A. and Welsh, D. 2017. Entrepreneurial intentions of young women in the Arab world: socio-cultural and educational barriers. *International Journal of Entrepreneurial Behaviour and Research*, 23, 880–902.

Meka, S. and Sanford, C. 2016. *My Turn to Speak: Vocies of Microfinance Clients in Benin, Pakistan, Peru and Georgia*. The Smart Campaign.

Mihalič, T. 2015. Tourism and economic development issues. *In:* Sharpley, R. and Telfer, D. (eds.), *Tourism and Development: Concepts and Issues*, 2nd edn. Bristol: Channel View Publications.

Minority Rights Group International. 2017. *Indonesia – Dayak* [Online]. Available: http://minorityrights.org/minorities/dayak/ [Accessed 18 June 2017].

Morrison, A. and Teixeira, R. 2004. Small business performance: a tourism sector focus. *Journal of Small Business and Enterprise Development*, 11, 166–173.

Moutinho, L., Ballantyne, R. and Rate, S. 2011. The new business environment and trends in tourism. *In:* Moutinho, L. (ed.) *Strategic Management in Tourism*. Wallingford: CABI.

Nabi, G., Walmsley, A. and Holden, R. 2013. Pushed or pulled? Exploring the factors underpinning graduate start-ups and non-start-ups. *Journal of Education and Work*, 10, 1–26.

North, D. 1990. *Institutions, Institutional Change and Economic Performance*. Cambridge: Cambridge University Press.

North, D. 1991. Institutions. *Journal of Economic Perspectives*, 5, 97–112.

OECD. 2001. *The Well-Being of Nations: The Role of Human and Social Capital*. Paris: OECD.

OECD. 2015. *Financing SMEs and Entrepreneurs 2015: An OECD Scoreboard*. Organization for Economic Co-operation and Development.

Peng, M. 2000. *Business Strategies in Transition Economies*. Thousand Oaks, CA: Sage.

Peng, M. 2001. How entrepreneurs create wealth in transition economies. *Academy of Management Executive*, 15, 95–108.

Peters, M. 2005. Entrepreneurial skills in leadership and human resource management evaluated by apprentices in small tourism businesses. *Education & Training*, 47, 575–591.

Potter, R. 2014. Measuring development: from GDP to HDI and wider approaches. *In:* Potter, R. and Desai, V. (eds.), *The Companion to Development Studies*, 3rd edn. London: Routledge.

Pusiran, A. K. and Xiao, H. 2013. Challenges and community development: a case study of homestay in Malaysia. *Asian Social Science*, 9, 1–17.

Russell, R. and Faulkner, B. 2004. Entrepreneurship, chaos and the tourism area lifecycle. *Annals of Tourism Research*, 31, 556–579.

Ryan, T., Mottiar, Z. and Quinn, B. 2012. The dynamic role of entrepreneurs in destination development, tourism planning and development. *Tourism Planning and Development*, 9, 119–131.

Schneider, F. and Enste, D. H. 2002. *The Shadow Economy: An International Survey*. New York: Cambridge University Press.

Schumpeter, J. 1934. *The Theory of Economic Development*. New York: Oxford University Press/Galaxy 1961.

Scott, R. W. 2001. *Institutions and Organizations*. Thousand Oaks, CA: Sage.

Seely, A. 2015. *VAT on Tourism*. London: House of Commons Library.

Shane, S. and Venkataraman, S. 2000. The promise of entrepreneurship as a field of research. *Academy of Management Review*, 25, 217–226.

Shaw, G. and Williams, A. 2010. Tourism SMEs: changing research agendas and missed opportunities. *In:* Pearce, D. and Butler, R. (eds.), *Tourism Research: A 20:20 Vision*. Oxford: Goodfellow Publishers.

Shone, M. 2011. Local government entrepreneurship in tourism development: the case of the Huruni District, New Zealand. *In:* Dredge, D. and Jenkins, J. (eds.) *Stories of Practice: Tourism Policy and Planning*. Farnham: Ashgate.

Smallbone, D. and Wyer, P. 2012. Growth and development in the small firm. *In:* Carter, S. and Jones-Evans, D. (eds.), *Entrepreneurship and Small Business: Principles, Practice and Policy*, 3rd edn. Harlow: Pearson.

Smallbone, D., Welter, F. and Ateljevic, J. 2014. Entrepreneurship in emerging market economies: contemporary issues and perspectives. *International Small Business Journal*, 32, 113–116.

Stinchcombe, A. L. 1965. Social structure and organizations. *In:* March, J. G. (ed.), *Handbook of Organizations*. Chicago, IL: Rand McNally.

Storey, D. J. 1994. *Understanding the Small Business Sector*. London: Routledge.

Szivas, E. and Riley, M. 1999. Tourism employment during economic transition. *Annals of Tourism Research*, 26, 747–771.

Thomas, R., Shaw, G. and Page, S. 2011. Understanding small firms in tourism: a perspective on research trends and challenges. *Tourism Management*, 32, 963–976.

Tourism Alliance. 2017. *Tourism After Brexit: A Post-Brexit Policy Agenda for the UK Tourism Industry*. London: Tourism Alliance.

UNCTAD. 2012. *Entrepreneurship Policy Framework and Implementation Guidance*. New York and Geneva: United Nations Conference on Trade and Development.

Von Mises, L. 1949. *Human Action*. New Haven: Yale University Press.

Walmsley, A. 2015. *Youth Employment in Tourism: A Critical Review*. Oxford: Goodfellow Publishers.

Walmsley, A. 2018. Policy decisions and tourism: unintended consequences or deliberate neglect – reactions to the ban on term time holidays in the UK's south west. *Journal of Policy Research in Tourism, Hospitality and Events.*

Wangchuk, R. 2008. *Homestays Benefit Local People and Threatened Species.* Ashoka Changemakers.

Wanhill, S. 2004. Government assistance for tourism SMEs: from theory to practice. *In:* Thomas, R. (ed.), *Small Firms in Tourism: International Perspectives.* London: Elsevier.

Weber, M. 1968. *On Charisma and Institution Building: Selected Papers.* Chicago: University of Chicago Press.

WEF. 2016. *The World Global Competitiveness Report 2016–2017.* Geneva: World Economic Forum.

West, G. P., Bamford, C. and Marsden, J. 2008. Contrasting entrepreneurial economic development in emerging Latin American economies: applications and extensions of resource-based theory. *Entrepreneurship Theory and Practice*, 32, 15–36.

World Tourism Organization. 2005. *Tourism, Microfinance and Poverty Alleviation.* Madrid: World Tourism Organization.

Yang, L. and Wall, G. 2008. Ethnic tourism and entrepreneurship: Xishuangbanna, Yunnan, China. *Tourism Geographies*, 10, 522–544.

Yi, C. 2016. Operators get specialised training as homestays boom. *Borneo Post Online* [Online]. Available: www.theborneopost.com/2016/09/11/operators-get-specialised-training-as-homestays-boom/ [Accessed 18 June 2017].

Chapter 11

Contemporary issues in entrepreneurship research

Introduction

The aim of this chapter is to review a selection of issues currently receiving increased attention either in the area of entrepreneurship, or that are of particular interest to entrepreneurship in tourism. The four issues that will be reviewed are ethnic minority entrepreneurship, lifestyle entrepreneurship, entrepreneurship education and smart tourism.

Learning outcomes

The learning outcomes for this chapter relate quite simply to an opening up to the reader of an initial awareness of the four issues outlined above. Specifically, at the end of the chapter the reader should be able to discuss:

- Why entrepreneurship might appeal to ethnic minorities.
- How different forms of lifestyle entrepreneurship explain the nature of much tourism entrepreneurship.
- The potential of entrepreneurship education in preparing tourism students for a changing labour market.
- The way smart tourism is developing and how it might shape the future of tourism in destinations.

Being familiar with these themes should provide the reader with a fuller understanding of the phenomenon of entrepreneurship in tourism.

Ethnic minority entrepreneurship in tourism

At least since Weber (2002, originally 1904/1905) drafted *The Protestant Ethic and the Spirit of Capitalism*, a strong case can be made that ethnicity plays an important role in entrepreneurship. Research on ethnic minority entrepreneurship (entrepreneurship displayed by those from ethnic minority groups), frequently focusing on immigrant entrepreneurs, has proliferated and in many societies rates of business start-up are higher among ethnic minorities than for the wider population. That ethnic minority businesses are also run differently has been discussed by Edelman et al. (2010), who review start-up and growth intentions of minority nascent entrepreneurs in the United States. Their results established the motivation to start a business did not differ between white and black entrepreneurs, but that differing motivations exist to grow a venture.

When considering ethnic minority entrepreneurship it is easy to overlook the variation within ethnic minority businesses, to see the world in terms of 'the majority' and 'the other'. The 'other', however, may consist of a large variety of ethnic minority groups, each with their own sectoral focus and self-employment statuses. Capotorti (1991:568) establishes that 'ethnic minority' is a diverse category with significant differences across ethnicities, characterised by

> a group numerically inferior to the rest of the population of a state, whose members being nationals of the state possess ethnic, religious or linguistic characteristics differing from those of the rest of the population. . . and show a sense of solidarity, directed towards preserving their culture, tradition, religion or language.

Within tourism, Adler and Adler's (2004) study of resort workers at five luxury resorts in Hawaii distinguished between four types of workers depending on their ethnicity:

- New immigrants (many from South East Asia) who undertake the most menial, low-paid jobs.
- The locals who provide a 'Polynesian flavour' to the resorts, but are 'trapped' in occupational hierarchies, in largely low and lower-managerial jobs.
- Seekers, frequently students from the mainland (US) but also Europe, take up temporary positions for lifestyle reasons, often seeking alternative experiences.
- The managers, university-educated, white, middle class, belong to the elite who usually 'fly in' also from the mainland and take up positions of seniority for two to three years as part of their occupational development.

To illustrate further, focusing on self-employment, Ram and Jones (2008) describe the historical landscape of ethnic minority businesses in the UK where ethnic Chinese are heavily involved in catering and where South Asians are heavily involved in textiles and convenience retailing, with both ethnic groups displaying higher self-employment rates than the ethnic white population. Self-employment rates among Afro-Caribbeans were, however, lower. Evidently, if one were only to look at the average for 'ethnic minority', rates of self-employment between 'White' and 'All Ethnic Groups' hardly differ (Office for National Statistics, 2014). A similar situation is described in New Zealand by de Vries et al. (2015) where business start-up rates among Chinese and Dutch ethnic minorities are above average.

The explanation as to why business formation among ethnic minorities is frequently above average has economic as well as cultural reasons. There is a large body of literature that discusses how ethnic minorities do not have the same access to resources (see also previous chapter), social networks and education and therefore are pushed into entrepreneurship for want of access to the career paths open to the majority ethnic population. Entrepreneurship can serve as a vehicle for social mobility where other avenues to achieve upward mobility remain closed.

Because tourism is characterised by low barriers to entry in relation to both human and financial capital, it might be regarded as a sector of choice for ethnic minorities who may not have access to either in equal measure to the indigenous population. This notion of tourism as a 'refuge sector' was identified by Szivas and Riley (1999) in a study that looked at Hungary in a period of transition from communism to market capitalism. Others such as Janta et al. (2011) found some evidence that for the immigrant Polish community in the UK tourism was seen as a refuge sector, but only by youth. Vaugeois and Rollins (2007) explored the notion of tourism as a refuge sector on Vancouver Island, an economy in transition (from resource-focused to greater diversification, including tourism). Here they confirmed the refuge hypothesis to a degree, but their study also demonstrated the complexity of this issue. Pechlaner et al. (2012) also confirmed the low barriers to entry argument to explain the attractiveness of tourism as a sector in the Tyrol region of the Alps. They also noted, however, that ethnic minorities could bring a unique skillset with them too. Rather than being pushed into tourism, 'the strongest motivational forces appear to be lifestyle and entrepreneurial – people moving into tourism for the positive attributes associated with the industry' (Vaugeois and Rollins, 2007:644).

Tourism as an employer does draw heavily on marginalised groups in society – including migrants (Baum, 2012), youth (Walmsley, 2015) and women (Baum, 2013) – but whether there are higher rates of ethnic minority entrepreneurship in tourism as compared to non-ethnic minority entrepreneurship generally is difficult to establish. What we can identify are cases where particular socio-economic circumstances have led to higher rates of ethnic minority entrepreneurship in tourism. Within this context Yang and Wall (2008:52) have argued that 'virtually no academic attention has been paid to entrepreneurship in ethnic tourism development'. This is slightly different to ethnic minority entrepreneurship in tourism, certainly where those developing ethnic tourism, that is tourism drawing on the culture of an ethnic group, are not from the same ethnic group as the culture that is being promoted. In fact, Yang and Wall (2008) are quite clear that many of the entrepreneurs in their study of Xishuangbanna Dai Autonomous Prefecture in Yunnan, China, were not from the ethnic minority population and as such were exploiting minority resources for their own benefit. The development of tourist areas more generally often witnesses the influx of non-local entrepreneurs (Butler, 1980; Barr, 1990).

Ethnic minority entrepreneurship in tourism remains an important and yet under-investigated phenomenon. Further research might usefully identify how different contexts support or hinder the establishment of ethnic minority businesses in tourism, how ethnic minority culture is being exploited and how ethnic minority entrepreneurs are competing with non-ethnic minority/or those from other ethnic minorities for the same tourist dollar.

Lifestyle entrepreneurship

Lifestyle entrepreneurship is endemic to tourism, which is why much of the literature on lifestyle entrepreneurship can be found in the tourism domain. This is one aspect of entrepreneurship where it is possible to argue, convincingly, that tourism is leading the field. If taking lifestyle to mean 'not primarily profit-focused' then most firms in tourism are lifestyle enterprises (Lee-Ross and Lashley, 2009, cite Thomas et al.'s (2000) study of around 1,300 operators of micro businesses in hospitality and tourism, which indicated that only approximately 10–15% of these micro-businesses were strongly motivated by economic incentives). In fact, standard business models that put at their heart typical goals of profit maximisation, market growth, or maximisation of shareholder value, and hence interpret and explain business operations through these lenses, fall wide of the mark in understanding the behaviour of the typical tourism SME, or the typical entrepreneur/small business owner. As Spence and Rutherford (2003:1) argue: 'It is often taken for granted that the small business owner/manager will behave almost as if the rational economic man [sic] of standard economics textbooks were real.' The study of small firms in tourism is necessarily a study of lifestyle firms.

This is not to say that profits (as a proxy for business success more generally) are unimportant to the typical tourism SME. Nonetheless, the purpose of many tourism firms as represented by the vision of the owner has a tendency to be more complex. Middleton et al. (2009:44) explain this as follows:

> Operating in a very local context, many of them (micro-businesses) are motivated as much, or more, by a mix of personal, quality of life and community goals, as by the economic/commercial rationale that dominates big business.

Recognition that entrepreneurs create tourism firms for a variety of reasons, not solely for sustained growth or profit maximisation, is no longer novel. Smith (1967) who conducted interviews with 150 entrepreneurs in the United States suggested early on that entrepreneurs could broadly be split into 'craftsmen' or 'opportunistic entrepreneurs'. Authors such as Ateljevic and Doorne (2000), who explored small tourism firms in New Zealand, Shaw and Williams (2004), who looked at lifestyle entrepreneurs in the south west of the UK, Marchant and Mottiar (2011), who investigated surfing businesses in Ireland, and Bredvold and Skålen (2016), who studied lifestyle entrepreneurs in tourism in Norway, have taken the analysis of entrepreneurial motivations in tourism beyond the purely economic. Indeed, it is precisely the non-economic motives that drive many tourism entrepreneurs that make the application of standard economic theory (with its profit orientation, and, still, assumption of rational behaviour) so difficult within the tourism sector (Dewhurst and Horobin, 1998). We have argued throughout this text that a key feature of the tourism–entrepreneurship relationship lies in tourism's low entry barriers. With regard to lifestyle entrepreneurship, it has been recognised (Snepenger et al., 1995) that tourism can be a driver of entrepreneurship based on something Snepenger et al. (1995) term 'travel stimulated entrepreneurial migration'. Here, individuals who visit a destination are so attracted by its appeal that they decide to return to set up a new life there, which frequently involves a tourism lifestyle firm.

Two recent studies of lifestyle entrepreneurs in tourism (Beaumont et al., 2016; Bredvold and Skålen, 2016) provide a clear insight into the complexities involved in distinguishing lifestyle entrepreneurs' motivations in tourism. Beaumont et al.'s (2016) study sought to promote further conceptual clarity of the notion of who is/is not a lifestyle entrepreneur in their review of surfing lifestyle businesses in Devon and Cornwall (counties in the south west of the UK). Following a number of earlier studies that had also sought to explore what it means to be a lifestyle entrepreneur, a twofold categorisation was adopted. Purists are those lifestyle entrepreneurs who place little or no value on economic success beyond being able to support their desired lifestyle. Not all lifestyle entrepreneurs are of this mindset, however. Beaumont et al. (2016) write of 'freestylers' as those lifestyle entrepreneurs that try to combine the profit orientation with a lifestyle orientation. Shaw and Williams (2004) equally identified this type of lifestyle entrepreneur in tourism who they term 'constrained entrepreneurs'. Of the 101 lifestyle surfing businesses that responded to Beaumont et al.'s (2016) survey, the majority were in fact freestylers (82%). Moreover, the study indicated that start-up motivations may change over time. To classify someone as a 'purist' or a 'freestyle lifestyle entrepreneur' is but a temporary classification. Beaumont et al.'s (2016) study showed that entrepreneurs' motivations changed; for some at least, there appears to have been a growing interest in business as the business 'took off'.

Bredvold and Skålen's (2016:103) study, which sought to understand how entrepreneurial identities are created, offers a fourfold classification of lifestyle entrepreneur narratives (see Table 11.1). The dimensions of their model are embeddedness versus independence and flexibility versus stability. Embeddedness refers to embeddedness within the socio-cultural environment, while independence refers to identity construction that attempts to break free from that environment. Stable identity construction reflects deeply rooted values in the individuals, whereas flexile identity construction refers to 'a more ambiguous and inconsistent internal grounding of identity'.

Bredvold and Skålen's (2016) research confirms what Beaumont et al.'s (2016) does in that lifestyle entrepreneurs in tourism combine commercial as well as lifestyle goals. Bredvold and Skålen's (2016) study furthermore illustrates how being true to cultural traditions can serve the business. Being a lifestyle entrepreneur in tourism does not have to mean not being able to innovate or find a niche for one's product – on the contrary. Ateljevic and Doorne's (2000) study showed how by not aligning themselves with an overly profit-driven motivation, lifestyle entrepreneurs were able to carve their own niches, their customers sharing similar motivations and values as the owners of these lifestyle firms. Furthermore, many of the firms in Ateljevic and Doorne's (2000) study introduced innovations in their markets, offering what we argue here could be regarded as more authentic tourism products and services. This in turn was seen to stimulate regional economic development. Based on these findings, policy-makers should not ignore lifestyle firms in their quest for economic development; it is not just the profit-driven, growth-oriented firms that can make a difference.

Table 11.1 Bredvold and Skålen's (2016:103) lifestyle entrepreneur narrative types

	Embedded	*Independent*
Flexible	The modern lifestyle entrepreneur narrative	The post-modern lifestyle entrepreneur narrative
Stable	The loyal lifestyle entrepreneur narrative	The freedom-seeking lifestyle entrepreneur narrative

On a final note, the notion of a lifestyle entrepreneur is likely to appeal to many prospective entrepreneurs as it may conjure up idyllic notions of managing one's lifestyle firm in tourism sat on a beach, sipping a margarita while answering emails. Of course, reality is not always this kind. A quote from one (would-be) lifestyle entrepreneur in Beaumont et al.'s (2016) study is sobering in this respect: 'My business takes up so much surf time it is stupid. I have less free time to go and find waves than when I worked 9–5 in an office.'

The study of the motivations, identities and challenges of combining profit-orientated with lifestyle aspirations is an area that is likely to appeal to tourism scholars for some time to come. If common media accounts are to be believed, Generation X (1966–1980 birth cohorts) are more likely to seek intrinsic rather than extrinsic rewards from work (Krahn and Nancy, 2014), and it is frequently suggested millennials (those born early 1980s to 2000) stress personal development and work–life balance (e.g., Hattke et al., 2017). The issue of self-employment might become more prevalent then as an increasing number of individuals seek non-standard forms of employment and meaning in their working lives.

Entrepreneurship education

> It has become fashionable to view entrepreneurship education as the panacea for stagnating or declining economic activity in both developed and developing countries.
>
> (Matlay and Carey, 2007:252)

According to Neck and Corbett (2018:9), entrepreneurship education is at a 'tipping point'. It has grown rapidly in the past 30 years, becoming fashionable, as the above quotation by Matlay and Carey (2007) suggests. However, research on entrepreneurship education has not kept pace, and indeed, according to Echtner (1995:121) there is a 'significant oversight' in tourism education's failure to address self-employment. We still do not know what should be taught, how it should be taught and how it might be assessed (Morris and Liguori, 2016). One area where progress has been made is in answering the question as to whether entrepreneurship can in fact be taught, which now appears to have been largely resolved in the affirmative (see also Chapter 7).

Entrepreneurship education (EE) has been defined by Neck and Corbett (2018:10) as 'developing the mindset, skill set, and practice necessary for starting new ventures'. Even though Neck and Corbett (2018) highlight venture creation, they also acknowledge that EE should deliver 'the life skills necessary to live productive lives even if one does not start a business'. We argue that EE is of relevance to tourism educators because of an increasingly dynamic graduate labour market that requires graduates with entrepreneurial skills and mindsets. With the shifting sands of the labour market, where loyalty to a firm is no longer a given as shorter-term employment relationships are built around an exchange of benefits and contributions (Clarke and Patrickson, 2008), in an era of protean (Hall, 2004), or boundaryless (Arthur and Rousseau, 1996) careers, where it is estimated, for example, that almost half of employees (in the UK) will quit and retrain completely after deciding a career isn't for them (Finnigan, 2015), tourism graduates who can display an entrepreneurial mindset are at a distinct advantage.

The expansion of higher education globally has raised concerns surrounding the under-employment of youth, many of who, it is claimed, are regarded as over-qualified for traditional tourism work. Leaving aside the debates as to whether these fears are justified or not, it is certainly true that governments have for some time considered promoting non-traditional avenues into graduate employment, be that in terms of sector focus (Elias and Purcell, 2003) or firm size, i.e., SMEs (Holden et al., 2007). An alternative avenue is that into self-employment and business start-up.

Much of the literature on entrepreneurship education focuses on preparing individuals to set up businesses. Literally hundreds of studies exist that have tried to assess the impact of entrepreneurship education along these lines. Nabi et al. (2017) conducted a systematic review of entrepreneurship education in higher education of more than 100 studies and identified four broad output measures:

- Attitudes towards entrepreneurship
- Skills and knowledge/feasibility/entrepreneurial intentions
- Actual business start-up
- Success of start-ups and broader social impacts of these start-ups.

Their study (Nabi et al., 2017) established that few studies outlined in any detail the pedagogical underpinning of the entrepreneurship education intervention they were researching. There appears to be more interest in outcomes, rather than how the outcomes were achieved.

Nabi et al. (2017) also identified a strong emphasis on 'soft' outcome measures rather than the 'hard' measures associated with actual business start-ups. This focus on soft measures, in particular entrepreneurial intentions, is understandable for both practical and theoretical reasons. In practice, the delivery of entrepreneurship education in HE is unlikely to result in immediate hard outcomes (business start-ups). Some students of EE may start a business immediately, others upon graduation, the majority some years after graduation. Identifying these outcomes requires a longitudinal approach and patience.

Intentions are the best predictor of behaviour (Bird, 1988) and so where behaviour cannot be observed immediately due to time lags, a focus on intentions is apposite (Krueger, 1993). Two models have predominantly been used (and sometimes adapted) in research on entrepreneurial intentions: Ajzen's Theory of Planned Behaviour (Ajzen and Fishbein, 1980) and Shapero's model of the Entrepreneurial Event (Shapero, 1982). In fact, these models have been used and discussed within the very limited tourism literature on entrepreneurship education/entrepreneurial intentions (e.g., Walmsley and Thomas, 2009; Gurel et al., 2010).[1] Both models, which to a degree overlap, have proven successful in explaining the development of entrepreneurial intentions (Krueger et al., 2000) and may serve therefore as assisting the development of entrepreneurship education if its aim is to inculcate entrepreneurial intentions.

Shapero's (1982) model focuses on perceived feasibility, perceived desirability and propensity to act as precursors to entrepreneurial intent. Ajzen's Theory of Planned Behaviour focuses on personal attitudes towards the behaviour, perceived social norms relating to the behaviour and perceived behavioural control. Entrepreneurship education may therefore stimulate entrepreneurial intentions if it enhances positive attitudes towards it (perceived desirability), and if it prepares students for the challenges necessary to successfully create a venture (perceived feasibility). It may also stimulate entrepreneurial intentions if it can help students overcome perceived negative social norms towards entrepreneurship, and if it can stimulate greater levels of confidence in one's ability to achieve the target behaviour (perceived behaviour control/propensity to act).

Entrepreneurship education that extends beyond, but also includes venture creation can be considered critical for the future of the tourism sector. We have already alluded to the dynamic business environment that requires individuals to demonstrate an entrepreneurial mindset and entrepreneurial effectiveness. These individuals are needed in all kinds of tourism firms, whether new start-ups or established. Furthermore, on the understanding that barriers to the creation of tourism firms are relatively low, and it is therefore regularly regarded by policy-makers as a sector of choice for rural diversification and poverty alleviation, entrepreneurship education may be regarded as a very powerful means of achieving policy goals.

Just how to develop entrepreneurship education for tourism remains an important issue that tourism educators as well as practitioners should consider, for the benefit of students/graduates and the industry. Evidence of 'what works' is scattered and will depend on what is trying to be achieved. We would not argue therefore that one approach is necessarily better than another, but that approaches to teaching entrepreneurship need to be adapted to suit the situation and might usefully adopt a range of approaches. Applying Béchard and Grégoire's (2005) as well as Fayolle and Gailly's (2008) insights into the pedagogy of entrepreneurship education, Nabi et al. (2017) classified four types of pedagogical approaches to entrepreneurship education:

- Supply model focusing on reproduction methods such as lectures, reading, and so forth.
- Demand model focusing on personalised/participative methods (e.g., interactive searches, simulations).
- Competence model focusing on communication, discussion, and production methods (e.g., debates, portfolios).
- Hybrid models (i.e., mixture of above).

Entrepreneurship education in tourism could include elements from all of the above approaches, i.e., align with the hybrid model. Because of entrepreneurship's action focus (e.g., Jones and Matlay, 2011; Neck and Corbett, 2018), we do, however, argue that students should be given opportunities to 'get their hands dirty', which might involve providing consultancy services to existing tourism firms, trying to set up their own business within parameters set by the education institution or using simulation software to create firms.

Smart tourism

Smart tourism as used here is an umbrella term for the increased integration of technology, particularly ICT, into the tourist experience. Smart tourism is a manifestation of innovation and entrepreneurship, and undoubtedly the adoption and tailored application of advances in ICT to tourism will continue to shape its very nature for some time to come. We have already seen (Chapter 5) how technological innovation is being used in tourism, from developments in AI to the use of social media in destination marketing, to the application of big data for marketing purposes and to track tourists' movements. There seems to be no sphere of tourism where technological developments are not having some impact. The reference here to smart tourism occurs because (a) it is unquestionably one of the 'hot topics' in tourism at present, and (b) it holds much scope for entrepreneurship in tourism, indeed potentially offers new business models. A cursory glance at text books in tourism published more than five years ago reveals limited, if any, mention of smart tourism, however.

Smart tourism 'encompasses touristic activities that are informed and supported by smart technology' (Gretzel et al., 2015a). The prefix 'smart' applies to technology that requires minimal human interaction, that has some special capability or connectivity (Gretzel et al., 2015b). In most circumstances it involves enhancing the tourist's experience via the integration of various aspects of the tourist's visit via the Internet of Things (for IoT to function there has to be the appropriate infrastructure, i.e., reliable and fast internet access, cloud computing and artificial intelligence technology; Guo et al., 2014).

The benefits to the tourist of smart tourism include:

- Ease of access to up-to-date information.
- An enhanced experience of attractions (e.g., having ready access to information about a gallery, museum and its exhibits). Extra value can be added to an exhibit or attraction, for example.
- Being able to navigate a destination and what it has to offer more easily.
- A more sustainable and user-friendly experience (rather than carting around numerous guide books and maps, everything can be accessed via smart technology on one's phone).

An area of growing interest in tourism relates to the coming together of smart technologies and destination management. Thus, the notion of smart destinations is now fairly common, and derives from thinking in the area of smart cities. Many destinations are adopting the logic underpinning smart destinations to gain a competitive edge, and in fact in some instances, such as in Tahiti, developing a smart destination is seen as a means to stimulate tourism demand at a time when visitor figures are in decline (Travel Startups, n.d.). A smart destination offers a number of advantages to the destination that include:

- the collection of customer/tourist data to help determine levels and patterns of demand
- a more sustainable form of tourism (optimal use of resources)
- an overall enhanced visitor experience, leading to a competitive edge
- branding opportunities (sharing of experiences via social media)
- stimulating demand for less well-known attractions.

It is important nonetheless to acknowledge that in certain circumstances smart tourism may not be welcomed. Technology is pervasive and can become addictive and so the promise of being able to integrate every element of one's experience via technology might be the last thing tourists want, or need. The idea that tourism serves as a form of escapism is certainly not new (e.g., Hiller, 1976) with tourism entrepreneurs recognising an opportunity to provide those needing to 'get away

Figure 11.1 'Getting away from it all'

Credit: Maurizio Costanzo, 'Phone Time', original in colour. https://creativecommons.org/licenses/by/4.0/

from it all' with 'digital detox'. Moreover, Gretzel et al. (2015b:562) recognise that there is much scope for research that looks at the benefits but also some of the dangers lurking behind the notion of smart tourism, such as '[p]rivacy concerns, the effects of technology-mediated life, information overload/the value of information'.

Summary

Akin to the approach adopted in Chapter 9, this chapter has in part moved away from an exclusive small firm focus. Rather, it has explored the relationship between entrepreneurship and tourism via a number of topics either currently 'in vogue' in entrepreneurship, or believed to be of particular importance to entrepreneurship in tourism. The issues covered are certainly not meant to be exhaustive of current developments, but serve to illustrate a selection of developments in the broader field of entrepreneurship in tourism. The first topic was ethnic minority entrepreneurship. Here it was recognised that entrepreneurship in tourism can offer a means of income generation for ethnic minorities otherwise excluded from higher level or professional roles in society. It was also recognised that the diversity within ethnic minorities is often overlooked, and that there is an ongoing danger that ethnic minority culture is exploited as a tourism asset by unscrupulous entrepreneurs.

Lifestyle entrepreneurship is a key aspect of entrepreneurship in tourism and is an area where it can be argued tourism is leading the way in terms of research focus (based on the amount of research on this topic offered within the tourism literature compared to that in the entrepreneurship literature). Because lifestyle considerations are important to many tourism entrepreneurs, standard economic perspectives of profit-orientation do not fully reflect the world of the tourism entrepreneur. Furthermore, motivations are not static; what might have been set up as a lifestyle venture can mutate into a profit-driven firm, just as much as profit motivations may cede to more lifestyle-orientated approaches.

Entrepreneurship education is going to play an increasingly important role in preparing tourism graduates for the realities of modern-day labour markets. Entrepreneurship education is not just about preparing individuals for starting businesses, although much research in this area has focused on this aspect. More broadly, it is understood as inculcating an entrepreneurial mindset in individuals, which should be of growing importance in increasingly competitive business environments.

Finally, we reviewed the notion of smart tourism. Although the importance of technology to tourism's development has long been recognised (and we have discussed the issue throughout the text), the rapid developments in ICT in particular are fundamentally reshaping many aspects of modern tourism. This is certainly the case if we look at the notion of smart tourism, where it is being applied by many destination management/marketing organisations in an attempt to become more competitive. Crucially, these technological advances provide much scope for innovation and entrepreneurship in tourism. It is, nonetheless, recognised that not all that glitters is gold, and for some tourists, smart tourism is the antithesis of what they desire. Smart tourism as an area of academic inquiry continues to gather pace, however (e.g., Xiang et al., 2015), and it is unlikely that this interest will wane in the near future.

Review questions/discussion points

1   Explain the difference between ethnic minority entrepreneurship in tourism and minority ethnic tourism development.
2   Why might you argue that lifestyle entrepreneurship is particularly relevant to tourism?
3   What are some of the challenges a lifestyle entrepreneur could face when setting up a tourism firm?
4   Rather than focusing on intent, what other measures of impact might you use to establish the impact of entrepreneurship education in tourism? What might the limitations of these other measures be?
5   If entrepreneurship education is 'all about practice', what role does theory play?
6   Consider how smart tourism may enhance or detract from your next holiday. Overall, do you think the move towards smart destinations adds to or detracts from a holiday?

Note

1   Although entrepreneurship education did not appear to have had an impact in Gurel et al.'s (2010) study.

References

Adler, P. and Adler, P. 2004. *Paradise Laborers: Hotel Work in the Global Economy*. New York: Cornell University Press.

Ajzen, I. and Fishbein, M. 1980. *Understanding Attitudes and Predicting Social Behaviour.* Englewood Cliffs, NJ: Prentice Hall.

Arthur, M. and Rousseau, D. M. 1996. *The Boundaryless Career: A New Employment Principle for a New Organizational Era.* Oxford: Oxford University Press.

Ateljevic, I. and Doorne, S. 2000. Staying within the fence: lifestyle entrepreneurship in tourism. *Journal of Sustainable Tourism,* 8, 378–392.

Barr, T. 1990. From quirky islanders to entrepreneurial magnates: the transition of the Whitsundays. *Journal of Tourism Studies,* 1, 26–32.

Baum, T. 2012. Migrant workers in the international hotel industry. *International Migration Papers.* Geneva: International Labour Office.

Baum, T. 2013. *International Perspectives on Women and Work in Hotels, Catering and Tourism.* Geneva: International Labour Office.

Beaumont, E., Walmsley, A., Woodward, E. and Wallis, L. 2016. The freestyle lifestyle entrepreneur: a tale of competing values. *British Academy of Management Conference 2016.* Newcastle: BAM.

Béchard, J. P. and Grégoire, D. 2005. Entrepreneurship education research revisited: the case of higher education. *Academy of Management Learning and Education,* 4, 22–43.

Bird, B. 1988. Implementing entrepreneurial ideas: the case of intention. *Academy of Management Review,* 13, 442–453.

Bredvold, R. and Skålen, P. 2016. Lifestyle entrepreneurs and their identity construction: a study of the tourism industry. *Tourism Management,* 56, 96–105.

Butler, D. 1980. The concept of a tourist area cycle of evolution: implications for management of resources. *Canadian Geographer,* 24, 5–12.

Capotorti, F. 1991. *Study on the Rights of Persons Belonging to Ethnic, Religious and Linguistic Minorities.* Geneva: United Nations.

Clarke, M. and Patrickson, M. 2008. The new covenant of employability. *Employee Relations,* 30, 121–141.

de Vries, H. P., Hamilton, R. and Voges, K. 2015. Antecedents of ethnic minority entrepreneurship in New Zealand: an intergroup comparison. *Journal of Small Business Management,* 53, 95–114.

Dewhurst, D. and Horobin, H. 1998. Small business owners. In: Thomas, R. (ed.), *The Management of Small Tourism and Hospitality Firms.* London: Cassell.

Echtner, C. 1995. Entrepreneurial training in developing countries. *Annals of Tourism Research,* 22, 119–134.

Edelman, L., Brush, C., Manolova, T. and Greene, P. 2010. Start-up motivations and growth intentions of minority nascent entrepreneurs. *Journal of Small Business Management,* 48, 174–196.

Elias, P. and Purcell, K. 2003. *Research Paper No.1 – Measuring Change in the Graduate Labour Market.* Employment Research Services Unit, University of the West of England, and Warwick Institute for Employment Research.

Fayolle, A. and Gailly, B. 2008. From craft to science: teaching models and learning processes in entrepreneurship education. *Journal of European Industrial Training,* 32, 569–593.

Finnigan, L. 2015. Britons in the workplace: the figures that lay bare the life of an average British employee. *The Telegraph,* 4 November 2015.

Gretzel, U., Sigala, M., Xiang, Z. and Koo, C. 2015a. Smart tourism: foundations and development. *Electronic Markets,* 25, 179–188.

Gretzel, U., Werthner, H., Koo, C. and Lamsfus, C. 2015b. Conceptual foundations for understanding smart tourism ecosystems. *Computers in Human Behaviour,* 50, 558–563.

Guo, Y., Liu, H. and Chai, Y. 2014. The embedding convergence of smart cities and tourism internet of things in China: an advance perspective. *Advances in Hospitality and Tourism Research,* 2, 54–69.

Gurel, E., Altinay, L. and Daniele, R. 2010. Tourism students' entrepreneurial intentions. *Annals of Tourism Research,* 37, 646–669.

Hall, D. 2004. The protean career: a quarter-century journey. *Journal of Vocational Behavior*, 65, 1–13.

Hattke, F., Homberg, F. and Znanewitz, J. 2017. Retaining employees – a study on work values of the millennial generation. *Academy of Management Proceedings*, 2017, 13968.

Hiller, H. 1976. Escapism, penetration, and response: industrial tourism and the Caribbean. *Caribbean Studies*, 16, 92–116.

Holden, R., Jameson, S. and Walmsley, A. 2007. New graduate employment in SMEs: still in the dark? *Journal of Small Business and Enterprise Development*, 14, 211–227.

Janta, H., Ladkin, A., Brown, L. and Lugosi, P. 2011. Employment experiences of Polish migrant workers in the UK hospitality sector. *Tourism Management*, 32, 1006–1019.

Jones, C. and Matlay, H. 2011. Understanding the heterogeneity of entrepreneurship education: going beyond Gartner. *Education & Training*, 53, 692–703.

Krahn, H. and Nancy, G. 2014. Work values and beliefs of 'Generation X' and ' Generation Y'. *Journal of Youth Studies*, 17, 92–112.

Krueger, N. F. J. 1993. The impact of prior entrepreneurial exposure on perceptions of new venture feasibility and desirability. *Entrepreneurship Theory and Practice*, 18, 5–21.

Krueger, N. F. J., Reilly, M. D. and Carsrud, A. L. 2000. Competing models of entrepreneurial intentions. *Journal of Business Venturing*, 15, 411–432.

Lee-Ross, D. and Lashley, C. 2009. *Entreprneurship & Small Business Management in the Hospitality Industry*. Oxford: Butterworth-Heinemann.

Marchant, B. and Mottiar, Z. 2011. Understanding lifestyle toursim entrepreneurs and digging beneath the issue of profits: profiling surf tourism lifestyle entrepreneurs in Ireland. *Tourism Planning and Development*, 8, 121–183.

Matlay, H. and Carey, C. 2007. Entrepreneurship education in the UK: a longitudinal perspective. *Journal of Small Business and Enterprise Development*, 14, 252–263.

Middleton, V., Fyall, A., Morgan, M. and Ranchhod, A. 2009. *Marketing in Travel and Tourism*. New York: Routledge.

Morris, M. H. and Liguori, E. 2016. Preface: teaching reason and the unreasonable. *In:* Morris, M. H. and Ligouri, E. (eds.) *Annals of Entrepreneurship Education and Pedagogy*. Northampton, MA: Edward Elgar Publishing.

Nabi, G., Liñan, F., Fayolle, A., Krueger, N. and Walmsley, A. 2017. The impact of entrepreneurship education in higher education: a systematic review and research agenda. *Academy of Management Learning and Education*, 16, 277–299.

Neck, H. and Corbett, A. 2018. The scholarship of teaching and learning entrepreneurship. *Entrepreneurship Education and Pedagogy*, 1, 8–41.

Office for National Statistics. 2014. *2011 Census Analysis: Ethnicity and the Labour Market, England and Wales*. Available: www.ons.gov.uk/peoplepopulationandcommunity/culturalidentity/ethnicity/articles/ethnicityandthelabourmarket2011censusenglandandwales/2014-11-13#characteristics-of-ethnic-groups-in-employment [Accessed 28 October 2017].

Pechlaner, H., Bo, G. and Volgger, M. 2012. What makes tourism an attractive industry for new minority entrepreneurs? Results from an exploratory qualitative study. *Tourism Review*, 67, 11–22.

Ram, M. and Jones, T. 2008. *Ethnic Minorities in Business*, 2nd edn. Milton Keynes: Small Enterprise Research Team, Open University.

Shapero, A. 1982. Social dimensions of entrepreneurship. *In:* C. Kent et al. (ed.), *The Encyclopedia of Entrepreneurship*. Englewood Cliffs, NJ: Prentice Hall.

Shaw, G. and Williams, A. 2004. From lifestyle consumption to lifestyle production: changing patterns of tourism entrepreneurship. *In:* Thomas, R. (ed.), *Small Firms in Tourism: International Perspectives*. London: Elsevier.

Smith, N. 1967. *The Entrepreneur and His Firm: The Relationship Between Type of Man and Type of Company*. East Lansing: Michigan State University.

Snepenger, D., Johnson, J. and Rasker, R. 1995. Travel-stimulated entrepreneurial migration. *Journal of Travel Research*, 34, 40–44.

Spence, L. and Rutherford, R. 2003. Small business and empirical perspectives in business ethics: an editorial. *Journal of Business Ethics*, 47, 1–5.

Szivas, E. and Riley, M. 1999. Tourism employment during economic transition. *Annals of Tourism Research*, 26, 747–771.

Travel Startups. n.d. *Travel Startups Incubator Partners with the Islands of Tahiti to Launch a Smart Tourism Nation* [Online]. Available: www.travelstartups.co/travel-startups-incubator-partners-with-the-islands-of-tahiti-to-launch-a-smart-tourism-nation/#9sXk0DyZW45gy1uG.99 [Accessed 06.06.2018].

Vaugeois, N. and Rollins, R. 2007. Mobility into tourism refuge employer. *Annals of Tourism Research*, 34, 630–648.

Walmsley, A. 2015. *Youth Employment in Tourism: A Critical Review*. Oxford: Goodfellow Publishers.

Walmsley, A. and Thomas, R. 2009. Understanding and influencing entrepreneurial intentions of tourism students. *In:* Ateljevic, J. and Page, S. (eds.), *Tourism and Entrepreneurship. International Perspectives*. Oxford: Elsevier.

Weber, M. 2002. *The Protestant Ethic and the Spirit of Capitalism and Other Writings*. New York: Penguin.

Xiang, Z., Tussyadiah, L. and Buhalis, D. 2015. Editorial: smart destinations: foundations, analytics, and applications. *Journal of Destination Marketing and Management*, 4, 143–144.

Yang, L. and Wall, G. 2008. Ethnic tourism and entrepreneurship: Xishuangbanna, Yunnan, China. *Tourism Geographies*, 10, 522–544.

Chapter 12

Conclusion

This chapter will summarise key discussions that have taken place with a view to highlighting issues that are likely to be of further interest to students, researchers, educators and policy-makers; issues that distinguish entrepreneurship in tourism from entrepreneurship in a generic sense. The purpose of this chapter is then to embed and reinforce key messages from the previous chapters as well as to highlight avenues for further research.

The aim of this book was to provide a critical, yet accessible, introduction to entrepreneurship in tourism. It has tried to straddle the line between rigour and relevance (Markusen, 2003), offering sufficient academic grounding without (hopefully!) getting lost in too much detail. The text was structured in such a way as to cover teaching in a typical 12–15-week semester. The first three chapters focused on key concepts in entrepreneurship, setting the foundation for the remainder of the book. Chapters 4 through 8 adopted a more micro, i.e., individual-firm focus, reviewing literature in the area of business plans, networking, financing a start-up, marketing, employment and strategic thinking/strategic entrepreneurship. From the perspective of someone considering starting and growing a business, these were the most practically oriented chapters. Chapters 9–11 took a more meso/macro approach, reviewing entrepreneurship's role as an agent of change and development at an industry and societal level. This does not mean these chapters are of no relevance to the individual firm, but the themes discussed will appeal more to those who require a bird's-eye view of developments in the field (e.g., policy-makers and scholars). Understandably then, these latter chapters are likely to be of greater interest to the public sector and quasi-public bodies/associations as well as students of entrepreneurship who want to get a greater appreciation of its role in society. Thus, we arrive at this final chapter, which is more speculative in that it seeks to offer, based on a review of key themes discussed in the book, the author's view of how entrepreneurship in tourism might develop in the future.

Because of the potential of a 'close coupling' (Langley, 1999) between tourism and entrepreneurship as was argued in Chapter 1, this text is timely. This is not to say, as is demonstrated throughout this book in fact, that entrepreneurship in tourism has been entirely neglected. However, these explorations have focused on specific features of the entrepreneurship–tourism nexus, for understandable reasons. This is the case, for example, in the edited works by Ateljevic and Page (2009) or more recently Brookes and Altinay (2015). These are very valuable contributions in their own right, and offer more detailed discussions of specific aspects of the tourism–entrepreneurship domain, but do not, and do not endeavour to, provide a coherent review of the subject as might typically be found in a single-authored text such as this. The two texts that come closest to what has been offered here in the sense that they are non-edited texts with a focus on entrepreneurship in tourism are those by Morrison et al. (1999) and Lee-Ross and Lashley (2009). Because of the inexorable pace of change in tourism relating to, for example, products, markets, consumer behaviour, industry structure as well as advances in research in both entrepreneurship and tourism, this text offers an updated perspective on the phenomenon of entrepreneurship in tourism. Indeed, the pace of change is such that developments in the areas of social enterprise, artificial intelligence, big data, the influence and use of social media, for example, are unsurprisingly not mentioned in Morrison et al.'s (1999) early contribution, but are similarly not covered in Lee-Ross and Lashley's (2009) more recent text either. This is indicative of the pace of change; much has happened in the past decade in tourism (only ten years ago Huang, 2008, was arguing how bed and breakfast businesses needed to engage with e-commerce, something that is today largely taken for granted).

The tourism–entrepreneurship nexus

Strong ties bind tourism and entrepreneurship. Many definitions of entrepreneurship suggest it is primarily about business start-up. Although this is arguably a contained view, it is nonetheless true that venture creation would, in most minds, constitute an entrepreneurial act. Most businesses start small and, if they do not fail, remain small. The structure of the tourism industry, the predominance of small firms, aligns closely then with the small-firm focus found in much entrepreneurship research. Moreover, barriers to entry in tourism are generally low. Certainly, small-scale entrepreneurship in tourism continues to provide an income to millions of people around the world, be that selling souvenirs, working as a tour guide, or offering a homestay. As well as low barriers to entry, these types of business, often undertaken informally, are woven into the fabric of the local community, which is one of the reasons why tourism may be regarded favourably by policy-makers.[1] This is particularly the case in emerging and/or developing countries as well as regions that have suffered economic decline, frequently including peripheral zones away from major conurbations where alternative sources of income are scant. The widespread belief on the part of governments around the world in entrepreneurship's key role in driving economic, and social, development is likewise becoming almost axiomatic.

We can add to this the fact that many people choose to set up businesses for lifestyle reasons. This is especially the case in tourism where the geographic location or the activity itself that is the focus of the lifestyle (e.g., lifestyle sport, hobby, etc.) accommodates the desire to pursue a lifestyle business.

From an academic perspective, entrepreneurship and tourism share many similarities in their development. Both are relatively recent additions to the pantheon of subjects now taught and studied at a tertiary level (and increasingly in schools too) despite both, in essence, being very human activities (both travel/mobility and creativity/invention) and on this basis have been in existence as long as humanity itself.

From a scholarly perspective, both tourism and entrepreneurship have fought for recognition, attempting to establish themselves as disciplines in their own right. Both subjects are in fact multidisciplinary, with knowledge contributing to and being influenced by areas such as economics, sociology, politics, anthropology and cultural studies. It is, we would argue, easier to place entrepreneurship in the broader discipline of economics than it is to place tourism in any existing discipline. This is certainly the case if entrepreneurship is taken to mean the commercialisation of an innovation. The impacts of tourism and entrepreneurship are nonetheless felt across society.

The role of entrepreneurial motivation in tourism

This text has confirmed that much of the generic literature on entrepreneurship still takes a classic view of entrepreneurship as driven by a profit motive and growth aspirations (e.g., Deakins and Freel, 2006; Marchant and Mottiar, 2011). In contrast, many tourism firms are driven by entrepreneurs, for whom the profit motive is important, but only to the extent that it ensures business survival and continuation. The business is a means to an end, not the end itself. Descriptions of owners of small firms such as lifestyle entrepreneurs (Beaumont et al., 2016; Shaw and Williams, 2004), freestyle entrepreneurs (Lewis, 2008) or non-constrained entrepreneurs (Shaw and Williams, 1998) are more accurate in describing the typical tourism entrepreneur than a characterisation of an entirely rational, profit-maximising individual. It is on these grounds that Morrison et al. (1999) suggest the majority of small businesses in the UK are in fact lifestyle firms. One imagines that this observation in the UK would also apply to most, if not all, developed economies.

The changing nature of careers and work, less job certainty, more precarious employment contracts, fewer 'jobs for life' and increasing number of individuals working in the 'gig economy' are placing increasing pressures on (tourism) employees to become more entrepreneurial in the shaping of their own careers. For many, employment in tourism has always been a dalliance; for example, for those seeking part-time work while still studying, or those between education and full-time work. Nonetheless, a desire for control over one's career and working life in an era of precarious employment may push individuals into tourism entrepreneurship, as much as the pursuit of an idealised lifestyle acts as a draw. Whether for push (i.e., mainly economic reasons relating to the supply of work) or for pull factors (a changing orientation in modern societies to work and careers that favours values associated with entrepreneurship) tourism is and will remain a sector of choice for many wanting to start and run their own business.

Erratic demand and susceptibility to environmental shocks

Fluctuations in demand, frequently severe, often following no discernible pattern, are a characteristic of much tourism particularly in emerging and developing economies. These fluctuations can be the result of a change in consumer preferences and tastes, or legislation, but similarly can be brought about by crises and disasters whether man-made (e.g., terrorism) or natural (flooding, drought, earthquakes, etc.). This uncertainty may inhibit entrepreneurship in tourism, or thwart it where it is beginning to grow. We have recognised that barriers to entry in tourism are low but this does not mean setting up and running a successful tourism firm is easy. Many are those who have sought 'the good life', either running a café for tourists, a small hotel or bed and breakfast establishment in some charming location, but with little knowledge of how to run a tourism firm. Unfortunately, for many of these individuals, this may have resulted in more than just financial losses, but related issues also (Dew et al., 2012, for example, found that financial disagreements are stronger predictors of divorce relative to other common marital disagreements).

There is some irony then that crises create opportunities also, and put pressure on the tourism entrepreneur to exploit them. Necessity is after all the mother of invention, and so the very susceptibility of tourism to shocks may in fact drive levels of innovation and entrepreneurship in the sector. This is an issue yet to be explored.

Entrepreneurship beyond the firm

A particular feature of entrepreneurship in tourism is its scope, which extends beyond the individual enterprise. If we look at entrepreneurship in other sectors, the supply side consists almost entirely of only loosely associated firms. But, in tourism, firms do not usually exist in isolation, they form part of a larger whole, combining to form destinations. These may be managed or marketed by destination management/ marketing organisations, whereby tourism SMEs often come together to form associations or alliances. This brings with it its own challenges in terms of governance and stakeholder management (e.g., Paddison and Walmsley, 2018) and can result in exclusion of certain groups (see the discussion of Guanxi in China, Chapter 4). Moreover, tourism is very much situation-dependent, its success relies on appropriate levels of infrastructure and the careful management of the natural and man-made environment to avoid the increasingly prevalent phenomenon of overtourism (or mass tourism). All of this means the tourism entrepreneur will need to be keenly aware of what is happening at the level of the destination and adapt his/her business strategies accordingly.

These peculiarities of tourism also result in an object of attention for entrepreneurship scholars other than the firm: the destination itself and/or its DMO. Studies that have been reviewed in this text such as those by Mariani et al. (2016) or Salas-Olmedo (2018), both focusing on destinations and how they are using innovations in tourism, are indicative of the kind of studies that are likely to proliferate in the next few years as destinations themselves become more innovative and entrepreneurial.

Intrapreneurship and firm growth

The need to innovate increases with the pace of environmental change. As theory in the area of strategic management makes clear, today's competitive advantage is tomorrow's threshold resource or competence. It is therefore crucial for owner/ managers of tourism firms to foster intrapreneurship (or corporate entrepreneurship). Some would argue the entire organisation needs to become entrepreneurial, to display an entrepreneurial orientation. This text has discussed this in a number of guises (e.g., the learning organisation, strategic entrepreneurship, strategic awareness capability).

Intrapreneurship in tourism is a topic that has received only limited attention, especially as it relates to a firm's stages of growth. In fact, theories of firm growth have scarcely been applied to tourism. Further research in tourism could seek to better understand the challenges and barriers to growth in tourism firms, dealing with issues such as maintaining an entrepreneurial orientation yet combined with increasing levels of bureaucracy. The impact of environmental factors in fostering growth and/or strategic renewal in tourism firms could be explored. For example, the impact of perceived risk of crises and disasters to growth ambitions (the assumption is that there will be less willingness to invest in capital assets the riskier the perceived environmental threats, whether natural or man-made) would be an interesting avenue for further study.

A further issue is the strategic measurement of performance in small tourism firms. How are businesses measuring performance, and how are the insights being used (or not) to promote growth? Case studies of pioneering tourism firms would be useful from both an organisation-internal perspective (how is an entrepreneurial orientation maintained) and external perspective (how are strategies leading to the development of new product–market combinations)?

This book would not be complete without recognising that despite the ongoing, and mounting, pressure on tourism firms to display entrepreneurial behaviour, exceptions to this rule will exist. Tourism is such a diverse phenomenon it would be naïve to believe that all firms in tourism face the same level of threats. Some tourism firms can be quite successful even though they are staid in their outlook and practices. Much will depend on levels of competition, and despite many tourism firms facing strong competition, levels of competition do vary. For example, in some locations geographical or legal constraints (e.g., building regulations in national parks or availability of reliable public transport) limit the extent of competitive rivalry. This should not detract, however, from the widespread changes the sector has witnessed and that will have some impact on all tourism firms. Furthermore, situations can change rapidly and so it is dangerous to rest too long on one's laurels on the assumption of environmental constancy.

Tourism employment

The opening lines of the Preface to the book, as well as this chapter, suggest we must all become entrepreneurs. While the focus of these exhortations to become more entrepreneurial relate in the main to the development of one's own career, the need to display entrepreneurial behaviour is all around us, including within a specific job role (Chapter 7 indicated that this also holds true for employees in an increasingly competitive business environment). It is becoming progressively difficult, and short-sighted, for a company to simply stand still, to do what it has always done and hope for the best. Creating an organisation therefore with an entrepreneurial orientation requires entrepreneurial employees who are provided with an environment that fosters entrepreneurial behaviour. Studies in tourism are beginning to emerge that focus on employment issues that the business literature has considered for some time, such as organisational learning and absorptive capacity. There is still much scope for further research here within the context of tourism.

The impact technology is having in tourism is receiving vast amounts of attention. From investigations into the sharing economy, digital marketing, big data, their analysis and artificial intelligence, there is little doubt this is a key theme, if not *the* theme in tourism at the time of writing (on the basis of the author's admittedly subjective perception of the themes apparent in recent conference calls). It is all the more surprising then that the human resource implications in tourism remain largely ignored. The more complex, unpredictable and tailored a task the less likely it will be replaced by AI. This is good news for some aspects of tourism, especially at the high end of the market, or where consumers appreciate a more 'authentic', place-specific experience. Nonetheless, as a sector it is not immune from developments in AI. Future research in tourism could explore the impact of AI on employees.

Small tourism firms and entrepreneurship

We broadly agree with Thomas et al.'s (2011) view of a continued absence of a coherent research agenda with regard to small firms in tourism. We would add that the same applies to research in entrepreneurship in tourism, which in part is a result of the former, certainly in relation to the entrepreneurial process and nascent entrepreneurship. There can be little doubt that to understand the supply side of tourism, one must understand the small tourism firm in all its manifestations.

Paradoxically, small tourism firms are regularly regarded as stifling growth and innovation, upholding outmoded business practices. At the same time, small firms are seen as hotbeds of innovation, driving growth and economic development. What these contrasting positions indicate is the unsatisfactory tarring of all small tourism firms with the same brush (we have argued the same with regard to employment practices; Walmsley, 2015). Chapter 6 discussed the issue of firm growth whereby it was recognised that there is no universal growth trajectory just as there is no typical small tourism firm. This may sound pedestrian and yet we do regularly encounter observations that seem to suggest otherwise.

Within the small firm context, much it seems will boil down to the nature of the owner/manager. The extent to which the firm grows, seeks to grow, innovates or provides an environment conducive to innovation will depend on owner/manager values, attitudes and motivation. The lesson for research in tourism is clear: to understand the small tourism firm is to understand its owner/manager.

The future of entrepreneurship research in tourism

What does the future hold for entrepreneurship research in tourism? Although we cannot say for sure, of course, what we can say is that there is certainly much scope for tourism researchers to draw on and apply theory from the field of entrepreneurship to tourism. We echo here what (Li, 2008) argued a decade ago, but in doing so recognise that advances in the field are not inevitable. Just as Thomas et al. (2011) suggest, research on small firms in tourism has advanced in piecemeal manner despite some promise at the turn of the millennium; only time will tell if we will witness a similar development with regard to research in entrepreneurship in tourism.

There are grounds for optimism, however. As technological developments continue to change the world we live in, tourism scholars are tackling with verve the research opportunities this presents.[2] We are, according to the World Economic Forum, now witnessing the Fourth Industrial Revolution, which is characterised by a convergence of technologies that is blurring the lines between the physical, digital, and biological spheres (World Economic Forum, 2016). Breakthroughs in technologies in areas such as artificial intelligence, the Internet of Things, biotechnology, 3D printing, blockchain and cloud computing continue to be made. Ongoing technological developments, many of which find application by entrepreneurs and intrapreneurs, will offer tourism scholars research opportunities aplenty.

Another area that may see growing interest is social entrepreneurship and more generally social innovation in tourism. Certainly, since the financial crisis of 2007/2008, concerns around the current economic system's ability to benefit all, including limiting environmental damage, have manifested themselves in politics and in consumer behaviour. Today, it might not seem as bizarre a question to ask 'For whom should corporations be run?' (Blair, 1998) as was the case pre-crisis. The area of social entrepreneurship has seen a proliferation of literature, referring both to conceptual and practical aspects of the phenomenon. Here too then tourism is able to draw a burgeoning body of literature in a contiguous field.

Tourism researchers should look beyond the boundaries of their own 'discipline' to enrich it, but should not dismiss tourism's potential to contribute to other disciplines too. Just as tourism research has led in the area of lifestyle entrepreneurship, tourism can enrich the broader field of entrepreneurship by providing examples of innovations in, for example, areas such as the sharing economy, in employment (for example in the gig economy), in the application of technology to services and the service encounter, as well as in innovative marketing practices. The relationship between entrepreneurship and tourism should continue to offer a fecund ground for scholarly endeavour.

Notes

1 We also note, however, that small-scale, informal economic activity in tourism can also be seen as inimical to overall economic development and therefore suppressed as Truong's (2018) example from Hanoi, Vietnam, demonstrates.
2 Judged by the number of conference calls the author has witnessed that seek to explore issues surrounding the impact of technological developments on the sector.

References

Ateljevic, J. and Page, S. 2009. *Tourism and Entrerpeneurship: International Perspectives.* London: Routledge.

Beaumont, E., Walmsley, A., Woodward, E. and Wallis, L. 2016. The freestyle lifestyle entrepreneur: a tale of competing values. *British Academy of Management Conference 2016.* Newcastle: BAM.

Blair, M. 1998. For whom should corporations be run? An economic rationale for stakeholder management. *Long Range Planning,* 31, 195–200.

Brookes, M. and Altinay, L. (eds.) 2015. *Entrepreneurship in Hospitality and Tourism: A Global Perspective.* Abingdon: Goodfellow.

Deakins, D. and Freel, M. 2006. *Entrepreneurship and Small Firms*. Berkshire: McGraw Hill.

Dew, J., Britt, S. and Huston, S. 2012. Examining the relationship between financial issues and divorce. *Family Relations: Interdisciplinary Journal of Applied Family Studies*, 61, 615–628.

Huang, L. 2008. Bed and breakfast industry adopting e-commerce strategies in eservice. *Service Industries Journal*, 28, 633–648.

Langley, A. 1999. Strategies for theorizing from process data. *Academy of Management Review*, 24, 691–710.

Lee-Ross, D. and Lashley, C. 2009. *Entrepreneurship & Small Business Management in the Hospitality Industry*. Oxford: Butterworth-Heinemann.

Lewis, K. 2008. Small firm owners in New Zealand: in it for the 'good life' or growth? *Small Enterprise Research*, 16, 61–69.

Li, L. 2008. A review of entrepreneurship research published in the hospitality and tourism management journals. *Tourism Management*, 29, 1013–1022.

Marchant, B. and Mottiar, Z. 2011. Understanding lifestyle toursim entrepreneurs and digging beneath the issue of profits: profiling surf tourism lifestyle entrepreneurs in Ireland. *Tourism Planning and Development*, 8, 121–183.

Mariani, M., di Felice, M. and Mura, M. 2016. Facebook as a destination marketing tool: evidence from Italian regional destination management organizations. *Tourism Management*, 54, 321–343.

Markusen, A. 2003. Fuzzy concepts, scanty evidence, policy distance: the case for rigour and policy relevance in critical regional studies. *Regional Studies*, 37, 701–717.

Morrison, A., Rimmington, M. and Williams, C. 1999. *Entrepreneurship in the Hospitality, Tourism and Leisure Industries*. Oxford: Butterworth-Heinemann.

Paddison, B. and Walmsley, A. 2018. New public management in tourism: a case study of York. *Journal of Sustainable Tourism*.

Salas-Olmedo, M. H., Moya-Gomez, B., Juan Carlos García-Palomares, J. C. and Gutierrez, J. 2018. Tourists' digital footprint in cities: comparing big data sources. *Tourism Management*, 66, 13–25.

Shaw, G. and Williams, A. 1998. Entrepreneurship, small business culture and tourism development. *In*: Debbage, K.G. and Ioannides, D. (eds.), *The Economic Geography of the Tourist Industry: A Supply-Side Analysis*. London: Routledge.

Shaw, G. and Williams, A. 2004. From lifestyle consumption to lifestyle production: changing patterns of tourism entrepreneurship. *In*: Thomas, R. (ed.), *Small Firms in Tourism: International Perspectives*. London: Elsevier.

Thomas, R., Shaw, G. and Page, S. 2011. Understanding small firms in tourism: a perspective on research trends and challenges. *Tourism Management*, 32, 963–976.

Truong, V. D. 2018. Tourism, poverty alleviation, and the informal economy: the street vendors of Hanoi, Vietnam. *Tourism Recreation Research*, 43, 52–67.

Walmsley, A. 2015. *Youth Employment in Tourism: A Critical Review*. Oxford: Goodfellow Publishers.

World Economic Forum. 2016. *The World Global Competitiveness Report 2016–2017*. Geneva: World Economic Forum.

Index

Page numbers in **bold** refer to figures, page numbers in *italic* refer to tables.